Translating the Language of Patents

This book is a guide to discovering and translating the language of patents in view of avoiding costly translation errors. Errors that might hinder the examination process for granting patents, or that might make patents undefendable in a context of litigation.

The 42 sections of this book each identify different provisions of the law for their relevance to translation. These provisions govern language uses, right down to the use of punctuation. Each of the sections present findings, both in terms of the provisions identified, and their specific significance to translation. Exemplified translations focus on French and English, but when there is a consensus across intellectual property systems, multilingual parallelism is highlighted. Wherever relevant, provisions of specific rules and regulations are presented and exemplified in the three official languages of the European Patent Office (EPO), English, French, and German, as well as three official languages of the United Nations World Intellectual Property Organization (WIPO), English, French, and Spanish.

Written by an experienced teacher, patent translator, and author of the blog, *Patents on the Soles of Your Shoes,* this is a rigorously researched, authoritative, and comprehensive guide for all students and translators working in legal translation. Accompanying e-resources are available on the Routledge Translation studies portal (routledgetranslationstudiesportal.com) including information on how to use this book in courses.

Françoise Herrmann, Phd, is currently a Lecturer at San Jose State University in California and at Kent State University in Ohio, thanks to the wizardry of online course delivery systems.

Translating the Language of Patents

Françoise Herrmann

Routledge
Taylor & Francis Group
LONDON AND NEW YORK

Designed cover image: phototechno, Getty Images

First published 2024
by Routledge
4 Park Square, Milton Park, Abingdon, Oxon OX14 4RN

and by Routledge
605 Third Avenue, New York, NY 10158

Routledge is an imprint of the Taylor & Francis Group, an informa business

British Library Cataloguing-in-Publication Data
A catalogue record for this book is available from the British Library

Library of Congress Cataloging-in-Publication Data
Names: Herrmann, Françoise (writer on patent law), author.
Title: Translating the language of patents / Françoise Herrmann.
Description: Abingdon, Oxon [UK] ; New York, NY : Routledge, 2024. |
Includes bibliographical references and index. |
Identifiers: LCCN 2023052419 (print) | LCCN 2023052420 (ebook) | ISBN 9781032729145 (hardback) | ISBN 9781032729251 (paperback) | ISBN 9781003423003 (ebook)
Subjects: LCSH: Patent laws and legislation. | Patents--Language.
Classification: LCC K1505 .H47 2024 (print) | LCC K1505 (ebook) | DDC 346.04/86--dc23/eng/20231117
LC record available at https://lccn.loc.gov/2023052419
LC ebook record available at https://lccn.loc.gov/2023052420

ISBN: 978-1-032-72914-5 (hbk)
ISBN: 978-1-032-72925-1 (pbk)
ISBN: 978-1-003-42300-3 (ebk)

DOI: 10.4324/9781003423003

Access the Support Material: routledgetranslationstudiesportal.com

Typeset in Times New Roman
by SPi Technologies India Pvt Ltd (Straive)

For the Shelf, the Sun, and the Action Hero.

Contents

Figures

Tables

Preface

This book is about translation, patents translation, and in particular the provisions of patent laws, regulations, and international agreements, which have linguistic impact on both the translation process and product. The unintended effect was a detailed characterization of the *language of patents*, precisely because this is a language *prescribed* by the provisions of such patent rules, regulations, and laws. Clearly however, translators turn to the law for *entirely different reasons* than lawyers, patent agents, examiners, inventors, and entrepreneurs.

For example, patent law professionals examine the *prior art* of an invention to find out whether the conditions of *novelty*, *inventive step* and *usefulness* have been met, for the crucial purposes of determining the *patentability* of an invention. Issues that admittedly have strictly nothing to do with translation. Still, patent translators also turn to the provisions of the law on *patentability* and *prior art*. However, when translators turn to the *prior art* found in patent applications, and in *International Search Reports* appended to patent applications, it is in the search for parallel and background texts. A search with the aim of immersing themselves into the target domain, to leverage terminology, stylistics, and most importantly, an understanding of the invention and its purpose. Clearly, these are two very different approaches to the processing of *prior art*.

Indeed, it is the premise of this book that translators might beneficially consult specific provisions of patent laws, rules and regulations, at the very least for the purpose of understanding the coherence of patent source texts, and most significantly for guaranteeing, beyond translation accuracy and appropriateness, the *compliance* of translations, with those provisions of patent laws, rules and regulations that apply. An irreducible difference in perspectives on the provisions of patent law, which should, by the same token, also settle any issues of territorial boundaries between legal and translation professions.

The driving force, originally motivating the selection of those provisions of patent law included in this book, was thus a true desire to prevent the layering of costly translation errors. Errors with consequences that may invalidate a patent application during the examination process, or that might make the invention un-defendable in case of litigation. For example, according to the provisions of the *Patent Cooperation Treaty*, *Article 46*, a translation error found to extend the scope of the invention results in *nullification of the original* international patent application. A consequence that places severe responsibility on translators.

In turn, consulting the law from a translator's perspective, in view of preventing translation errors, amounted to uncovering the prescriptions that govern the *language of patents*. Prescriptions that translators must heed. Prescriptions that sometimes even override traditional grammatical rules. For example, the structure, form, and content of patent claims are *exclusively* specified in patent regulations, down to punctuation, capital letters, and the definition of a legal sentence. Likewise, but on a discursive level, the disclosure of an invention, in exchange of patenting rights, is also completely regulation-driven, considering that the provisions of the law clearly determine both the content *and* the order in which an invention is recited. Thus, the *language of patents* distinctly, and repeatedly, emerged in a *speech act* perspective as language uses *performing the prescriptions of the law*. Language uses, sometimes quite unique, calling for explicitness that might only be sourced in the coherence of the provisions of the law. Most significantly, language uses that are *also* required to perform the requirements of the law *in translation*.

Unintended as it was to characterize the *language of patents*, this book is replete with additional takeaways of significant interest to patents translation. Indeed, more than one question perhaps lurking in the patent translator's mind, is likely to find an answer in this book. For example, a general question begging for a legal explanation might be lingering about: *why* patents grant *negative rights* to exclude others from making, using, or producing an invention, rather than *positive rights* for inventors or their assignees to produce, market and license their inventions? Or a more specific question might remain as to: *why* so many preferences, such as "*preferred, more preferred* and *most preferred*" are recited in patents, regardless of the domain of invention? These are just two questions that this book definitely answers explicitly. Answers found incidentally to pertinent questions, which are nonetheless secondary to the primary purpose of this book. The primary purpose of this book being to examine the sorts of constraints that the provisions of patent laws and international agreements place on language use, *a fortiori* on translation, with the stated purpose of preventing errors.

What transpires also from this book is that the focus on the provisions of the law, with direct impact on translation, tends to offset some of the known complexity of patent source texts (ST). Patent ST-complexity essentially arises from the subject matter of inventions, at the frontier of any given field, whether physics, chemistry, biochemistry, apparel production, orthopedic implant surgery or other. However, understanding how any single invention is recited, and claimed, regardless of the domain, including the specifics of the formulations, and the details of what is included in the disclosure, provides a framework. A framework that, in turn, reduces some of the unknown, and thereby facilitates the understanding of the invention. An invention which, by definition, charts a hitherto *unknown* portion of knowledge, at the horizon of any given field.

The curated provisions of patent rules, regulations, and laws, which appear in this book, are organized into 42 different sections, each time analyzed for their specific implications in the translation process. Within each section, examples are provided. Examples extracted from specific patents, and/or from case law, cited in legal journals, and in the United States Patent and Trademark Office (USPTO) *Manual of Patent Examination Procedure* (MPEP). The focus is essentially on the language used in US *utility* patents, but unexclusively. Wherever relevant, the *European Patent Cooperation Treaty* (EPC) is invoked, in reference to corresponding language use in European (EP) patents. Likewise, the *Patent Cooperation Treaty* (PCT) is also invoked, in reference to corresponding language use in World Intellectual Property Organization (WIPO) patents. Corresponding counterparts of the US MPEP, found in administrative instructions and guidelines at the European Patent Office (EPO), and the World Intellectual Property Organization (WIPO), are also cited, wherever suitable, as a source of clarification and interpretation for the selected provisions of patent laws, rules, regulations, and international agreements. In certain sections of this book, the parallelism of the language used in US, European, and World Intellectual Property patents, is also explicitly highlighted, via the consensus on intellectual vs. real property that exists in governing patent laws, rules, regulations, and international agreements.

To facilitate navigation of the highlighted provisions of laws, rules and regulations, selected for their relevance to translation, each section of this book includes its own references to citations of both the law and exemplary patents. Three Appendices are also provided at the end of the book, each Appendix compiling the complete list of citations, according to patent granting authority (USPTO, EPO, and WIPO). References to the *Patent Cooperation Treaty* (PCT), in some instances, are cited in French, English and Spanish, official languages of WIPO. Whereas references to the *European Patent Convention* (EPC), in some instances, are cited in English, French and German, the official languages of the European Patent Office.

Three disclaimers are hereby incorporated in this book. The first disclaimer is that this book is *not* intended to provide any sort of legal advice. This book specifically addresses translators engaging in translation, in particular patent translators, and those translators with an interest in patent translation, or seeking to specialize in this domain. The second disclaimer is that this book does not seek to be exhaustive in the presentation of provisions of patent rules and regulations for their linguistic impact on translation. A practical cut-off point is required for the completion of any book. The third disclaimer is that this book does not seek to derail science in its exposure, for example, of the transgenic animal industry. Likewise, this book does not seek to diminish the unquestionable advances of the pharmaceutical industry in connection to the development of patented drugs. A small section on *patent controversies* was added to this book for the reasons put forward in the discussion of their relevance to translation—*strictly* in abstraction of any other presupposed agenda.

Finally, several people have pointed out that this work is actually *ex-rated*. *Ex-rated*—because the study took shape within the context of developing and teaching, several patent translation courses, at the NYU School of Professional Studies (SPS), where I am now an ex-NYU Adjunct. As a result, this book was written under the umbrellas of both SJSU and Kent State, where I am currently teaching, and where I have the privilege to explore patents translation.

San Francisco, July 2023

Acknowledgements

I stand on the shoulders of giants. Expert patent translators who published two edited volumes of *The American Translators Association (ATA) Patent Translator's Handbook*, one of which specifically covers Japanese patents. Two *Handbooks* that have stood the test of time since they were published, now more than 25 and 15 years ago respectively. Contrary to other domains of professional translation, the literature on patents translation is truly scant. Thus, I would like to thank the authors of the *Handbooks* for their insights, which generously informed both the preparation of my patent translation courses at New York University (NYU), and the research for this book.

Even as I began teaching patents translation, and blogging about the ubiquity of patents in everyday life, I could not have ever imagined writing this book. But now that this book is written, I hope that in many ways the work will simply be a worthy supplement to the *Handbooks*. Mostly, I hope that the 2007 *Handbook* authors will have forgiven me for not having first brought to fruition an updated, edited edition of the 2007 *Handbook*. The truth of the matter is that this book took me all over the map, before coming into sharp focus.

I would also like to thank all the participants in my NYU patents translation courses, who both encouraged and challenged me. I was encouraged because some of the participants in my courses were professional lawyers. Law professionals, who were used to referring directly to the provisions of laws and regulations. However, they were also genuinely surprised by an approach that consisted in examining, in detail, the language uses invoked to *perform* the requirements of applicable laws, in view of analyzing the impact of laws on translation. The lawyers who participated in the classes were pleasantly surprised because this take on the law was certainly not the usual (lawyer's) way of turning to the provisions of laws and regulations. However, for the purposes of translation, they generously agreed that this approach also made a lot of sense.

This endorsement, coming from representatives of the legal profession, in turn encouraged me to pursue the corpus-based research project underlying this book, which initially systematically informed the course content and methodology. Indeed, under other circumstances, it might have been quite presumptuous of me to turn to the law for answers that I was after all *diverting* for the purposes of teaching patents translation. However, both method and approach were clearly well received, just as such an approach would be applauded, much later, within the context of ATA Conference presentations.

Participants in my NYU patents translation courses were also my biggest challengers. Challengers, because they asked important questions. Questions that fed directly into the mapped-out corpus-based research process, as they learned to research the language uses they found, performing the requirements of the law, just as I had for the preparation of the courses. I also found myself switching translation direction (from French into English, to English into French), when my NYU French medical translation course participants also demanded a course on patents translation, in the other direction.

Looking back to designing a French patents translation course, upon student-request, the process gave me many insights on what could possibly compare from one patenting system to another. However, I also found myself starting from scratch a second time, searching for answers on what impacted translation in the codes and regulations. Only this time, I was searching in French, essentially at the *Institut National de la Propriété Industrielle* (INPI) in France, and also the *Office de la Propriété Intellectuelle du Canada* (OPIC), with an occasional Francophone foray in West Africa, at the *Organisation Africaine de la Propriété Intellectuelle* (OAPI), considering that at least one, State Department employee, and course participant, hailed from Cameroon. A second time, turning to the law for information on what governed recitation, and what mattered to translation, a second time with a different set of patent laws, in a different language, in three different francophone continents.

For the opportunity to design my first, fully online, Master's Program, French to English, 16-week patents translation course, which had to be approved by the New York Board of Education, I am deeply thankful to Dr. Milena Savova, former Director of the Master's in Science Program in Translation, at NYU. After, having prepared a complete, French to English, 16-week, fully online, Master's course in French Medical Translation, I will always remember when Milena told me that I had a much bigger task, *shortly* ahead, which was to teach the Masters course in Patents Translation (French to English), a course that had never been taught before at NYU. I was thrilled, but I clearly had not understood what I had gotten myself into, nor had I understood that I was *not* teaching French medical translation the following semester.

For the subsequent opportunity to also teach French patents translation, in the former NYU French Translation Certificate Program, and the generous encouragements received, I am also deeply grateful to Steven Gendell, former Coordinator of the NYU French Translation Certificate program, Flaubert translator, and teacher *extraordinaire*.

San Francisco, July 2023

Acronyms and abbreviations

AppFT	Patent Application Full-Text and Image Database
ATA	American Translators Association
ART	Antiretroviral therapies
AR	Augmented Reality
AU	Australia
CBE	Convention sur le brevet européen (French abbreviation for European Patent Convention)
CFR 37	Code of Federal Regulations, Title 37
CIPO	Canadian Intellectual Property Office
DOI	Digital Object Identifier
EP	European patent
EPC	European Patent Convention
EPO	European Patent Office
DE	Germany
FDA	Food and Drug Administration
FIT	Fédération Internationale des Traducteurs [International Federation of Translators]
FR	France
GMOs	Genetically Modified Organisms
GMCs	Genetically Modified Crops
GURTs	Genetic Use Restriction Technologies
HT	herbicide tolerant (crop)
HR	herbicide resistant (crop)
IR	insect resistant (crop)
INID codes	Internationally agreed Numbers for the Identification of bibliographic Data
INPI	Institut National de la Propriété Industrielle (French national patent office)
IPEA	International Preliminary Examining Authorities
IPC	International Patent Classification system
IP	Intellectual Property
ISA	International Search Authority (delivering opinion on patentability of WO patent application)

ISR	International Search Report
JPO	Japanese Patent Office
KI	knock-in (mice)
KO	knock-out (mice)
MPEP	Manual of Patent Examination Procedures
MT	machine translation
MX	Mexico
NP	Noun Phrase
NZ	New Zealand
OA	Organisation Africaine (French African patent)
OPIC	Office de la propriété intellectuelle du Canada (Canadian IP Office)
OMPI	Office Mondial de la Propriété Intellectuelle (French acronym for WIPO)
PatFT	Patent Full-Text and Image Database
PCT	Patent Cooperation Treaty
PP	prepositional phrase
SI	Système International (French abbreviation for International System of measurements)
SISA	Supplementary International Search Authority
SSR	Single Sentence Rule
ST	Source TextT-
GURT	Trait-specific Genetic Use Restriction Technology
TK	Traditional Knowledge
TT	Target Text
URL	Uniform Resource Locator
USC 35	United States Code, Title 35
USD	United States Design (patent)
USPTO	United States Patent and Trademark OfficeV-
GURT	Variety-specific Genetic Use Restriction Technology
VP	verb phrase
WIPO	World Intellectual Patent Organization
WO	World Organization (patent)

1 Corpus of laws, rules, regulations, international agreements, and administrative instructions

Patents are complex documents. Complex because they are regulated. In other words, almost all aspects of a patent, including such processes as drafting, filing, examining, granting, and litigating in cases of infringement, are informed by the provisions of a dedicated branch of the law. Patent law, a branch that subsumes the rules, regulations and international agreements, governing patents. A dedicated branch, administered by national and international patent offices. The following Table 1.1 brings together the corpus of selected laws, rules, regulations, and international agreements, together with the administrative instructions and guidelines for interpretation, whose selected provisions have informed the corpus-based research, underlying this book.

Implications for translation

The question of relevance to translation arises immediately, since such rules, regulations, and administrative guidelines, listed in Table 1.1, and more selectively in each of the following sections of this book, *clearly* belong to the domain of law. However, relevance to translation is the very question that is answered in this book, where the main premise is that an *understanding* of the provisions of specific rules, regulations and administrative guidelines *must* inform the translation process, to prevent the layering of costly translation errors. Prevention *a fortiori*, considering that the correction of patent translation errors is an arduous, sometimes impossible task (Holthaus, 2019). For example, uninformed choice of the verbs *comprising* vs. *consisting of*, per the provisions of US, European and WIPO rules, might inadvertently result in *closing* a claim, thereby making an invention highly vulnerable to infringement. Therefore, such rules, regulations and guidelines have *everything* to do with translation, even if translators consult them for reasons *vastly* different from those of lawyers, patent agents, inventors, entrepreneurs or even legislators. Indeed, the task of this book was precisely to select, and make explicit how such specific rules, regulations and international conventions impact the translation process; how selected provisions of patent rules and regulations have *direct* linguistic consequences on language uses, even governance on the choices that translators make every step of the way, to completing a patent translation.

DOI: 10.4324/9781003423003-1

Table 1.1 Corpus of laws, rules, regulations, international agreements, and administrative instructions

United States Patent and Trademark Office (USPTO)	*European Patent Office (EPO)*	*UN World Intellectual Property Organization (WIPO)*
US Constitution (1787)	European Patent Convention (EPC)	Patent Cooperation Treaty (PCT)
United States Code Title 35 (*USC35*)	European Guidelines for Examination	Regulations under the PCT
US Code of Federal Regulations Title 37 (*CFR37*)		WIPO Standards, Recommendations and Guidelines
USPTO Manual of Patent Examination Procedure (*MPEP*)		Administrative Instructions under PCT

For translation, such a systematic analysis of selected provisions of rules and regulations with linguistic impact, is not without unintended purpose, considering that the result amounted to a functional definition of the *language of patents*. A language governed by certain rules *outside* of traditional grammar, inclusive of syntax, semantics, and morphology. Thus, the implications of a focus on the above-mentioned rules and regulations, for the purpose of informing the translation process, also include a characterization of *the language of patents*. An identification of the prescriptive rules, in this case, which govern language use, and that *must* become part of a patent translator's competence, in view of producing accurate, appropriate, and equally important, *compliant* translations from a legal perspective.

References

Administrative instructions under the Patent Cooperation Treaty. https://www.wipo.int/pct/en/texts/ai/ai_index.html

European Patent Convention (EPC). https://www.epo.org/law-practice/legal-texts/html/epc/2020/e/index.html

European Guidelines for Examination. https://www.epo.org/law-practice/legal-texts/html/guidelines/e/index.htm

Holthaus, H. (June 25, 2019). The Impact of Errors in Patent Translation. In *the ATA Law Division BLAWG*. www.linkedin.com/pulse/impact-errors-patent-translation-patent-and-technical-translator

Regulations under the Patent Cooperation Treaty. https://www.wipo.int/pct/en/texts/rules/rtoc1.html

US Constitution [Transcript]. https://www.archives.gov/founding-docs/constitution-transcript

US Code Title 35—Patents. https://www.uspto.gov/web/offices/pac/mpep/mpep-9015-appx-l.html

US Code of Federal Regulations Title 37. https://www.uspto.gov/web/offices/pac/mpep/mpep-9020-appx-r.html

USPTO Manual of Patent Examining Procedure (MPEP). https://www.uspto.gov/web/offices/pac/mpep/index.html

WIPO Patent Cooperation Treaty (PCT). https://www.wipo.int/pct/en/texts/articles/atoc.html

WIPO Standards. https://www.wipo.int/standards/en/part_03_standards.html

2 What is a patent?

For those who are just starting their patent translation journey, or those who might have been thrown into patent translation without any background information on the genre, the following succinct preliminaries provide basic information on patents, their long history and function. Most importantly, these preliminaries clearly identify the *source text* that is most often translated in the domain of patents translation, so that everyone might start on the same page.

A simple definition of patents is elusive. Elusive, considering that patents, in the United States, belong to a separate 300-year-old branch of US Law, administered today by more than 10,000 people, at the United States Patent and Trademark Office (USPTO). Thus, the following points selectively highlight essential aspects of the definition of patents. Selected essential aspects of a patent, which together might function to answer the *not-so-simple* question: *What is a patent*?

Provisions for a patenting and copyright system in the United States date as far back as the *United States Constitution*, in 1787, at the founding of the Union. Indeed, the provisions of *Article 1*, *Section 8*, setting forth the Powers of Congress, specify particularly, on Line 8, that Congress shall have the Power:

> [...] To promote the Progress of Science and useful Arts, by securing for limited Times to Authors and Inventors the exclusive Right to their respective Writings and Discoveries [...]

Scrolling forward to the 1950s, past the eighteenth-century *US Constitution* that set forth the promotion of Intellectual Property, and the nineteenth-century legislative process, *Title 35 of the United States Code* codified all previous six US Federal Patent Acts. A codification where the provisions of *Section 101* set forth the basic idea of a US *patent*, in terms of *inventions patentable*:

> Whoever invents or discovers any *new* and *useful* process, machine, manufacture, or composition of matter, or any *new* and *useful* improvement thereof, may obtain a patent therefor, *subject to the conditions and requirements of this title.*
>
> [italics mine]

DOI: 10.4324/9781003423003-2

Thus, an inventor might obtain a patent for the discovery of new and useful inventions, including improvements, providing certain conditions and requirements are met.

Implications for translation

The above statute and its origins in the United States Constitution of 1787 point to a clearly definable *patent* genre, whose prescriptions are codified in a separate branch of the law. A *genre* where translation specialization is possible, with a welcome breadth of topic. A welcome breadth of topic, considering that the specification "*any new and useful process, machine, manufacture or composition of matter*" plus improvements, cuts across all domains of human invention. Whether human invention pertains to science, technology, engineering, medicine, pharmaceuticals, cosmetics, or fashion, plus more. Indeed, such breadth of inventive activity gives room for patent translators even to specialize in one or several domains of invention, while still working within the clearly separate *genre* of patents.

References

35 USC 101—Invention patentable. https://www.uspto.gov/web/offices/pac/mpep/mpep-9015-appx-l.html#d0e302376

US Constitution—Article I Section 8 Line 8 (1787). https://www.archives.gov/founding-docs/constitution-transcript

3 When is a patent?

The conditions and requirements that must be met for obtaining a US patent are generally known as the conditions of *patentability*. US conditions and requirements of *patentability* include: *utility, novelty* and *non-obviousness. Utility* is set forth in *Title 35* of the *United States Code Section 101* cited above, in the repetition of the terms "*new and useful*" and further specified in the *Manual of Patent Examination Procedure (MPEP) Section 2107* as an assertion of "*specific and substantial utility that is credible to a person of ordinary skill in the art*". The remaining two conditions: *novelty* and *non-obvious subject matter* are respectively set forth in *Title 35 USC Sections 102* and *103*.

The provisions of *Title 35 USC Section 102* set forth the condition of *novelty* as follows:

> A person shall be entitled to a patent unless—
> (1) the claimed invention was patented, described in a printed publication, or in public use, on sale, or otherwise available to the public before the effective filing date of the claimed invention [...]

whereas the provisions of *Title 35 USC Section 103* set forth the condition of *non-obviousness* as follows:

> A patent for a claimed invention may not be obtained [...] if the differences between the claimed invention and the prior art are such that the claimed invention as a whole would have been obvious before the effective filing date of the claimed invention to a person having ordinary skill in the art to which the claimed invention pertains.

In a nutshell, regarding *novelty* and *non-obviousness*, it is not enough for an invention to be new. The invention must also be *non-obvious* to a person having ordinary skill in the relevant art. Consider, for example, the significant inventive step taken in Sir James Dyson's *bladeless* fan. No fan ever existed without blades, prior to Dyson's *bladeless* fan. Indeed, no one could even conceive of moving air in a room without the movement of blades. The fact of the matter is that the prior art of fan inventions was exclusively focused on blade design,

DOI: 10.4324/9781003423003-3

Table 3.1 Patentability terminology (English and French)

Conditions of patentability (English)	*Critères de brevetabilité (français)*
novelty	*nouveauté*
non-obviousness	*inventivité*
utility	*application industrielle*

until Sir James Dyson, a knighted British engineer, invented the *air multiplier* technology that drives the *bladeless* fan, and all of its subsumed inventive parts. A game-changing technology, since such technology is far safer (especially for children and pets), far more efficient and pleasant, with none of the turbulence and noise associated with blade fans.

Implications for translation

The conditions of *patentability* are crucial to inventors, and their representatives, when filing for a patent. In contrast, *patentability* is unrelated to translation. However, an *understanding* of *patentability*, and the conditions that apply, will simplify the task of translating any communication that might arise between examiners and applicants, related to the issue of *patentability*, and the degree to which conditions are met. Likewise, *understanding* of the terms related to *patentability* will facilitate locating established translations that perform the same function, as well as any differences that might exist in the concept of *utility*. For French patents, for example, the corresponding terms in use for referring to the *conditions of patentability—novelty*, *non-obviousness*, and *utility*—are, respectively, *critères de brevetabilité, nouveauté*, *inventivité*, and *application industrielle*, as listed in Table 3.1.

References

35 USC 101—Invention patentable. https://www.uspto.gov/web/offices/pac/mpep/mpep-9015-appx-l.html#d0e302376

35 USC 102—Conditions of patentability: novelty. https://www.uspto.gov/web/offices/pac/mpep/mpep-9015-appx-l.html#al_d1fbe1_234ed_52

35 USC 103—Conditions of patentability: non-obvious subject matter. https://www.uspto.gov/web/offices/pac/mpep/mpep-9015-appx-l.html#al_d1fbe1_19797_b0

MPEP Section 2107—Guidelines for examination of applications for compliance with the utility requirement. [R-11.2013]. https://www.uspto.gov/web/offices/pac/mpep/s2107.html

4 What does a patent do?

Contrary to popular belief, a patent does *not* grant the right to produce or sell an invention. A patent grants inventors, their assignees or heirs, the *right to exclude others* from producing, or using the invention without some form of authorization or a license. Thus, a patented invention protects inventors. The patent enables inventors to recoup the costs, or time spent inventing, testing, and bringing their invention to market. Time to recoup afforded by the right to prevent others from engaging in the same activity for a given period of time.

The right to exclude others is specified in the provisions of *Title 35 USC Section 154 (a) 1*, as follows:

> Every patent shall contain a short title of the invention and a grant to the patentee, his heirs or assigns, of the right to exclude others from making, using, offering for sale, or selling the invention throughout the United States or importing the invention into the United States, and, if the invention is a process, of the right to exclude others from using, offering for sale or selling throughout the United States, or importing into the United States, products made by that process [...]

Whereas the *reason* for excluding others, in abstraction of economic considerations, is essentially explained, in *Section 301 of the MPEP*, regarding *Ownership/Assignability of Patents and Applications*. A reason, which lies in preventing conflicts *internal* to the legal system, specified as follows:

> [...] Ownership of the patent does not furnish the owner with the **right** to make, use, offer for sale, sell, or import the claimed invention because there may be other legal considerations precluding same (e.g., existence of another patent owner with a dominant patent, failure to obtain FDA approval of the patented invention, an injunction by a court against making the product of the invention, or a national security related issue). [...]

In other words, a conflict would exist, if for example, positive patenting rights were granted to inventors, enabling them to start manufacturing a product that

DOI: 10.4324/9781003423003-4

had not (yet) obtained an authorization to market, from the Food and Drug Administration (FDA).

Implications for translation

Violation of the inventor's exclusive rights to *exclude others* from using, producing and/or marketing a patented invention without authorization or license, gives rise to *patent infringement cases*. The court documents produced in connection with such legal action might also fall under the purview of patents translation, depending on the client, or the case.

References

35 USC 154 (a) 1—Contents and term of patent: provisional rights. https://www.uspto.gov/web/offices/pac/mpep/mpep-9015-appx-l.html#d0e303482

MPEP Section 301—Ownership/assignability of patents and applications. [R-10.2019]. https://www.uspto.gov/web/offices/pac/mpep/s301.html

5 When is a patent a source text for translation?

Prior to passing the tests of *invention patentable*, in view of obtaining rights to exclude others from using, producing, or marketing an invention, the inventor or applicant must file an application that *discloses* the invention. The *disclosure* requirement is explained in *Section 608* of the USPTO *Manual of Patent Examination Procedure* (MPEP), as follows:

> To obtain a valid patent, a patent application as filed must contain a full and clear *disclosure of the invention* in the manner prescribed by 35 U.S.C. 112(a). The requirement for an adequate disclosure ensures that the public receives something in return for the *exclusionary rights* that are granted to the inventor by a patent.

Implications for translation

It is the disclosure of the invention, together with the claims to the invention, found in patent applications, which comprise the essential source texts in the domain of patents translation. Regardless of the invention category, whether bird feed, space engine stage, therapeutic molecule, or shoe sole, inventors are required to *disclose* their invention, according to numerous specific rules and regulations, examined in detail further into this book. A rule-governed disclosure, which both constrains and standardizes the way in which an invention is recited. A disclosure that, in turn, offers a source text with specific rule-governed features, invoking recurring languages uses for translation.

References

35 USC 112 (a)—Best mode requirement and obligation to disclose. https://www.uspto.gov/web/offices/pac/mpep/mpep-9015-appx-l.html#d0e302824912

MPEP Section 608—Disclosure. [R-11.2013]. https://www.uspto.gov/web/offices/pac/mpep/s608.html

DOI: 10.4324/9781003423003-5

6 The Person Having Ordinary Skill in the Art (PHOSITA)

According to the provisions of *Title 35 USC Section 103*, previously cited, even if an invention fulfils all the conditions of *novelty* and *utility*, a patent still might not be obtained. Indeed, for a product, process, machine, composition of matter, or improvement to count as a *patentable invention*, it must also be *non-obvious*, roughly in the sense of *ingenious*, to *a Person Having Ordinary Skill In The Art (PHOSITA)*, a.k.a. *l'homme du métier* in French.

Thus, a corollary question to the issue *of non-obviousness* in the examination of the *patentability* of an invention is the determination of *who* would decide on *non-obviousness*. The provisions of the *MPEP Section 2141.03* shed the following light on the level of *ordinary skill in the art* needed, or on the knowledge attributed to a *PHOSITA*. Most importantly, the provisions of *MPEP Section 2141.03* clearly specify that the *PHOSITA* is not a real person, but a hypothetical one. In other words, the *PHOSITA* is *a standard* used in the determination of non-obviousness (Hill & Pate, 2022).

> The person of ordinary skill in the art is a hypothetical person who is presumed to have known the relevant art at the time of the invention. Factors that may be considered in determining the level of ordinary skill in the art may include: (A) "type of problems encountered in the art"; (B) "prior art solutions to those problems"; (C) "rapidity with which innovations are made"; (D) "sophistication of the technology"; and (E) "educational level of active workers in the field". In a given case, every factor may not be present, and one or more factors may predominate.
>
> [*MPEP 2141.03*]

As a result, for an invention to become patentable, it is *not enough for the invention to be new* and *useful*. An act of invention, called an *inventive step*, must have taken place. An act that appears *non-obvious* to a hypothetical *PHOSITA*, at the time of the invention. In other words, the novel product, process, machine, composition of matter, or improvement must subsume *more* than the ordinary skill of a hypothetical person involved in the art, at the time of the invention. The work of an *inventor*, whether by extraordinary insight or systematic research, must have intervened.

DOI: 10.4324/9781003423003-6

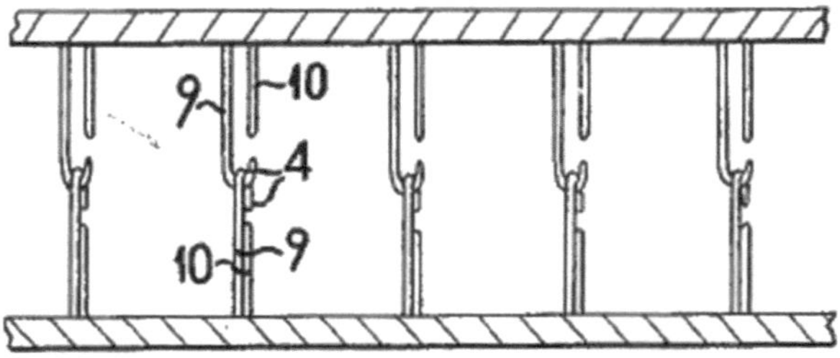

Figure 6.1 Velcro™ hook and loop invention (US2717437)

A famous example of an *inventive step*, or *non-obviousness* occurred for the Velcro™ invention. Prior to G. de Mestral's Velcro™ invention, many sorts of fasteners existed. Ties, bows, zippers, hooks… but no one ever thought of emulating the sort of attachment that exists when the burrs of *Burdock* thistles burrow inside pets' fur, or stubbornly cling onto clothing. The manufacture of fabric with a *hook* side, which attaches to a *loop* side, was a completely unknown process, which was also completely *un-thought of*, even to those various persons skilled in the art of fasteners. Indeed, it was so odd, and *non-obvious* to *everyone*, that it took years for Velcro™ to actually become a commercially viable product, initially for use only on scuba diving equipment.

Implications for translation

Inventive steps and the *condition of non-obviousness* relative to the *PHOSITA*, invoked for determining the *patentability* of an invention, are tasks and processes unrelated to translation. However, it is well worth the effort to understand the concept of *non-obviousness*, precisely because *non-obviousness* resolves the apparent contradiction between *improvement* and *invention*, as well as the confusion between *novelty* and *invention*.

In other words, *improvements*, though not entirely new, might also be inventions when they fulfill the conditions of *patentability*, especially *non-obviousness* of that part which is new and improved, relative to the prior art. For example, consider the buzz and anticipation that surrounds the new and improved functionalities of the iPhone each year, whether it is Touch ID, Face ID, or the Always-On functionalities, each of which are patented inventions. Conversely, a process, product, machine, or composition of matter that is new, is not necessarily an invention, unless the condition of *non-obviousness* is fulfilled. For example, consider the new colors regularly added to the product line of iPhone Silicone Cases, or to the iWatch Classic Silicone bands, none of which new colors are inventions, although the original bands and cases were patented.

Thus, such underlying concepts as *novelty*, *non-obviousness* relative to a *PHOTISA*, and *invention* <u>must</u> be grasped for understanding patent source texts, together with their associated conversations. For example, conversations surfacing as translation jobs, between the patent granting authority and the client. Conversations at this juncture, which might essentially involve examination of patent applications for their *patentability*.

References

35 USC 102—Conditions of patentability: novelty. https://www.uspto.gov/web/offices/pac/mpep/mpep-9015-appx-l.html#al_d1fbe1_234ed_52

35 USC 103—Conditions of patentability: non-obvious subject matter. https://www.uspto.gov/web/offices/pac/mpep/mpep-9015-appx-l.html#al_d1fbe1_19797_b0

Hill, G.K. and A.J. Pate. (Sept. 24, 2022). Avoiding confusion of PHOSITA (Person Having Ordinary Skill in the Art). American Intellectual Property Association (AIPLA). https://www.aipla.org/list/innovate-articles/avoiding-confusion-of-phosita

MPEP Section 2141.03—Level of ordinary skill in the art. [R-10.2019]. https://www.uspto.gov/web/offices/pac/mpep/s2141.html#d0e209300

Cited patent

MESTRAL, George de (1955). Velvet type fabric and method of producing same (Patent No. US2717437). United States Patent and Trademark Office (USPTO). https://image-ppubs.uspto.gov/dirsearch-public/print/downloadPdf/2717437

7 Prior art

What is the *prior art* in a patent? What purpose does it have? What role does it play for translators?

The prior art of a patent essentially incudes, but is not limited to:

- patents, including published and abandoned patent applications, which count as "prior public knowledge or prior public availability" [*MPEP 901.01*]
- foreign patent documents [*MPEP 901.05*]
- non-patent publication or other printed materials [*MPEP 901.06*]

Together, this material will be used to assess the *patentability of an invention*, in particular whether the claimed invention meets the conditions of *novelty*. *Novelty* is specified in the *United States Federal Code Title 35*, *Section 102*, essentially as *the absence of description* "[...] *in a printed publication, or in public use, on sale, or otherwise available to the public before the effective filing date of the claimed invention* [...]".

Implications for translation

What translators need to know about the *prior art* of a patent is entirely different from what inventors or examiners are seeking to find out, in view of determining the *patentability* of an invention. For translators, the *prior art* of a patent is *the best source of documentary information available* concerning the invention.

Prior art information is conveniently recited right at the beginning of a patent specification, in the (regulated) section addressing the *Background of the invention*. In this dedicated section of the specification, the *prior art*, such as patents, patent applications, articles, book chapters or conference papers, will be cited within the context of a narrative, designed to clearly highlight the problems associated with the state of the prior art, and how the invention is seeking to resolve such known problems. For translators, this section is most useful, since the *prior art* information provided is usually enough to *gist* what

DOI: 10.4324/9781003423003-7

the invention is about. The *prior art* references provided also supply extra resources, such as:

- additional documentary information for understanding the invention and associated terminology.
- model patents or patent applications in the target language, if the cited *prior art* patents have already been translated.
- and keywords for further *googling*—if necessary.

For typical examples of prior art, explicitly incorporated as *Background of the invention*, in the narrative of the patent specification, consider for example the extract included below, from the patent, US6102245, titled *Drinking vessel with valve*. A patent awarded to the well-known British industrial designer, Mandy Haberman, for the Anywayup cup™ invention, called a *sippy* cup in the United States.

> Trainer cups (that is a cup or mug provided with a lid having a mouthpiece—usually a spout—associated there with) are well known and have been designed to bridge the gap between use of a baby's feeding bottle and use of a normal cup or glass by a young child. Such a trainer cup will often be a child's first step in learning to feed itself. As this period in a child's development will usually coincide with the cutting of its first teeth, quite apart from the child's inherent difficulty in handling what is new to it which may lead to the cup inadvertently being knocked over, the irritability characteristic of teething allied with the natural exuberance of young children tends to exacerbate what is frequently a noisy and messy experience.
>
> The existence of the lid may reduce or at least delay the effect of knocking the cup over but will not deter a child from shaking the cup violently up and down. Neither will the lid delay spillage for very long if the cup is knocked over. Notwithstanding that trainer cups of this kind have been known for a very lengthy period of time, I am unaware of any practical arrangement for overcoming these self-evident problems.
>
> In the somewhat different field of babies feeding bottles, I have myself designed arrangements in which a valve interrupts the flow of fluid from the interior of the bottle through a teat or other mouthpiece (see for example my U.S. Pat. Nos. 2,131,301 and 2,169,210). Bottles to my design have achieved some commercial success particularly in the rather specialized field of feeding babies with sucking problems.
>
> Other arrangements proposing valved feeding bottles such as U.S. Pat. Nos. 4,135,513, 3,704803 and 4,339,046 and UK Patents 460 274 and 1253398 have been proposed in the patent literature but I am not aware that any of these proposals have proved of practical utility. I am not

aware of any of them having been marketed. Nevertheless, it is clear that there have been a series of proposals by different workers for the valving of babies feeding bottles.

References

MPEP Section 901.01—Canceled matter in U.S. patent files. [R-08.2017]. https://www.uspto.gov/web/offices/pac/mpep/s901.html#d0e110030

MPEP Section 901.05—Foreign patent documents. [R-08.2017]. https://www.uspto.gov/web/offices/pac/mpep/s901.html#d0e110750

MPEP Section 901.06—Nonpatent Publications. [R-08.2012]. https://www.uspto.gov/web/offices/pac/mpep/s901.html#d0e113237

35 USC 102—Conditions for patentability: novelty. https://www.uspto.gov/web/offices/pac/mpep/mpep-9015-appx-l.html#d0e302383

Cited patent

Haberman, M.N. (2000). Drinking vessel with valve (Patent No. US6102245). United States Patent and Trademark Office (USPTO). https://image-ppubs.uspto.gov/dirsearch-public/print/downloadPdf/6102245

8 The International Search Report (ISR)

For an inventor filling an international application for a *Patent Cooperation Treaty* (PCT) patent, designated WO, the preliminary examination process will be based on an *International Search Report* (ISR), combined with an opinion, regarding fulfilment of the conditions of *patentability*: *novelty*, *inventive step*, and *industrial applicability*.

The PCT ISR is carried out on *prior art* in the language of publication, or in the language of the translation of the international application. Per the provisions of the PCT *International Search and Preliminary Examination Guidelines*, Section 17.52:

> An international application filed in Arabic, Chinese, English, French, German, Korean, Japanese, Portuguese, Russian or Spanish, is published in any one of those ten languages, designated official publication languages for PCT patents. An international application filed in any other language is published in the language of the translation, into one of the ten, above-cited, official publication languages.

Just for information, the PCT, governed by the United Nations, World Intellectual Property Organization (WIPO), comprising 156 signatory states (in 2022), offers an opportunity to file a single international patent application. A single patent application that secures protection within any (or all) designated member states, instead of having to file separate applications, in each of the contracting states, to obtain protection. For more details on the examination process of *Patent Cooperation Treaty* (PCT) WO patents, see the *PCT Examination Guidelines, Chapt. 2 Overview of the International Stage*, listed in the below reference section.

Implications for translation

For translators, the *International Search Report* (ISR) serves an entirely different purpose than that, which motivates the examination process, carried out to determine the *patentability* of an invention. As a document containing the results of a *prior art* search, conveniently listed in a report, published together

DOI: 10.4324/9781003423003-8

with International WO-designated patents and patent applications, the ISR functions as another *invaluable documentary source of information.*

Unlike references to the *prior art*, included in the narrative at the beginning of a patent application, informing the *Background of the invention*, the *International Search Report* (ISR) is delivered, to WIPO and the applicant, by the International Search Authorities (ISAs). International Search Authorities are selected signatory state patent offices, variously designated to carry out the international search of prior art, and to deliver an opinion on the *patentability* of the invention. The International Search Report (ISR), which is appended to the patent, after the claims section, lists the patents and publications retrieved in the search. The patents and publications retrieved are indexed according to a series of categories, summarizing the International Search Authority opinion. See Table 8.1 below for the key to the categories of prior art documents, cited in an ISR.

In sum, for patent translators, the information contained within the International Search Report is invaluable. This information also serves purposes different from those invoked for inventors and patent examiners. The patents and printed materials cited in an ISR (see sample in Table 8.2), variously indexed to reflect the authority's opinion on *patentability*, offer perfect documentary resources. Resources for further understanding an invention and its dedicated terminology, or for finding target language models, when the referenced materials are already translated. In general, the ISR citations might also offer a starting point for additional dictionary- or google-based searches.

Table 8.1 Categories of cited prior art documents in a PCT ISR (International Search Report)

International Search Report categories for cited documents	
* Special categories of cited documents "A" document defining the general state of the art which is not considered to be of particular relevance "E" earlier document but published on or after the international filing date "L" document which may throw doubts on priority claim(s), or which is cited to establish the publication date of another citation or other special reason (as specified). "O" document referring to an oral disclosure, use, exhibition or other means "P" document published prior to the international priority date claimed	"T" later document published after the international filing date or priority date and not in conflict with the application but cited to understand the principle or theory underlying the invention "X" document of particular relevance; the claimed invention cannot be considered novel or cannot be considered to involve an inventive step when the document is taken alone "Y" document of particular relevance; the claimed invention cannot be considered to involve an inventive step when the document is combined with one or more other such documents, such combination being obvious to a person skilled in the art "&" document member of the same patent family

Table 8.2 Sample International Search Report (ISR) for WO2007088279

INTERNATIONAL SEARCH REPORT

International application No
PCT/FR2007/000187

A. CLASSIFICATION OF SUBJECT MATTER
INV. A47J37/04 A47J36/16 A47J43/07

According to International Patent Classification (IPC) or to both national classification and IPC

B. FIELDS SEARCHED

Minimum documentation searched (classification system followed by classification symbols)
A47J

Documentation searched other than minimum documentation to the extent that such documents are included in the fields searched

Electronic data base consulted during the international search (name of data base and, where practical, search terms used)
EPO-Internal

C. DOCUMENTS CONSIDERED TO BE RELEVANT

Category*	Citation of document, with indication, where appropriate, of the relevant passages	Relevant to claim No.
X	FR 2 871 042 A (SEB SA SOCIETE ANONYME) 9 December 2005 (2005-12-09) page 5, line 22 - page 30; claims 4,7; figures 2-4	1-17, 23-29
X	US 2002/027175 A1 (CAPP RAND) 7 March 2002 (2002-03-07)	1,3-7, 10,12, 15-17, 20-29
Y	paragraphs [0043] - [0046]; figures 1,2	18,19
Y	US 2004/065211 A1 (MCNAIR JOHN DUNCAN) 8 April 2004 (2004-04-08) paragraph [0043]; figures 1,2,4	18,19
X	US 2005/223906 A1 (XU ZHAOXIA ET AL) 13 October 2005 (2005-10-13) paragraphs [0018] - [0128]; figures 1,2	1-12,16, 22-29

☐ Further documents are listed in the continuation of Box C. ☒ See patent family annex.

* Special categories of cited documents :

"A" document defining the general state of the art which is not considered to be of particular relevance
"E" earlier document but published on or after the international filing date
"L" document which may throw doubts on priority claim(s) or which is cited to establish the publication date of another citation or other special reason (as specified)
"O" document referring to an oral disclosure, use, exhibition or other means
"P" document published prior to the international filing date but later than the priority date claimed

"T" later document published after the international filing date or priority date and not in conflict with the application but cited to understand the principle or theory underlying the invention
"X" document of particular relevance; the claimed invention cannot be considered novel or cannot be considered to involve an inventive step when the document is taken alone
"Y" document of particular relevance; the claimed invention cannot be considered to involve an inventive step when the document is combined with one or more other such documents, such combination being obvious to a person skilled in the art.
"&" document member of the same patent family

Date of the actual completion of the international search	Date of mailing of the international search report
6 June 2007	13/06/2007

Name and mailing address of the ISA/	Authorized officer
European Patent Office, P.B. 5818 Patentlaan 2 NL - 2280 HV Rijswijk Tel. (+31-70) 340-2040, Tx. 31 651 epo nl, Fax: (+31-70) 340-3016	Van Bastelaere, Tiny

Form PCT/ISA/210 (second sheet) (April 2005)

The sample ISR shown in Table 8.2 is extracted from the T-Fal® Actifry (low-fat fryer) patent application, WO2007088279, titled *Cooking appliance with stirring means and associated method.*

References

Patent Cooperation Treaty (PCT) *International Search and Preliminary Examination Guidelines*. Part I Introduction and Overview. Chapt. 2 Overview of the International Search Stage. https://www.wipo.int/pct/en/texts/ispe/2_10_12.html

PCT—*International Search and Preliminary Examination Guidelines*. Part V. Written opinion/international preliminary examination report. Chapt. 17.52 Language of the written opinion and the international preliminary examination report. https://www.wipo.int/pct/en/texts/ispe/17_09_55.html#_17_52

Cited patent

Goderiaux, A. and J-C. Bizard (2007). Cooking appliance with stirring means and associated method (Patent Application No. WO2007088279). World Intellectual Property Organization (WIPO). https://patentscope.wipo.int/search/en/detail.jsf?docId=WO2007088279&_cid=P22-LNJ5WO-15053-1

9 Internationally agreed Numbers for the Identification of bibliographic Data (INID) codes

INID is an acronym that stands for Internationally agreed Numbers for the Identification of bibliographic Data. INID numbers appear on the cover sheets of *all* patents, whether *Patent Cooperation Treaty* (WO), *European Patent Convention* (EP), African (OA), or individual country patents such as US patents, or patents designated GB, FR, DE, AU, NZ, MX, or other, and filed nationally, respectively in Great Britain, France, Germany, Australia, New Zealand, or Mexico. According to the USPTO *Manual of Patent Examination Procedure* (MPEP) *Section 901.05(b)*, INID codes provide:

> … a means whereby the various data appearing on the first page of patent and like documents or in patent gazettes can be identified without knowledge of the language used and the laws applied.

Examples of INID codes are the following:

(54) Title of the invention
(71) Name(s) of applicant(s)
(72) Name(s) of inventor(s)
(73) Names of grantee(s) holder(s), assignee(s), or owner(s)
(25) Language in which the application was originally filed
(22) Date(s) of filing the application(s)
(57) Abstract or claim

Thus, the information listed on a patent bibliographic cover sheet is indexed, in each instance, by an INID code. For example, the line of information immediately following INID code (54) might be safely assumed to refer to the *title of the invention*, whether the information appears in Pinyin-, Cyrillic-, Arabic-, or Latin-character print.

Implications for translation

INID codes are also particularly useful for translators, albeit for reasons opposite to those set forth in the provisions of the USPTO MPEP. The fact of the

DOI: 10.4324/9781003423003-9

matter is that the key to INID codes offers a small corpus of standardized multilingual terminology, officially translated into the six major (working) international languages of the UN (English, French, Chinese, Russian, Spanish, and Arabic). Thus, when hesitating between the terms *compte-rendu, resumé* and *abrégé* for translating the term "Abstract" into French, all that is needed is access to the key to the INID code (57) in French (e.g., found in the French version of the World Intellectual Property Organization [WIPO] Standard ST. 9, referenced below). Likewise for Spanish terminology, which might be found in the corresponding Spanish version of the same WIPO Standard ST. 9, also referenced below. For US patents, the key to INID codes in English is copied from the English version of the WIPO Standard ST. 9, in the provisions of the *MPEP Section 901.05(b)*.

Standardized translations of the INID code designations found on patent coversheets, together with their standardized circled reference numbers, also enable translators to prepare templates for their translations, which saves time, complies with filing regulations, and looks terrific. To obtain a font with circled numbers that look like INID codes, beyond the circled number 20, available in Microsoft Word Symbols, download a free *CombiNumerals* font suitcase from the *Font Space*. (See Appendix I for instructions.)

References

MPEP Section 901.05 (b)—Other significant data. [R-08.2012]. https://www.uspto.gov/web/offices/pac/mpep/s901.html#d0e112731

OMPI ST. 9—Recommandation concernant les données bibliographiques. [French]. https://www.wipo.int/standards/fr/pdf/03-09-01.pdf

OMPI Norma ST. 9—Recomendación relativa a los datos bibliográficos contenidos en los documentos de patente y en los CCP o en documentos relacionados con ellos. [Spanish]. https://www.wipo.int/standards/es/pdf/03-09-01.pdf

Font Space—*CombiNumerals*. http://www.fontspace.com/category/numbers,circles

WIPO Standard ST. 9—Recommendation concerning bibliographic data on and relating to patents and SPCS. https://www.wipo.int/export/sites/www/standards/en/pdf/03-09-01.pdf

10 Title of the invention—INID code (54)

The provisions of *Title* 37 *CFR Section 1.72(a)* supply guidance as follows, regarding the title of an invention to be disclosed in a US patent application. Note that the maximum title length is actually quite long, considering that 500 characters is anywhere between 100 and 150 words.

> The title of the invention may not exceed 500 characters in length and must be as short and specific as possible. [...] Unless the title is supplied in an application data sheet (§ 1.76), the title of the invention should appear as a heading on the first page of the specification.

Regarding the title of an invention, the provisions of the *MPEP* further specify that certain words may *not* be used at the beginning of a title:

> The words listed below are not considered as part of the title of an invention, these words should not be included at the beginning of the title of the invention and will be deleted when the Office enters the title into the Office's computer records, and when any patent issues. The term "new" will not be deleted when it is a part of a proper name, such as "New York". Similarly, the term "design" will not be deleted when it is a part of a term, such as "Design-aiding apparatus...".
>
> - A
> - An
> - The
> - Improved
> - Improvement(s) in/for/of
> - New
> - Novel
> - Related to
> - Design
> - Design for/of (a)
> - Ornamental design
> - Ornamental

DOI: 10.4324/9781003423003-10

Considering that an application might be translated to English, which might be filed for European protection, according to the *European Patent Convention* (EPC), or elsewhere in the world, via the World Intellectual Property Organization (WIPO), under the *Patent Cooperation Treaty* (PCT), would the same requirements apply for the invention titles of international (WO) or (EP) patents? Below, the provisions for two more patent title regulations, respectively for European (EP) patents, filed via the European Patent Office, and world (WO) patents, filed via the United Nations World Intellectual Property Organization (WIPO).

European (EP) patents

The *European Patent Convention* (EPC) *Rule 41(2)(b)* omits word counts, opting instead for content, and provides the following guidelines for invention titles:

> [...] the title of the invention, which shall clearly and concisely state the technical designation of the invention and shall exclude all fancy names; [...]

If "fancy names" raises questions, then the *European Guidelines for Examination* further clarify the provisions of the *EPC Rule 41(2)(b)*, and in general what to omit from titles, as follows:

(1) Personal names, fancy names, the word "patent" or similar terms of a non-technical nature which do not serve to identify the invention should not be used.
(2) The abbreviation "etc.", being vague, should not be used and should be replaced by an indication of what it is intended to cover.
(3) Titles such as "Method", "Apparatus", "Chemical Compounds" alone or similar vague titles do not meet the requirement that the title must clearly state the technical designation of the invention.
(4) Trade names and trademarks should also not be used. The Receiving Section, however, need only intervene when names are used which, according to common general knowledge, are trade names or trademarks.

World Intellectual Property Organization (WO) patents

Regulations under the *Patent Cooperation Treaty* (PCT) specify word count, in *Rule 4.3* as follows:

> The title of the invention shall be short (preferably from two to seven words when in English or translated into English) and precise.

The provisions of WIPO Standard ST. 15 supply substantial additional guidelines for the wording of titles, including examples, indexing each of the guidelines. In the dedicated reference section below, references to the provisions of WIPO Standard ST. 15 are also listed for French and Spanish.

Finally, the provisions of PCT regulations, *Rule 37.2*, specify that when the title is "missing or found defective", and the applicant does not supply a new one, the International Search Authority provides a title for the invention in the language of publication.

Implications for translation

Beyond the USPTO, EPO and WIPO guidelines for invention titles cited above, National patent offices also set forth their own regulations and examination procedures for the invention titles of patent applications filed nationally. The point is that all aspects of a patent application, reciting and claiming an invention, are *regulated*, right down to the selection words, permitted or not, and even punctuation. An understanding of such constraints, placed on source and target patent texts, prevents translators from walking into a "mine field". For invention titles in particular, precision and concision are probably the most common guidelines. Common guidelines augmented with specific characters counts, terms to avoid, and an understanding of how consistency in the choice of terminology is going to play out in the disclosure of the invention, considering the notions of *ascertainability* and *attendance* explicated further into this book.

References

37 CFR 1.72(a)—Title and abstract. https://www.uspto.gov/web/offices/pac/mpep/mpep-9020-appx-r.html#d0e320224

European Patent Convention. Part III. Chapt. II. Rule 41(2)(b) Request for grant. https://www.epo.org/law-practice/legal-texts/html/epc/2020/e/r41.html

European Guidelines for Patent Examination. Part A. Chapt. III. 7.1 Requirements (for Titles). https://www.epo.org/law-practice/legal-texts/html/guidelines/e/a_iii_7_1.htm

MPEP Section 606—Title of Invention [R-10.2019]. https://www.uspto.gov/web/offices/pac/mpep/s606.html

OMPI Norme ST. 15—Principes directeurs sur la rédaction des titres d'invention dans les documents de brevet [French]. https://www.wipo.int/export/sites/www/standards/fr/pdf/03-15-01.pdf

OMPI Norma ST.15—Directrices para la redacción de títulos de invenciones en documentos de patentes [Spanish]. https://www.wipo.int/export/sites/www/standards/es/pdf/03-15-01.pdf

Regulations under the PCT—Rule 4.3 Title of the invention. https://www.wipo.int/pct/en/texts/rules/r4.html

Regulations under the PCT—Rule 37 Missing or defective title. https://www.wipo.int/pct/en/texts/rules/r37.html#_37

WIPO Standard ST. 15—Guidelines for the wording of titles of inventions in patent documents [English]. https://www.wipo.int/export/sites/www/standards/en/pdf/03-15-01.pdf

11 Grantee, holder, assignee, or owner of a patent —INID code (73)

Patents have the attributes of personal property. This means that once the patent is awarded to an inventor, he or she who now owns the patent, may grant or assign their rights, in part or in whole, in their capacity of *grantor* or *assignor*. The patent is then assigned to a designated person (legal or natural), who becomes the *grantee*, *assignee*, *holder*, or *owner*, depending on the case. In turn, the new *grantee*, *assignee*, *holder*, or *owner* holds the patent rights to exclude others, until the patent is again re-assigned, or until it becomes public domain. The patent becomes public domain upon expiration of the 20-year protection period for US *utility* and *plant* patents, and 15-year protection period for US *design* patents.

In certain cases, inventors assign their patenting rights to the *applicant*. This is the case, for example, when the *applicant* is a company or university. Thus, inventors might assign their rights to the University or Company, in charge of the application process, and the management of company or institutional patent portfolios. In other cases, such as in an estate, patents might also be transferred. For example, this was the case with some of the Charles Miller shoe patents of the 1930s. These early twentieth-century patents are annotated as having been granted to him, the inventor on record. Then, the patents were transferred to his widow, Ida Gordon Miller, *Executrix* of his estate upon his death. In turn, his widow, Ida Gordon Miller, assigned the patents to the I. Miller & Sons Company, in her *assignor* capacity. See, for example, the bibliographic information quoted below, for US2138385, titled *Elastic top shoe*.

> 2,138,385
> ELASTIC TOP SHOE
> Charles Miller, Long Island City, N. Y., Ida Gordon
> Miller, executrix of said Charles Miller, deceased,
> assignor to I. Miller & Sons, Inc., Long Island City, N. Y.,
> a corporation of New York.
> Application March 5, 1935, Serial No. 9371.

Incidentally, the I. Miller & Sons Company crafted exquisite shoes for performance artists at the turn of the twentieth century. The I. Miller & Sons

DOI: 10.4324/9781003423003-11

Company then created comfortable *and* beautiful shoes for the patrons of the arts, particularly for women. Some of the shoes were even created in collaboration with André Perugia, the famous, early twentieth-century, French shoe designer. A French shoe designer with an impressive patent portfolio of designs, sometimes also serving as the historic archive of their combined, and then much celebrated *avant-garde* talents.

From a bibliographic perspective, according to the provisions of WIPO Standard ST. 9, the terms *grantee*, *assignee*, *holder* and *owner*, designating INID code (73) are all synonymous, in that they each refer to the person who currently "owns" the patenting rights, even if they are each the result of clearly different processes of patent ownership, or of the transfer of ownership. Per the provisions of *Section 301* of the *MPEP*, regarding the *Ownership/Assignability of Patents and Applications*, the terms *assignment*, *ownership*, *licensing*, *individual* and *joint ownership*, are clearly defined as follows.

> ***Assignment*** means a transfer by a party of all or part of its right, title, and interest in a patent […]
>
> ***Ownership*** of a patent gives the patent owner the right to exclude others from making, using, offering for sale, selling, or importing into the United States the invention claimed in the patent. *35 U.S.C. 154(a)(1)* […]
>
> ***Licensing***—As compared to assignment of patent rights, the licensing of a patent transfers a bundle of rights which is less than the entire ownership interest, e.g., rights that may be limited as to time, geographical area, or field of use. […]
>
> ***Individual ownership***—An individual entity may own the entire right, title, and interest of the patent property. This occurs where there is only one inventor, and the inventor has not assigned the patent property.
>
> ***Joint ownership***—Multiple parties may together own the entire right, title, and interest of the patent property. […]

Implications for translation

For translation, the above definitions of different types of patent ownership, assignment or transfer of ownership, serve to inform the translator's understanding of key patent transaction processes. In turn, such background information will facilitate locating correct translations. Although in the case of the

Table 11.1 WIPO Standard ST. 9 English and French terminology for INID code (73)

WIPO Standard ST. 9 for INID code (73)	*OMPI Norme ST. 9 pour le code INID (73)*
grantee	*(légataire)*
holder	*titulaire*
assignee	*cessionnaire*
owner	*propriétaire*

UN World Intellectual Property Organization (WIPO) Standard ST. 9, INID code designations already exist in documents drafted in the six official languages of the United Nations. French terminology for INID code (73) appears in Table 11.1.

References

MPEP Section 301—Ownership/assignability of patents and applications [R-10.2019]. https://www.uspto.gov/web/offices/pac/mpep/s301.html

OMPI ST. 9—Recommandation concernant les données bibliographiques. [French]. https://www.wipo.int/standards/fr/pdf/03-09-01.pdf

OMPI Norma ST. 9—Recomendación relativa a los datos bibliográficos contenidos en los documentos de patente y en los CCP o en documentos relacionados con ellos. [Spanish]. https://www.wipo.int/standards/es/pdf/03-09-01.pdf

WIPO Standard ST. 9—Recommendation concerning bibliographic data on and relating to patents and SPCS. https://www.wipo.int/export/sites/www/standards/en/pdf/03-09-01.pdf

Cited patent

Miller, G. (1938). Elastic top shoe (Patent No. US2138385). United States Patent and Trademark Office (USPTO). https://image-ppubs.uspto.gov/dirsearch-public/print/downloadPdf/2138385

12 The patent application

The main purpose of the patent application is to obtain patent rights to *exclude* others from using, selling, reproducing, or manufacturing an invention (per the previously cited statutory provisions of *Title 35 USC Section 154 (a) 1)*.

Once filed, the patent application will be examined to determine whether the invention fulfills all the *conditions of patentability* previously discussed, and whether other aspects of form, structure and content are compliant. For example, the application will be examined for compliance with such statutes as *the enablement requirement* and the *best mode requirement*, each of which are explained in dedicated sections, further into this book, for their implications in the translation process. A lengthy patent examination process, culminating in the decision to grant, or to deny the patent. An examination process termed *patent pendency* that takes up to three years in the United States, considering the backlog of applications, unless expedited under special humanitarian award conditions. Incidentally, this backlog in the patent examination process is at the origin of the label "*Patent pending*" found on so many marketed products. A label indicating that the product, or some aspect of the product, such as the process, is still under examination for a patent award.

The application will also be assessed, in view of determining the patent maintenance fees that will be due each year for the full duration of the patent's 20- or 15-year protection period. Fees are due for 20 years to maintain protection for both US *utility* and *plant* patents. Fees are due for 15 years to maintain protection for US *design* patents.

Succinctly, the contents, form, and structure of a patent application are governed by specific provisions of: 1. *Federal Patent Law, Title 35 of the United States Code* (35 USC); 2. *Administrative Regulations, Title 37 of the Code Federal Regulations* (37 CFR) and; 3. Supplementary administrative rules for interpretation of both statutes and regulations, drafted in the USPTO *Manual of Patent Examination* Procedure (MPEP). As a result, regardless of the invention in question, a patent application typically comprises the following documents, among other filing requirements, such as the Inventor's Oath (*MPEP 602.1*):

- an application data sheet (*37 CFR 1.76*)
- an abstract of the invention (*37 CFR 1.72(b)*)

DOI: 10.4324/9781003423003-12

- a description or specification of the invention (*37 CFR 1.71*)
- at least one drawing (*37 CFR 1.81, 1.83, 1.84*), and
- a claims section (*37 CFR 1.75*), which clearly lays out the scope of the patent protection requested.

The patent application, in particular the abstract, the specification and claims sections, must also comply with rules and regulations, specifying the form and style of the materials submitted. For example, the following rules and regulations specify the use of:

- Arabic numerals [*37 CFR 75(f)*]
- punctuation [*MPEP 608.1(m)*]
- line spacing [*37 CFR 1.52b(2)i*]
- font type and size [*37 CFR 1.52b(2) ii*], and
- indentations [*37 CFR 1.75 (i)*]

Implications for translation

The above far-from-exhaustive introduction to patent applications, from a regulatory perspective, clearly stresses an important point. Translating patents not only involves an understanding of the subject matter of the invention, whether about hybrid engines, or quick release medication. Translating patents is also advantageously informed by an understanding of the regulations that control the ways in which inventions are legally disclosed, recognized, and registered.

An inventor cannot disclose an invention for patenting purposes in the same way that findings are disclosed in scientific papers, or industrial prototypes in white papers. Inventors are obligated to follow all the legal requirements and regulations for presenting and qualifying their invention. In turn, such an understanding of exactly which rules and regulations are controlling *also* becomes crucial for patent translators. At the very least, those rules and regulations which have linguistic impact must also inform the translation process, in view of preventing a potential layer of translation error.

One preliminary example of the linguistic impact of the rules that must inform the translation process concerns any changes that might be brought to the indentations of a patent claim. Translators trained to edit target texts for readability in translation might mistakenly wish to re-organize the content of a long claim, or worse, re-word the claim. While such an approach might be legitimate in other domains of translation, this approach would no doubt result in a patent translation error. Error, because according to the provisions of *Title 37 CFR Section 1.75 (i)*, each of the indentations in a claim are required to correspond to the different steps or components of the process, product or composition of matter being claimed, providing that such steps or components exist in the invention. Regulated indentations that will have applied each time the steps or components were invoked in the body of the source application, especially in the sections reciting the *Brief summary of the invention*, the *Detailed description of the invention*, and/or in the *Abstract*. Legally significant indentations, which are meaningful to the recitation of the invention, and whose meaning must be retained in the translation, precisely in view of preserving the legitimacy of the translation.

References

37 CFR 152—Language, paper, writing, margins, compact disc specifications. https://www.uspto.gov/web/offices/pac/mpep/mpep-9020-appx-r.html#d0e318327

37 CFR 1.71—Detailed description and specification of the invention. https://www.uspto.gov/web/offices/pac/mpep/mpep-9020-appx-r.html#d0e320131

37 CFR 1.72(b)—Title and abstract. https://www.uspto.gov/web/offices/pac/mpep/mpep-9020-appx-r.html#d0e320224

37 CFR 1.75—Claim(s). https://www.uspto.gov/web/offices/pac/mpep/mpep-9020-appx-r.html#d0e320269

37 CFR 1.76—Application data sheet. https://www.uspto.gov/web/offices/pac/mpep/mpep-9020-appx-r.html#plt_d0e320348

37 CFR 1.81—Drawings required in patent application. https://www.uspto.gov/web/offices/pac/mpep/mpep-9020-appx-r.html#aia_d0e320940

37 CFR 1.83—Content of drawing. https://www.uspto.gov/web/offices/pac/mpep/mpep-9020-appx-r.html#d0e320967

37 CFR 1.84—Standards for drawings. https://www.uspto.gov/web/offices/pac/mpep/mpep-9020-appx-r.html#d0e320999

Manual of Patent Examining Procedure (MPEP). https://www.uspto.gov/web/offices/pac/mpep/index.html

MPEP Section 301—Ownership/Assignability of Patents and Applications. I. Ownership. [R-10.2019]. https://www.uspto.gov/web/offices/pac/mpep/s301.html

MPEP Section 602.01—Naming the inventor; inventor's oath or declaration. [R-07.2022]. https://www.uspto.gov/web/offices/pac/mpep/s602.html#ch600_d1ff64_24f27_297

MPEP Section 608.01 (a)—Arrangement of the application. [R-07.2022]. https://www.uspto.gov/web/offices/pac/mpep/s608.html#d0e43582

MPEP Section 608.01 (h) and (m)—Mode of operation of invention. [R-11.2013]. https://www.uspto.gov/web/offices/pac/mpep/s608.html#d0e44799

MPEP Section 2164—The Enablement Requirement. [R-11.2013]. https://www.uspto.gov/web/offices/pac/mpep/s2164.html

US Code Title 35—Patents. https://www.uspto.gov/web/offices/pac/mpep/mpep-9015-appx-l.html

US Code of Federal Regulations Title 37. https://www.uspto.gov/web/offices/pac/mpep/mpep-9020-appx-r.html

13 Disclosure of the invention

The document disclosing an invention, together with the claims section in the patent application process, is the source text that comprises the distinctive aspects of patents translation.

Why disclose an invention?

To obtain a patent (i.e., the rights to *exclude* others from using, producing, or manufacturing, and licensing an invention), inventors are first required to *disclose* their invention to a patent-granting institution. Patent-granting authorities include such entities as the *United States Patent and Trademark Office* (USPTO), the *European Patent Office* (EPO), the United Nations *World Intellectual Property Organization* (WIPO), the French *Institut National de la Propriété Industrielle* (INPI), the *Japanese Patent Office* (JPO), and many others. According to the *Manual of Patent Examination Procedure* (MPEP) *Section 608*, the purpose of the disclosure is to:

> … make sure that the public receives something in return for the exclusionary rights that are granted to the inventor in a patent.

For US patents, the disclosure of an invention is governed by the many different provisions set forth in the *Federal Code Title 35*, the *Code of Federal Regulations Title 37*, and as interpreted in the USPTO *Manual of Patent Examination Procedure* (MPEP). Likewise, elsewhere outside of the United States, inventions are disclosed according to the provisions of corresponding laws and regulations, such as those cited in Table 1.1, for the *United Nations World Intellectual Property Organization* (WIPO), and the *European Patent Office* (EPO).

As a result, an understanding of the rules and regulations, controlling the disclosure of an invention, is useful for patents translators, since such rules and regulations provide a framework for understanding *how* the content of a patent is structured and ordered, *regardless* of the invention-at-hand, whether self-cleaning cement or super moisturizing lipstick formulas. Below, some of the most important rules and regulations, governing disclosure, followed by their implications for translation.

DOI: 10.4324/9781003423003-13

Disclosure rules and regulations

Provisions for the disclosure of an invention, within the context of what is also termed the patent specification, are set forth in the *United States Code Title 35 Article 112* (a) as follows, for the most general terms:

> (a) IN GENERAL—The specification shall contain a written description of the invention, and of the manner and process of making and using it, in such full, clear, concise, and exact terms as to enable any person skilled in the art to which it pertains, or with which it is most nearly connected, to make and use the same, and shall set forth the best mode contemplated by the inventor or joint inventor of carrying out the invention.
>
> [*35 USC 112(a)*]

The general provisions of the statute cited above, which require inventors to describe their invention in such detail that it might be produced and used by *any person skilled in the art*, are further detailed in *Title 37 of the Code of Federal Regulations* (e.g., *Sections 1.71, 1.73, 1.74*), and various subsections of the *MPEP Section 608*, outlined below. Each provision intended to further specify the different parts of the description of an invention, and their recitation order.

Specifically, inventors are required to address the below-listed bulleted points in their disclosures, and to include the information in the ordered arrangement that the rules invoke, *regardless of the domain of invention*. In other words, whether the invention relates to toothpicks, taco shell production, saxophones, fish feed, or aircraft turbines, the following rules will function to frame the ordered narrative, disclosing the invention.

- ***Background of the invention***: Per the provisions the *MPEP Section 608.01(c)*, the *Background of the invention* includes: (1) a statement of the domain of the invention or field to which the invention belongs, using the *International Patent Classification* (IPC) of inventions as reference, *and* (2) one or several paragraphs, concerning the *state of the prior art*, in which the invention arises. Specifically, the compact survey of the *prior art* serves to highlight the problematic situation, in which the need for the invention emerges. For example, the Quick Response (QR) Code invention disclosed in the patent, EP0672994, titled *Method and apparatus for reading an optically two-dimensional code*, recites an invention that arises in a situation, where the QR code *raises the bar* on barcodes. The invention *raises the bar* because the QR code processes *350 times more* information than a barcode. Information that a QR code also decodes *20 times faster* than a barcode.
- ***Brief summary of the invention***: Per the provisions the *MPEP Section 608.01(d)*, the *Brief summary of the invention* is where the claimed object of the invention is briefly described, including "the exact nature, operation and

purpose of the invention" as claimed. Conventionally, the *Brief summary of the invent*ion is often a *verbatim* recitation of the first claim of the patent, because of the *ascertainability* and *antecedence* requirements that govern the interpretation of claim terminology. Requirements that will be examined further into this book for their important relevance in the translation process. In any event, the *Brief summary of the invention* precedes the *Brief description of the drawings* and the *Detailed description of the invention*, in the ordered arrangement, in which an invention is disclosed.

- ***Brief description of the drawings***: Per the provisions of the *MPEP Section 608.01(f)*, the *Brief description of the drawings* includes the figure drawing numbers. Figure drawing numbers, which will be referenced in the *Detailed description of the invention*, together with any of the numbers or letters, indexing the component parts of the figures. Specifically, the *Brief description of the drawings* comes with the added provision that "no single reference character [is] being used for two different parts or for a given part and a modification of such part."
- ***Detailed description of the invention***: Per the provisions the *MPEP Section 608.01(g)*, the *Detailed description of the invention* is recited in light of each of the drawings and their component parts. The recitation of the invention is also required to include sufficient detail to *enable* any person skilled in the art to make and use the invention, without undue experimentation, per the provisions of the statute *Title 35 USC Section 112(a)*, cited earlier. Accordingly, the *Detailed description of the invention* must include an *embodiment* of the invention [37 *CFR 1.71 (b)*] that satisfies the *enablement requirement* (*MPEP 2164*), whereby any person skilled in the art is *enabled* to make and use the invention. Thus, the recitation of the *Detailed description of the invention* invokes more than just one or several *examples* of the invention. The *Detailed description of the invention* must include an *enabling* and *complete embodiment* of the invention, per the provisions of *Title 37 CFR 1.71 (b)*. Provisions regarding *enablement* and *embodiments*, which will be examined further into this book, for their separate relevance to translation.

Implications for translation

For patent translators, the implications of the above-cited, non-exhaustive list of rules and regulations, governing the disclosure of an invention, are *invaluable*. Even though translators turn to the rules and regulations governing the disclosure of an invention for purposes *entirely* different from those that exist for law professionals, inventors, and entrepreneurs, seeking to disclose their inventions in view of obtaining a patent.

First, the provisions of these rules and regulations, together with the ordered arrangement of the information they invoke for each invention, provide *a very predictable narrative*. In turn, this predictability (i.e., knowing what to expect in the disclosure of an invention) is most helpful in domains that are often far out and complicated. Far out domains, considering that inventions are precisely intended to map new territory. Regardless of the invention in question, whether it is a new formula for shampoo, new shock-proof soles for sports shoes, or a new complication for a timepiece, the recitation will follow the ordered arrangement, and regulated steps of disclosure, in such a way that the details of the invention will fall in place. In other words, the predictability of the narrative, disclosing an invention, provides a welcome measure of *familiarity*, which frees a fair amount of cognitive space to figure out the new details of an often-complex invention.

Secondly, the information invoked in the first few pages of a patent specification, where the domain of the invention is specified, and the prior art is examined, in view of highlighting the problematic situation that the invention seeks to resolve, is crucial to the understanding of the invention as whole, and to the rest of the detailed disclosure. Indeed, the information invoked by just three of the patent specification disclosure rules (the *Background of the invention*, the *Brief summary of the invention* and the *Brief description of the drawings*), together with the ordered arrangement in which the information is presented, is often the very best source of documentary information that the translator needs for an understanding of the source text. Often, no better summary, or overview, of the invention exists, and just this information will suffice to gist the essential context of the invention for translation purposes. Otherwise, the initial sections of the recitation of the invention are also purported to contain the very best source of references for further research in the specified domain, especially when specific patents, articles, or chapters, are cited as part of the overview of the prior art.

Thirdly, anyone translating patents will have noticed how some of the actual language uses tend to recur, even across quite disparate domains of invention. Recurring language uses, such as for example the very first sentence of a patent, which always *relates* the invention to its domain in the International Patent Classification (IPC) system. The fact of the matter is that such recurring language uses are performing the requirements of the rules and regulations, governing the disclosure of *all* inventions. Thus, such recurring language uses should come as no surprise. Indeed, they are to be expected, considering that the rules and regulations, governing the disclosure of inventions apply to all patents—whether the patent is protecting the formulation of paint pigments, or the manufacture of bended wood to make furniture.

In sum, for the above-mentioned reasons, it is fair to say that the rules and regulations that govern the process of disclosing an invention also inform the translation process, in more than one significant way. At the very least, such rules and regulations for disclosing an invention provide a predictable and ordered recitation framework, supporting an understanding of the invention at hand. On another level, the rule-governed narrative invokes specific recurring language uses, functioning to perform the requirements of the law and applicable rules and regulations. Recurring language uses, such as those invoked to *describe* the *background of an invention*, to *highlight* the *problematic situation* in which an invention arises, *to summarize* an invention, to *introduce drawings*, and then *to cross-reference* the description of an invention with the drawings. Recurring language uses, amplifying the number of matches retrieved from term bases, to facilitate the patent translation process. Recurring language uses examined in detail further into this book.

References

35 USC 112 (a) to (f)—Specification. https://www.uspto.gov/web/offices/pac/mpep/mpep-9015-appx-l.html#d0e302824912

37 CFR 1.71 (a), (b), and (c)—Detailed description and specification of the invention. https://www.uspto.gov/web/offices/pac/mpep/mpep-9020-appx-r.html#d0e320131

37 CFR 1.73—Summary of the invention. https://www.uspto.gov/web/offices/pac/mpep/mpep-9020-appx-r.html#d0e320249

37 CFR 1.74—Reference to drawings. https://www.uspto.gov/web/offices/pac/mpep/mpep-9020-appx-r.html#d0e320259

MPEP Section 2164—The enablement requirement. [R-11.2013]. https://www.uspto.gov/web/offices/pac/mpep/s2164.html

MPEP Section 608.01 (a)—Arrangement of the application. [R-07.2022]. https://www.uspto.gov/web/offices/pac/mpep/s608.html#d0e43582

MPEP Section 608.01 (c)—Background of the invention. [R-07.2022]. https://www.uspto.gov/web/offices/pac/mpep/s608.html#d0e44561

MPEP Section 608.01 (d)—Brief summary of invention. [R-07.2015]. https://www.uspto.gov/web/offices/pac/mpep/s608.html#d0e44589

MPEP Section 608.01 (f)—Brief description of drawings. [R-10.2019]. https://www.uspto.gov/web/offices/pac/mpep/s608.html#d0e44626

MPEP Section 608.01 (g)—Detailed description of invention. [R-10.2019]. https://www.uspto.gov/web/offices/pac/mpep/s608.html#d0e44731

MPEP Section 608.01 (h)—Mode of operation of invention. [R-11.2013]. https://www.uspto.gov/web/offices/pac/mpep/s608.html#d0e44799

MPEP Section 608—Disclosure. [R-11.2013]. https://www.uspto.gov/web/offices/pac/mpep/s608.html

14 Global consensus on disclosing inventions

The way in which an invention is disclosed is not only remarkably predictable in United States patents. The disclosure of an invention is also remarkably predictable in European and International *Patent Cooperation Treaty* patents, despite significant and obvious differences across legal systems. Such remarkable predictability, even across national frontiers, occurs because the disclosure of inventions is regulated in a *consensual* way. Indeed, an almost 600-year history of intellectual property informs the rules and regulations, which have evolved to govern the disclosure of inventions everywhere. A 600-year history, beginning with the *Parte Veneziana*, the Venetian Patent Statute, enacted by the Senate of Venice in 1474, recognizing, and organizing the fifteenth-century glass artisan guilds of the Republic of Venice (Comino et al., 2017).

Countless *Letters Patent* have also been preserved and archived. For example, *Letters Patent* granted to Cambridge University Press, signed by Henry VIII in 1534, or those granted to the Saint-Gobain Glass Manufactory, signed by Louis XIV, the Sun King of France, in 1665. Historical documents where the basic tenets of intellectual property were already set forth in writing. Specifically, the basic tenets consisted in the disclosure of an invention, in exchange for patenting rights to exclude others. To be fair, the rules and regulations that now govern the disclosure of inventions carry little resemblance to the historical manuscripts just mentioned. Nonetheless, present-day regulations are *clearly* rooted in a traceable past, in terms of purpose, and the essence of procedure and process. The fact of the matter is that patents today continue to offer protection to inventors, in exchange for the disclosure of their inventions. A protection that consists in excluding others from copying, manufacturing, or marketing the invention for a certain set time period, during which the inventor might recoup costs, and continue to engage in research.

To further drive the point of consensus-driven predictability, even across national legal systems, the below Table 14.1 offers a comparison of the way in which inventions are disclosed, according to rules and regulations selected from the *US Code of Federal Regulations (Title 37)*, the *European Patent Convention* (EPC) and the World Intellectual Property Organization (WIPO) *Patent Cooperation Treaty* (PCT).

DOI: 10.4324/9781003423003-14

Table 14.1 Consensus on the provisions for disclosing inventions according to selected US, European, and World Intellectual Property rules and regulations

USPTO—US *utility* patents	EPO—EP patents	WIPO—WO patents
Source: Title 37 CFR Art. 1.71 to 1.76. https://tinyurl.com/5n732ew6	**Source**: European Patent Convention Part III. Chapt. II. Rule 42 – Content of the description. https://tinyurl.com/37cs84px	**Source**: Regulations under the PCT – Rule 5 – The Description. https://tinyurl.com/4c5pc3xv
Detailed description and specification of the invention **[37 CFR 1.71]** The specification must include a written description of the invention or discovery and of the manner and process of making and using the same, and is required to be in such full, clear, concise, and exact terms as to enable any person skilled in the art or science to which the invention or discovery appertains, or with which it is most nearly connected, to make and use the same. **[37 CFR 1.71a]** The specification must set forth the precise invention for which a patent is solicited, in such manner as to distinguish it from other inventions and from what is old. It must describe completely a specific embodiment of the process, machine, manufacture, composition of matter or improvement invented, and must explain the mode of operation or principle whenever applicable [...].	(1) The description shall: (a) specify the technical field to which the invention relates; (b) indicate the background art which, as far as is known to the applicant, can be regarded as useful to understand the invention, draw up the European search report and examine the European patent application, and, preferably, cite the documents reflecting such art; (c) disclose the invention, as claimed, in such terms that the technical problem, even if not expressly stated as such, and its solution can be understood, and state any advantageous effects of the invention with reference to the background art; (d) briefly describe the figures in the drawings, if any; (e) describe in detail at least one way of carrying out the invention claimed, using examples where appropriate and referring to the drawings, if any;	**5.1** *Manner of the Description* (a) The description shall first state the title of the invention as appearing in the request and shall: (i) specify the technical field to which the invention relates; (ii) indicate the background art which, as far as known to the applicant, can be regarded as useful for the understanding, searching and examination of the invention, and, preferably, cite the documents reflecting such art; (iii) disclose the invention, as claimed, in such terms that the technical problem (even if not expressly stated as such) and its solution can be understood, and state the advantageous effects, if any, of the invention with reference to the background art; (iv) briefly describe the figures in the drawings, if any;

(*Continued*)

Table 14.1 (*Continued*)

USPTO—US *utility* patents	EPO—EP patents	WIPO—WO patents
[37 CFR 1.71b] Title and abstract **(b)** The title of the invention may not exceed 500 characters in length and must be as short and specific as possible. […]	(f) indicate explicitly, when it is not obvious from the description or nature of the invention, the way in which the invention is industrially applicable.	(v) set forth at least the best mode contemplated by the applicant for carrying out the invention claimed; this shall be done in terms of examples, where appropriate, and with reference to the drawings, if any; where the national law of the designated State does not require the description of the best mode but is satisfied with the description of any mode (whether it is the best contemplated or not), failure to describe the best mode contemplated shall have no effect in that State;
[37 CFR 1.72] Summary of the invention A brief summary of the invention indicating its nature and substance, which may include a statement of the object of the invention, should precede the detailed description. Such summary should, when set forth, be commensurate with the invention as claimed and any object recited should be that of the invention as claimed.	(2) The description shall be presented in the manner and order specified in paragraph 1, unless, owing to the nature of the invention, a different presentation would afford a better understanding or be more concise.	
[37 CFR 1.73] Reference to the drawings When there are drawings, there shall be a brief description of the several views of the drawings and the detailed description of the invention shall refer to the different views by specifying the numbers of the figures and to the different parts by use of reference letters or numerals (preferably the latter).	[Intentionally left blank.]	(vi) indicate explicitly, when it is not obvious from the description or nature of the invention, the way in which the invention is capable of exploitation in industry and the way in which it can be made and used, or, if it can only be used, the way in which it can be used; the term "industry" is to be understood in its broadest sense as in the Paris Convention for the Protection of Industrial Property.
[37 CFR 1.74] Claims **[37 CFR 1.75]** Application data sheet **[37 CFR 1.76]**		(b) The manner and order specified in paragraph (a) shall be followed except when, because of the nature of the invention, a different manner or a different order would result in a better understanding and a more economic presentation.

Implications for translation

The striking consensus on the way in which inventions are disclosed in patent applications worldwide, and across a large portion of history, according to rules and regulations with shared notions about intellectual property, creates a *prodigious multilingual parallel corpus of patent texts*. A vast corpus, in an extensive array of languages, covering the full scope of characterized invention domains. To be more precise regarding the existing volume of patent documents, at just three patent-granting authorities: an ever-growing corpus of approximately 120 million patents are stored at the EPO, 43 million at the WIPO, and 11 million at the USPTO. A significant corpus of patents, where regardless of the domain of a particular invention, whether fish feed, therapeutic molecule, or irrigation system, different inventions are disclosed in a variety of official filing and publication languages, according to the rules cited in the above Table 14.1. Inventions disclosed in print, where one or several documents might serve as translation models or parallel texts, both in terms of terminology and/or the discursive way in which the inventions are recited.

As a result, it is no understatement when expert patent translators suggest that *patents* are the best source of information for background and model texts, as well as terminology. The fact of the matter is that both inventors *and* examiners also turn to patents, and cite patents as *prior art*.

References

37 CFR 1.71 (a), (b), (c)—Detailed description and specification of the invention. https://www.uspto.gov/web/offices/pac/mpep/mpep-9020-appx-r.html#d0e320131

37 CFR 1.72 (a), (b)—Title and abstract. https://www.uspto.gov/web/offices/pac/mpep/mpep-9020-appx-r.html#d0e320224

37 CFR 1.73—Summary of the invention. https://www.uspto.gov/web/offices/pac/mpep/mpep-9020-appx-r.html#d0e320249

37 CFR 1.74—Reference to drawings. https://www.uspto.gov/web/offices/pac/mpep/mpep-9020-appx-r.html#d0e320259

37 CFR 1.75—Claim(s). https://www.uspto.gov/web/offices/pac/mpep/mpep-9020-appx-r.html#d0e320269

37 CFR 1.76—Application data sheet. https://www.uspto.gov/web/offices/pac/mpep/mpep-9020-appx-r.html#plt_d0e320348

Comino, S., Galasso, A. and C. Graziano (2017). The Diffusion of New Institutions: Evidence from Renaissance Venice's Patent System. National Bureau of Economic Research (NBER) Working Paper No. 24118 December 2017. JEL No. K23,N23, O33,O34. https://www.nber.org/system/files/working_papers/w24118/w24118.pdf

European Patent Convention—Part III. Chapt. II. Rule 42 Content of the description. https://new.epo.org/en/legal/epc/2020/r42.html

Humphreys, F. (March 29, 2018). Conservation of the Cambridge University Press Archive: Framing the Letters Patent. Blog: Cambridge University Library Special Collections. https://specialcollections-blog.lib.cam.ac.uk/?p=15977#:~:text=Granted%20by%20Henry%20VIII%20in,all%20manner%20of%20books

Letters patent of 26 Henry VIII, 1534-07-20. Reference Code: GBR/0265/UA/Luard 162. https://archivesearch.lib.cam.ac.uk/repositories/2/archival_objects/21253
Letters Patent signed by Louis XIV, the Sun King of France, in 1665. Archives Saint-Gobain Glass Manufactory. https://archives.saint-gobain.com/ressource/xviie/1665/1665-louis-xiv-fonde-la-manufacture-royale-des-glaces-miroirs-linstigation-de
Regulations under the PCT—Rule 5 The Description. https://www.wipo.int/pct/en/texts/rules/r5.html#_5

15 Language uses invoked to perform the requirements of the law

The global consensus on intellectual *versus* real property, clearly expressed in the provisions of the rules and regulations that govern the way in which inventions are recited and claimed, creates predictability and recurrence. Predictability and recurrence in the organization of the content, and in the form and function of the documents drafted to file for a patent. Most significantly, predictability and recurrence exist in the very language uses that are invoked to carry out the requirements of the applicable rules and regulations.

As shown in Table 14.1 in Section 14, strong correspondences exist between the provisions of *US Federal Regulations* (*Title 37)*, the WIPO *Patent Cooperation Treaty* (PCT) and the *European Patent Convention* (EPC), regarding the disclosure of an invention. Requirements that inventors worldwide must satisfy, whether their invention pertains to wavy ramen noodles, a sunscreen formula, or an orthopedic implant. Requirements that subsume specific language uses to perform the functions of describing, summarizing, and claiming an invention, according to the provisions of the rules and regulations that apply. Specific recurring language uses, through which the disclosure of the invention becomes compliant.

Implications for translation

The following is an exemplified analysis of some of the recurring and varying language uses that are invoked to perform the requirements of applicable patent rules and regulations. This analysis is carried out using *Speech Act Theory* (Austin, 1975). A theory that is particularly useful both to *the language of patents* and to translation. *Speech Act Theory* is useful to t*he language of patents* (and more generally to *the language of law*, as in Marmor, 2014) because this is a language that quintessentially "does things in the world". The *language of patents* is a prescriptive language, replete with rules, regulations and language uses that are essentially and deeply *performative*. *Speech Act Theory* is also useful to translation because once the relevant requirements of the law are identified, explained and understood for what the requirements "say and do",

DOI: 10.4324/9781003423003-15

it is easy to find examples of recurring and varying language uses within patents that are performing the requirements of identified and relevant patent rules and regulations, applicable to all patents. In turn, translation is also facilitated, because translation involves finding target languages uses that are performing the same (and understood) requirements of the law, this time in the target language.

Thus, the following analysis seeks to identify the source text language uses, ushering compliance with patent rules and regulations. Language uses, which *a fortiori* are *also* required to perform the requirements of applicable rules and regulations *in translation*. In other words, beyond *accurate* and *appropriate translations*, it is a basic premise of this book that *compliant translations* are also of paramount importance, considering the high costs of error in patents translations, and the difficulty, if not impossibility, of fixing translation errors. Compliant in the sense of properly *performing* the requirements of relevant patent rules and regulations.

The first sentence of the disclosure

Translators can safely assume that the very first sentence describing an invention, whether in French, German, Spanish, Arabic, Chinese, Russian or Portuguese, to name just a few official languages, will *always* function to *relate* the invention to the technical or scientific domain. A connection between invention-at-hand and domain of invention, as officially classified in the *International Patent Classification* (IPC), that satisfies the provisions of patent rules and regulations shown in Table 14.1 in the previous section. Specifically, satisfying the provisions of the *PCT Rule 5.1a(i)*, the *EPC rule 42.1a*, or *Title 37 CFR Section 1.71* [as further interpreted in the *MPEP Section 608.01(c)*, and respective *Guidelines for the examination* of European and World patents], depending on the patent-granting authority. As a result, the first sentence of a patent, regardless of the filing language, contains very specific and predictable language uses performing the provisions of applicable rules and regulations, which might be easily leveraged in term bases. Specifically, for example, the verbs 'relates to' and 'concerns' are recurring for the first sentence in English, connecting the invention to its domain. Whereas, in French, the verbs *concerner* and *porter*, as well as the expression *a trait à* are recurring language uses performing the abovementioned provisions of the *European Patent Convention*, the *Patent Cooperation Treaty* and the *Code of Federal Regulations (Title 37)* that apply.

Table 15.1 Predictable first sentences of a disclosure (EN<>FR)

This invention relates to ...	*Cette invention a trait à ...*
This invention concerns ...	*Cette invention concerne ...*
	Cette invention porte sur ...

Background of the invention

Likewise, applying a linguistic analysis on language uses invoked to perform the requirements of applicable rules and regulations, this time regarding the *Background of the invention*, per the provisions of the *Code of Federal Regulations* (CFR), the *Patent Cooperation Treaty* (PCT), and the *European Patent Convention* (EPC), cited above in Table 14.1, translators should expect certain terms to recur across domains of invention. Terms that will be used to recite the state-of-the-prior-art and current unresolved problems. For example, the following terms should be expected to recur: 'prior art', 'background or context of the invention'; patent citations followed by the verbs ' discloses' and 'recites', or the uncommon use of the verb 'teaches' with an inanimate subject, such as 'US4538922 teaches'; reference to 'those having skill in the art' (to the PHOSITA mentioned previously), and the expression 'said', as in 'said invention', functioning as a determiner in reference to an antecedent. Whereas, in French, the following corresponding terms should be expected to recur: *art antérieur*, *arrière-plan ou contexe de l'invention*, *le document US538922 A4 enseigne*, in an equally unusual way with an inanimate subject, *l'homme du métier*, and *leditl laditel lesdit(e)s*, referring to an antecedent. All of which are *predictable* language uses, invoked to perform the requirements of disclosing the background state-of-the-prior-art, in which the invention-at-hand arises, *regardless* of the language used for filing the patent application, or the type of invention.

Additionally, translators should expect the section on the *Background of the invention*, inclusive of the *teachings* of previous or related patents, to conclude with one of more sentences, specifying exactly how the invention arises to resolve, or improve upon, the previously recited problems of the *prior art*. Concluding sentences precisely invoked to perform the specific requirements of the *Patent Cooperation Treaty*, the *European Patent Convention* and the *Code of Federal Regulations*, listed in Table 14.1. Regulatory requirements further

Table 15.2 Sample predictable language uses for reciting the prior art of an invention (EN<>FR)

prior art	*art antérieur*
background or context of the invention	*arrière-plan ou contexte de l'invention*
Patent citations such as:	Citations de brevets telles que:
US123456 recites …	*le document (brevet) récite …*
US123456 discloses …	*le document (brevet) divulgue …*
US123456 teaches …	*le document US538922 A4 enseigne …*
References to *those having skill in the art*	Références à *l'homme du métier*
Use of '*said*' functioning as a determiner, referring back.	Usage des déterminants *leditl laditel lesdit(e)s.*
Examples:	Exemples:
said invention	*ladite invention*
said aspect of the invention	*ledit aspect de l'invention*

explicated in the *Guidelines for Examination* of patent applications, such as, for example, in the *MPEP Section 608.01(c)*, for US patents, as follows:

> Where applicable, the problems involved in the prior art or other information disclosed which are solved by the applicant's invention should be indicated.

To illustrate just how language uses are invoked to perform this requirement of the disclosure of an invention, the following concluding sentences, listed in Table 15.3, were extracted from the initial section of the disclosure, reciting the background *state-of-the-prior-art*, in several different US, European (EP) and

Table 15.3 Varying language uses invoked to disclose how an invention arises to solve a problematic situation of the prior art

Accordingly, in view of above-described problems encountered in the related art, a principal object of the present invention is to provide a novel two-dimensional code capable of assuring an excellent accuracy in the reading operation and bringing an excellent data ratio (i.e., a ratio of a data area to the whole code area).
EP0672994—*Method and apparatus for reading an optically two-dimensional code.*

A real need therefore exists for nice-tasting complete foods and nutritional supplements, designed to be consumed directly without prior dilution in water, prepared from dairy products, easy to enrich with vitamins and minerals, having a high energy value, containing, as fat, only refined fat, capable of containing products which are sensitive to oxidation such as vitamins, which have a low osmotic pressure so as to avoid side effects such as diarrhea in undernourished subjects.
US20040052918A1—*High energy complete food or nutritional supplement, method for preparing same and uses thereof.*

Therefore, there is a need to provide furniture, and a method of manufacturing the same, in which the furniture is manufactured of a small number of different types of parts, thereby simplifying construction. There is also a need to provide furniture, and a method of manufacturing the same, in which the furniture is sturdy. There is further a need to provide furniture, and a method of manufacturing the same, in which the furniture is aesthetically pleasing. There is a further need to provide furniture which is ergonomically sound and comfortable. The present invention is directed toward filling those needs.
US5284380A—*Furniture comprising laminated slats and methods of manufacturing such furniture.*

The objects assigned to the invention are therefore intended to remedy the various disadvantages listed above and to provide a food cooking apparatus that allows for a uniform and uniform cooking of food by particularly efficient riddling of the latter during the course of cooking.
WO2007088279—*Cooking appliance with stirring means and associated method.*

None of the pet toys discussed above includes interlocking arms that form an enclosure over a recess in the pet toy for receiving treats. In the present invention, the interlocking arms engage the pet by requiring the pet not only to remove the treat from the recess but also to disengage the interlocking arms to access the recess. In addition, none of the pet toys discussed above forms the same shape as the present invention when the arms are interlocked, thereby causing the toy to spiral when thrown and further stimulating the pet during a game of fetch.
US20130087104—*Pet toy with interlocking arms and recess for treat.*

World Intellectual Property Organization (WO) patents, *among countless*. In other words, concluding sentences that specify exactly how the invention arises to resolve, or improve upon the recited problems of the prior art, extracted from patents and patent applications, governed by *US Federal Regulations*, the *European Patent Convention* (EPC) and the *Patent Cooperation Treaty* (PCT).

Source text sentences, indicating precisely how the invention arises to solve problems of the prior art, at the conclusion of the section on the *Background of the invention*, per the provisions of *MPEP Section 608.01(c)*, and equivalent for the EPC (e.g., *Guidelines for Examination in the EPO*, Part F., *Chapt II. 4.3*) and PCT (e.g., *International Search and Preliminary Examination Guidelines Part II, Chapt. 4.04*). Source text sentences that will *also* be required to perform the *same functions in the target text*. A translation task that is greatly facilitated, when prompted by a clear understanding of the governing provisions of rules and regulations, and of how language use might *vary* to perform such regulatory requirements.

Disclosing the brief description of the drawings

Title 37 of the Code of Federal Regulations, Section 1.74 specifies that:

> When there are drawings, there shall be a brief description of the several views of the drawings and the detailed description of the invention shall refer to the different views by specifying the numbers of the figures, and to the different parts by use of reference letters or numerals (preferably the latter).

Thus, when the *brief description of the drawings* is disclosed, such a *brief description* precedes the subsequent *detailed description of the invention*, where the drawings are referenced in support of the detailed disclosure.

As a result, when applying a linguistic analysis on *language uses, performing the requirements of rules* and *regulations*, no one should be surprised to find a recurring sentence in the specification, such as those cited in Table 15.4, functioning to introduce the way in which drawings are referenced in the detailed description of the invention, per the provisions of *Title 37 CFR Section 1.74*. The fact of the matter is that regulations governing the disclosure of an invention apply to *all* patents. In turn, this sets up legitimate expectations for recurring language uses, performing the requirements of rules and regulations, in each case, for reach invention.

Additionally, when there is a consensus on specific regulatory provisions, across legal systems, such as the case for disclosing inventions, and particularly for this example concerning the disclosure of patent figure drawings, then recurring language uses, performing consensual regulatory provisions, are also expected to occur. In any event, more than one patent translator will have been acutely aware of the "repetitions" from one patent to another—if not completely *verbatim* at this juncture, then in meaning, and even for the most disparate set of inventions.

Table 15.4 Examples of language uses performing the provisions of Title 37 CFR Section 1.74 with EPC and PCT equivalents, in English, French, and Spanish

The invention will be better understood, and other advantages will become apparent on reading the detailed description of an embodiment given as an example, the description being illustrated by the attached drawing in which: FIG. 1 shows a perspective representation of a hand intended for a humanoid robot. FIGS. 2a, 2b, and 2c represent a spreader of the hand in different plan views […]	L'invention sera mieux comprise et d'autres avantages apparaîtront à la lecture de la description détaillée d'un mode de réalisation donné à titre d'exemple, description illustrée par le dessin joint dans lequel: La figure 1 représente en perspective une main destinée à équiper un robot à caractère humanoïde. Les figures 2a, 2b, et 2c représentent un palonnier de la main dans différentes vues en plan […]	La invención se comprenderá mejor y otras ventajas surgirán con la lectura de la descripción detallada de un modo de realización dado a título de ejemplo, descripción ilustrada por el dibujo adjunto en el que: La figura 1 representa en perspectiva una mano destinada a equipar un robot de carácter humanoide. Las figuras 2a, 2b, y 2c representan un distribuidor de la mano en diferentes vistas en planta […]
US2016325437—*Actuation of a hand intended for being provided on a humanoid robot.*	**FR3016542A1**—*Actionnement d'une main destinée à équiper un robot à caractère humanoïde.*	**ES2685961T3**—*Accionamiento de una mano destinada a equipar un robot de carácter humanoide.*
Other objects and advantages of the invention appear in greater detail in the following description made with reference to the accompanying drawings, given as illustrative and non-limiting examples, and in which: FIG. 1 is a front view looking down, showing the inside of a cooking appliance constituting a first embodiment of the invention. FIG. 2 is an exploded view showing the FIG. 1 appliance. FIG. 3 is a plan view showing the appliance of FIGS. 1 and 2 […]	D'autres objets et avantages de l'invention apparaîtront plus en détails à l'aide de la description qui suit, en référence aux dessins annexés donnés à titre d'exemples illustratifs et non limitatifs dans lesquels: La figure 1 illustre, selon une vue plongeante de face, l'intérieur d'un appareil de cuisson conforme à un premier mode de réalisation de l'invention. La figure 2 illustre, selon une vue éclatée, l'appareil illustré à la figure 1 […]	Otros objetivos y ventajas de la invención se mostrarán de forma más detallada por medio de la descripción que viene a continuación, en referencia a los dibujos anexos dados a título de ejemplos ilustrativos y no excluyentes en los que: La figura 1 ilustra, según una vista de frente desde arriba, el interior de un aparato de cocción de acuerdo con un primer modo de realización de la invención. La figura 2 ilustra, según une vista desplezada, el aparato ilustrado en la figura 1 […]
US9498083B2—*Cooking appliance with stirring means and associated method.*	**WO2007088279A1**—*Appareil de cuisson avec moyen de remuage et procédé afférent.*	**ES2362025T3**—*Aparato de cocción con medio de removido y procedimiento correspondiente.*

(*Continued*)

Table 15.4 Examples of language uses performing the provisions of Title 37 CFR Section 1.74 with EPC and PCT equivalents, in English, French, and Spanish

The manner in which the present invention is carried out will be more fully understood from the following description, taken in connection with the accompanying drawing, in which: FIG. 1 shows a front view of an aerogenerator according to the invention. FIG. 2 shows a perspective view of an exemplary turbine of the invention which can be used in the aerogenerator of FIG. 1 [...] **US2015108762A1**—*Aerogenerator comprising a trunk and a plurality of branches extending from this trunk.*	L'invention sera mieux comprise et d'autres buts, avantages et caractéristiques de celle-ci apparaîtront plus clairement à la lecture de la description qui suit et qui est faite au regard des dessins annexés, sur lesquels: La figure 1 représente, selon une vue de face, un aérogénérateur selon l'invention. La figure 2 représente, selon une vue en perspective, un exemple de turbine selon l'invention pouvant être utilisée sur l'aérogénérateur de la figure 1 [...] **FR2988144A1**—*Aérogénérateur comprenant un tronc et une pluralité de branches s'étendant à partir de ce tronc.*	[Intentionally left blank. No Spanish patent family member for the WindTree aeronegerator invention.]

Accordingly, the examples in Table 15.4 are variations in language uses, performing the provisions of *Title 37 CFR Section 1.74* and equivalent *EPC Rule 42.1 (d, e)* and *PCT Rule 5.2 (iv, v)* cited previously in Table 14.1. Exemplary sentences, disclosing the list of figures relative to the *detailed description of the invention*, where they will be referenced more extensively. The examples, *among countless*, are extracted from three different patent families with members in English, French, and Spanish, where available.

An additional example of language use performing the provisions of *Title 37 CFR Section 1.74* is provided in Table 15.5. This example is extracted from one of André Perugia's famous 1929 shoemaking patents. An example, *also among many*, that serves to reiterate the point about *consensus across history*. A 600-year consensus in the matter of intellectual *versus* real property, and particularly regarding the disclosure of inventions, as previously explained.

The examples cited above of the varied language uses, performing the requirements of *Title 37 CFR Section 1.74*, and consensual equivalents, matter significantly for translation, in as much *as the target text also needs to perform the requirements of rules and regulations*. Thus, an understanding of the

Table 15.5 Early twentieth-century language uses performing the provisions of Title 37 CFR Section 1.74, in English and French

The manner in which the present invention is carried out will be more fully understood from the following description, taken in connection with the accompanying drawing, in which: Fig. 1 is a perspective view of a shoe embodying the present invention; and Fig. 2 is a fragmentary plan view of the shoe, shown in Fig. 1. [...] **US1798271**—*Shoe closure. (Perugia, 1929)*	Le dessin annexé représente à titre d'exemple une forme d'exécution de l'objet de l'invention. La fig. 1 montre en perspective une chaussure suivant l'invention. La fig. 2 est une vue partielle à plus grande échelle dans laquelle on a supposé que l'une des patelettes n'était pas encore fixée sur la tige de la chaussure. [...] **FR680710**—*Perfectionnements à la fabrication des chaussures. (Perugia, 1929)*

underlying provisions of applicable rules and regulations, generating the language uses, becomes crucial to preventing misinterpretation and error. The *brief description of drawings* in a patent is disclosed relative to the *detailed description of an invention*, because this is where the drawings will further support an *enabling* description.

Safeguarding the scope of the invention in the detailed description of the invention

According to the provisions of the *MPEP Section 2111* on *Claim interpretation*, the claims to an invention must be given "*their broadest reasonable interpretation consistent with the specification*". As a result, the specification includes, whether by convention and/or judge's writ, a *safeguard* sentence or paragraph, at the very conclusion of the disclosure of the invention, which functions to *expand* the scope of the description of the invention provided. This safeguard is provided because the specification to an invention cannot possibly exhaustively describe the full scope of the invention. Consider, for example, the countless applications of Amazon's One-Click™ check out invention. No specification of the invention could ever exhaustively describe all the possible and potential uses. Thus, inventors are able to avoid importing limitations of the specification into the claims section, which might otherwise be construed from having only described one or even several embodiments of the invention, per the disclosure requirements. This variously expressed safeguard addresses the matter of claims interpretation directly, by explicitly making it clear that the description is *unlimited* to the particular embodiment of the invention provided.

Below, Table 15.6 brings together a series examples, providing an array of language uses, both horizontally across domains of invention, and vertically across history, which safeguard the provisions of patent law regarding the *broadest reasonable interpretation of claims*. The examples are extracted from a

Table 15.6 Varying language uses invoked to safeguard the broadest reasonable interpretation of claims

<table>
<tr><td>Any other means of attaching the tabs may also be resorted to without departing from the spirit of the present invention.
US1798271—Shoe closure. (Perugia, 1929)</td><td>Bien entendu, on pourrait, au lieu de fixer les pattelettes sur le dessus de la tige, comme représenté, les fixer intérieurement, mais l'aspect de la chaussure serait moins séduisant.
FR680710—Perfectionnements à la fabrication des chaussures. (Perugia, 1929)</td></tr>
<tr><td>Obviously, these angular values are given purely by way of example. Other values are of course possible.
US2016325437—Actuation of a hand intended for being provided on a humanoid robot. [English version]</td><td>Il est bien entendu que ces valeurs angulaires ne sont données qu'à titre d'exemple. D'autres valeurs sont bien entendu possibles.
FR3016542B1—Actionnement d'une main destinée à équiper un robot à caractère humanoïde. [French version]</td></tr>
<tr><td>Of course, the case may be executed in any other desired manner and any other inner or outer mechanism may serve for driving the tracing stylus without thereby widening the scope of the invention as defined in the accompanying claims.
US3055113A—Tracing device. (Etch A Sketch® 1962)</td><td>Bien entendu toute autre structure pourrait être donnée au boitier, et tout autre mécanisme intérieur ou extérieur pourrait servir à mouvoir le stylet-traceur, sans pour cela sortir du cadre de l'invention.
FR1242870—Dispositif traceur. (1960)</td></tr>
<tr><td colspan="2">Variations and modifications of the invention may be suggested by reading the specification, and studying the drawings, which are within the scope of the invention. For example, the jacket may comprise any one of a number of soft materials other than plastic foam. The outside shape of the jacket may be cylindrical as shown in Fig. 4 instead of spherical. The outside surface of the spherical toy-ice cream maker may be decorated. Other possible materials could include foam rubber, neoprene or urethane. I therefore wish to define the scope of the invention by the appended claims.
US5857351A—Play ball ice-cream maker.</td></tr>
<tr><td colspan="2">While there has been shown and described what is considered to be preferred embodiments of the invention, it will, of course, be understood that various modifications and changes in form or detail could readily be made without departing from the spirit of the invention. It is therefore intended that the scope of the invention not be limited to the exact forms described and illustrated, but should be construed to cover all modifications that may fall within the scope of the appended claims.
US2014201026—Personalized customer shopping experience.</td></tr>
<tr><td colspan="2">While the present disclosure has been described with reference to various embodiments, it will be understood that these embodiments are illustrative and that the scope of the disclosure is not limited to them. Many variations, modifications, additions, and improvements are possible. More generally, embodiments in accordance with the present disclosure have been described in the context of particular embodiments. Functionality may be separated or combined in blocks differently in various embodiments of the disclosure or described with different terminology. These and other variations, modifications, additions, and improvements may fall within the scope of the disclosure as defined in the claims that follow.
US2015015475A1—Multi-function input device.</td></tr>
</table>

variety of patents, covering inventions in unelated domains, in both English and French when the patent family is multilingual.

For experienced patent translators, the above cited recurring variation in language uses, concluding the description of an invention, is immediately recognizable. An understanding of how this conclusion performs to safeguard the requirements of patent law, considering the broadest possible interpretation of claims, guarantees that translations will also target performance of the same requirement.

The language of patents

The above exemplification of recurring language uses, invoked to perform various provisions of the consensual rules and regulations, governing the disclosure of inventions, together with many additional terms, are part of the *language of patents*. A language sometimes called "*patentese*" because so many of the terms defy proper understanding without contextual explanation, in reference to the purpose of patent rules and regulations. *Patentese*, also because such language uses seldom, if ever, occur elsewhere in the same way, as will become even more evident for the claims section, explicated further into this book. A language invoked to perform the requirements of the law, one rule, one regulation, one provision at a time. A language, once translated, that is also prescribed to perform the requirements of the law.

Essentially however, the consensus that exists on intellectual property, in particular for patents, is a *blessing* for translation. A true *blessing*, because the consensual rules and regulations for disclosing inventions create a distinctly identifiable *multilingual* genre, or text type, with clearly identifiable language uses, invoked to perform the specific, regulation-driven, functions of disclosure. In turn, this much predictability creates a multilingual framework for understanding sometimes complex inventions, freeing up much cognitive space for researching and *gisting* the subject matter of an invention-at-hand. This much specified predictability in language uses, governed by consensual provisions of patent rules and regulations, then forms the generative syntax of a language, termed *the language of patents*, applicable to any invention, whether pet toys, premature infant incubators, or wind tunnel fans (without blades). A generative syntax, whose combination rules, found in specific provisions of patent law, once acquired, enable translators to feel at home in the domain of patent translation.

References

37 CFR Articles 1.71 to 1.76. https://www.uspto.gov/web/offices/pac/mpep/mpep-9020-appx-r.html#d0e320131

Austin, J. L. (1975). *How to Do Things with Words*. Cambridge, MA: Harvard University Press.

European Patent Convention—Part III. Chapt. II. Rule 42 Content of the description. https://new.epo.org/en/legal/epc/2020/r42.html

European Patent Organization Guidelines for Examination—Part F. Chapt II. 4.3 Background art. https://new.epo.org/en/legal/guidelines-epc/2023/f_ii_4_3.html

Marmor, A. (2014). *The Language of Law*. Oxford, UK: Oxford University Press.
MPEP Section 2111—Claim Interpretation; Broadest Reasonable Interpretation. [R-10.2019]. https://www.uspto.gov/web/offices/pac/mpep/s2111.html
MPEP Section 608.01 (c)—Background of the Invention. [R-07.2015]. https://www.uspto.gov/web/offices/pac/mpep/s608.html#d0e44561
Regulations under the PCT—Rule 5 The Description. https://www.wipo.int/pct/en/texts/rules/r5.html#_5
WIPO International Search and Preliminary Examination Guidelines—Part II. Chapt. 4.05 Background art. https://www.wipo.int/pct/en/texts/ispe/4_02_27.html#_4_05

Cited patents

Adoni, S.M. et al. (2014). Personalized customer shopping experience (Patent Application No. US2014201026). United States Patent and Trademark Office (USPTO). https://image-ppubs.uspto.gov/dirsearch-public/print/downloadPdf/20140201026
Angus, D.P. & R.D. Angus (1999). Play ball ice-cream maker. (Patent No. US5857351A). United States Patent and Trademark Office (USPTO). https://image-ppubs.uspto.gov/dirsearch-public/print/downloadPdf/5857351
Bordereaux, A. & J-C. Bazard (2016). Cooking appliance with stirring means and associated method (Patent No. US9498083B2). United States Patent and Trademark Office (USPTO). https://image-ppubs.uspto.gov/dirsearch-public/print/downloadPdf/9498083
Bordereaux, A. and J-C. Bisar (2011). Aparato de cocción con medio de removido y procedimiento correspondiente (Patenta No. ES2362025T3). Oficina Española de Patentes y Marcas (OEPM). https://worldwide.espacenet.com/patent/search/family/037056447/publication/ES2362025T3?q=ES2362025T3
Brined, A. and M. Leanne (2004). High energy complete food or nutritional supplement, method for preparing same and uses thereof (Patent Application No. US2004 0052918A1). United States Patent and Trademark Office (USPTO). https://image-ppubs.uspto.gov/dirsearch-public/print/downloadPdf/20040052918
Chaize, P. (1960a). Dispositif traceur. (Patent No. FR1242870). Institut National de la Propriété Industrielle (INPI). https://worldwide.espacenet.com/patent/search/family/048744471/publication/FR1242870A?q=FR1242870
Chaize, P. (1960b). Dispositif traceur. (Patent No. FR1242870). Institut National de la Propriété Industrielle (INPI). https://worldwide.espacenet.com/patent/search/family/048744471/publication/FR1242870A?q=FR1242870
Ely, C.M. and F.R. Rothkopf (2015). Multi-function input device (Patent Application No. US2015015475A1). United States Patent and Trademark Office (USPTO). https://image-ppubs.uspto.gov/dirsearch-public/print/downloadPdf/20150015475
Gehry, F. (1994). Furniture comprising laminated slats and methods of manufacturing such furniture. (Patent No. US5284380A). United States Patent and Trademark Office (USPTO). https://image-ppubs.uspto.gov/dirsearch-public/print/wedownloadPdf/5284380
Godeau, A. & J-C. Bazard (2007). Appareil de cuisson avec moyen de remuage et procédé affèrent. (Patent Application No. WO2007088279A1). World Intellectual Property Office (WIPO). https://patentscope.wipo.int/search/en/detail.jsf?docId=WO2007088279&_cid=P22-LNKN86-41125-1
Grandjean, A. (1962). Tracing device (Patent No. US3055113A) United States Patent and Trademark Office (USPTO). https://image-ppubs.uspto.gov/dirsearch-public/print/downloadPdf/3055113

Hara, M. et al. (1995). Method and apparatus for reading an optically two-dimensional code (Patent No. EP0672994). Européen Patent Office. https://worldwide.espacenet.com/patent/search/family/012640203/publication/EP0672994A1?q=EP0672994

Laville, J. et al. (2016). Actuation of a hand intended for being provided on a humanoid robot. [English version] (Patent Application No. US2016325437). United States Patent and Trademark Office (USPTO). https://image-ppubs.uspto.gov/dirsearch-public/print/downloadPdf/20160325437

Laville, J. et al. (2018.) Accionamiento de una mano destinada a equipar un robot de carácter humanoide (Patenta No. ES2685961T3). Oficina Española de Patentes y Marcas (OEPM). https://worldwide.espacenet.com/patent/search/family/050639718/publication/ES2685961T3?q=ES2685961T3

Laville, J. et al. (2019). Actionnement d'une main destinée à équiper un robot à caractère humanoïde. [French version] (Patent No. FR3016542B1). Institut National de la Propriété Industrielle (INPI) https://worldwide.espacenet.com/patent/search/family/050639718/publication/FR3016542B1?q=FR3016542B1

Michaud-Larivière, J. (2013). Aérogénérateur comprenant un tronc et une pluralité de branches s'étendant à partir de ce tronc (Patent No. FR2988144A1). Institut National de la Propriété Industrielle (INPI). https://worldwide.espacenet.com/patent/search/family/047080760/publication/FR2988144A1?q=FR2988144A1

Michaud-Larivière, J. (2015). Aerogenerator comprising a trunk and a plurality of branches extending from this trunk (Patent Application No. US2015108762A1). United States Patent and Trademark Office (USPTO). https://image-ppubs.uspto.gov/dirsearch-public/print/downloadPdf/20150108762

Perugia, A. (1929a). Perfectionnements à la fabrication des chaussures. (Patent No. FR680710). Institut National de la Propriété Industrielle (INPI). https://worldwide.espacenet.com/patent/search/family/009022421/publication/FR680710A?q=FR680710

Perugia, A. (1929b). Shoe closure (Patent No. US1798271). United States Patent and Trademark Office (USPTO). https://image-ppubs.uspto.gov/dirsearch-public/print/downloadPdf/1798271

Williams, S. et al. (2013). Pet toy with interlocking arms and recess for treat. (Patent Application No. US20130087104). United States Patent and Trademark Office (USPTO). https://image-ppubs.uspto.gov/dirsearch-public/print/downloadPdf/20130087104

16 The Enablement Requirement

The statutory *Enablement Requirement* is specified in the provisions of the *Federal Code Title 35 Section 112 (a)*, in regards the patent specification, as follows:

> The specification shall contain a written description of the invention, and of the manner and process of making and using it, in such full, clear, concise, and exact terms as to *enable* any person skilled in the art to which it pertains, or with which it is most nearly connected, to make and use the same, and shall set forth the best mode contemplated by the inventor or joint inventor of carrying out the invention.
>
> [italics mine] [*35 USC 112 (a)*]

It follows, according to further explanation provided in the provisions of the *MPEP Section 2164*, that for a patent claim to be valid, claims must be supported by an *enabling* disclosure of the invention. In other words, claims to an invention must be supported by a disclosure of the invention that comprises enough details for any person skilled in the art to be *enabled* to reproduce the invention, without undue experimentation.

Implications for translation

The *Enablement Requirement* addresses those persons skilled in the art, offering inventors an overarching framework for what to include in the recitation of an invention. For translators, understanding that this requirement applies to all patent specifications increases predictability, which in turn facilitates understanding of the invention at hand, and consequently of the translation task. However, beyond specifically informing predictability in the process of translating patent specifications, *appropriation* of the concept of *enablement* is really what permeates every page of this book.

Again, the basic premise of this book is that certain rules and regulations governing the drafting and filing of patents have *direct* linguistic impact on the translation process. As a result, understanding of those specific rules and regulations is *enabling* for translation, especially when such understanding prevents

DOI: 10.4324/9781003423003-16

costly errors. For example, translators are *enabled* in their pre-translation tasks when they know that the best source of background information may be found in the first few paragraphs of the patent, reciting the invention relative to the prior art, as well as in the search report at the end of a *Patent Cooperation Treaty* (PCT) patent. Likewise, translators are *enabled* when they understand that each claim in a patent "begins with a capital letter and ends with a period" per the provisions of *MPEP Section 608.01(m)*, no matter how many words, paragraphs or even pages appear between the "capital letter" and the "period". In this case especially, as discussed further into this book, understanding of the "single-sentence rule" (SSR) potentially prevents rejection of a patent application, due to invalidation of the translated claims.

Thus, once again for *entirely* different reasons, both legal professionals and translators turn to the provisions of the law, in this case the *Enablement Requirement*. Fulfilling the *Enablement Requirement* for legal professionals means that the patent specification contains an embodiment with sufficient detail to enable any person skilled in the art to reproduce the invention, without undue experimentation. Whereas in translation a certain amount of diversion occurs, considering that *enablement* might mean as much understanding as possible of the provisions of patent rules and regulations with a direct linguistic impact. An *enablement* that informs the translation process, in view of producing translations that are not only *appropriate* and *accurate*, but also *compliant* in their performance of the applicable requirements of rules and regulations.

References

35 USC 112(a)—Specification. https://www.uspto.gov/web/offices/pac/mpep/mpep-9015-appx-l.html#d0e302824912

37 CFR 1.71(a)—Detailed description and specification of the invention. https://www.uspto.gov/web/offices/pac/mpep/mpep-9020-appx-r.html#d0e320131

MPEP Section 2164—The Enablement Requirement. [R-11.2013]. https://www.uspto.gov/web/offices/pac/mpep/s2164.html

MPEP Section 608.01(m)—Form of claims. [R-10.2019]. https://www.uspto.gov/web/offices/pac/mpep/s608.html#d0e45061

17 Embodiment *vs.* example

The logophile translator might ask: Does one have to use the term *embodiment* as in the expression "*an embodiment of the invention*"? Wouldn't the term *example* work just as well?

With all due respect to those translators who might have cringed at the personification of inventions, the short answer is yes, *embodiment* is the correct term. The term *example* is wanting—when translating a patent. Besides, how would one explain and translate the following excerpt from a patent description where co-occurrence of both terms clearly arises?

> DETAILED DESCRIPTION Various non-limiting embodiments of the present disclosure will now be described to provide an overall understanding of the principles of the structure, function, and use of the apparatuses, systems, methods, and processes disclosed herein. One or more examples of these non-limiting embodiments are illustrated in the accompanying drawings. Those of ordinary skill in the art will understand that systems and methods specifically described herein and illustrated in the accompanying drawings are non-limiting embodiments.
>
> Excerpt WO2017156187—*Disdrometer having acoustic transducer and methods thereof.*[1]

The long answer, and reason for the distinction, is that only the description of a complete *embodiment of the invention* performs the *enablement requirement* of a patent specification. The purpose of the *enablement requirement* of a patent is that the invention must be described in sufficient detail for any person skilled in the art *to be enabled* to make and use the invention, *without undue experimentation* [*MPEP Section 2164.01*]. This is also the reason why a claimed invention must be supported by an *enabling* disclosure of the invention. In empirical research the *embodiment* of an invention would loosely address the *reproducibility* principle.

Thus, an *embodiment of the invention*, per the following provisions of *Title 37 CFR Section 1.71(a, b)*, is *more than just 'an example'*.

(a) The specification must include a written description of the invention or discovery and of the manner and process of making and using the

DOI: 10.4324/9781003423003-17

> same, and is required to be in such full, clear, concise, and exact terms as *to enable any person skilled in the art or science to which the invention or discovery appertains, or with which it is most nearly connected, to make and use the same.*
>
> (b) [...] *It must describe completely a specific embodiment of the process, machine, manufacture, composition of matter or improvement invented,* and must explain the mode of operation or principle whenever applicable. *The best mode contemplated by the inventor of carrying out his invention must be set forth.*
>
> [italics mine]

Indeed, the disclosure of an invention need not even include a *working* or *prophetic example* if the disclosure is otherwise *enabling*. In other words, if the disclosure includes the description of a complete *embodiment of the invention*, per the provisions of the *MPEP Section 2164.02*, then no need for an example, based on precedence set forth in an appeal that upheld a decision taken for the Borkowski et al., patent application (Application of Borkowski, 422 F.2d 904, 164 U.S.P.Q. (BNA) 642 (C.C.P.A. 1970)), as follows:

> The specification need not contain an example if the invention is otherwise disclosed in such manner that one skilled in the art will be able to practice it without an undue amount of experimentation.

The required *embodiment of the invention* must also describe the *best mode* envisioned by inventors for carrying out their invention. The *best mode* functions as an extra safeguard against incomplete disclosure of invention, per the provisions of *Title 35 USC Section 112(a)*, and more specifically per the provisions of the above-cited provisions of *Title 37 CFR Section 1.71 (b)*.

Implications for translation

The implications pertain to the legal differences between the terms 'example' and 'embodiment'. Two terms that might otherwise incorrectly be construed as synonymous. Two terms which translate respectively in French to *exemple* versus *mode de réalisation*, without bringing up any notions of personification.

Even though a glossary is likely to provide the term *embodiment* as the correct translation for *mode de réalisation*, no glossary is equipped to prevent translators from selecting a supposedly better sounding, less repeated, or ultimately, "simply" a personally *preferred* term, without personification, such as "example". This is perhaps because a glossary is unlikely to provide a contrastive regulatory explanation. A contrastive regulatory reason, according to which the *embodiment* of an invention is different from an *example* in that *only* an embodiment fulfils *the* statutory *enablement requirement* in the specification of an invention.

In other words, *only* an *embodiment* of the invention, *required* in the disclosure of an invention, as set forth in *Title 37 CFR Section 1.71 (b)*, is deemed to provide the level of detail to *enable* those skilled in the art to make or use the invention. Such clear difference also explains why translators might find both terms—*example and embodiment*—co-occurring in the same patent sentence or paragraph, as quoted previously for the patent WO2017156187, titled *Disdrometer having acoustic transducer and methods thereof*.

At the end of the day, the term "*embodiment*" in reference to the disclosure of an invention may not appeal to the *literati*, because of the denoted personification. However, in the absence of alternative legal terminology, the term "*embodiment*", as specified in the *Code of Federal Regulations*, *Title 37 CFR Section 1.71(b)*, is here to stay, both in source English patent texts, and as translated terminology, in patent translations to English.

Call to order! Motion for synonyms <u>*denied*</u>.

Note

1 A disdrometer is an instrument used to measure the drop-size distribution and velocity of falling hydrometeors. In other words, an instrument able to measure the difference in size, velocity, and distribution of rain, hail, and soft hail (graupel).

References

35 USC 112 (a) to (f)—Specification. https://www.uspto.gov/web/offices/pac/mpep/mpep-9015-appx-l.html#d0e302824912

37 CFR 1.71 (a) and (b)—Detailed description and specification of the invention. https://www.uspto.gov/web/offices/pac/mpep/mpep-9020-appx-r.html#d0e320131

Application of Borkowski, 422 F.2d 904, 164 U.S.P.Q. (BNA) 642. (C.C.P.A. 1970). https://casetext.com/case/application-of-borkowski

MPEP Section 2164—The Enablement Requirement. [R-11.2013]. https://www.uspto.gov/web/offices/pac/mpep/s2164.html

MPEP Section 2164.01 (a)—Undue experimentation factors. [R-08.2012]. https://www.uspto.gov/web/offices/pac/mpep/s2164.html#d0e215360

MPEP Section 2164.02—Working example. [R-11.2013]. https://www.uspto.gov/web/offices/pac/mpep/s2164.html#d0e215531

Cited patent

Wolf, L. et al. (2017). Disdrometer having acoustic transducer and methods thereof (Patent No. WO2017156187). World Intellectual Property Organization (WIPO). https://patentscope.wipo.int/search/en/detail.jsf?docId=WO2017156187&_cid=P22-LNL3DS-83944-1

18 The Best Mode Requirement

The detailed description of an invention is usually replete with expressions stating various degrees of preference, such as those listed in Table 18.1:

Table 18.1 Sample language uses invoked to disclose the best mode

preferably	*de préférence*
more preferably	*davantage de préférence*
even more preferably	*encore davantage de préférence*
most preferably	*de préférence parmi toutes*

For example, within the context of the patent reciting the Plumpy'Nut® Ready-to-Use Therapeutic Food (RUTF) for humanitarian purposes (a nutritionally augmented peanut butter, packaged in squeeze pouches, with the capacity to bring severely malnourished children back to life), the disclosure specifies:

> [0019] The subject of the present invention is therefore a complete food or a nutritional supplement rich in lipids, containing not more than 10%, preferably not more than 5% and still more preferably not more than 2% water with respect to its weight, [...]
>
> [US20040052918A1—*High energy complete food or nutritional supplement, method for preparing same and uses thereof.*]

The explanation for this expression of escalating preferences, typical of patents, lies in the statutory *best mode requirement*, which specifies, according to US Patent Law *Title 35 USC Section 112 (a)*:

> The specification ... shall set forth the best mode contemplated by the inventor or joint inventor of carrying out the invention.

DOI: 10.4324/9781003423003-18

A statutory requirement clarified in the *MPEP Section 2165*, as follows:

> The best mode requirement is a safeguard against the desire on the part of some people to obtain patent protection without making a full disclosure as required by the statute. The requirement does not permit inventors to disclose only what they know to be their second-best embodiment, while retaining the best for themselves.

Thus, the *best mode requirement* means that inventors are obligated to disclose, not only their invention in exchange for patent protection, but the best mode of the invention. In other words, inventors cannot keep what they know to be the best mode of an invention to themselves, and only disclose what they know to be the second best, for *enablement* purposes.

In turn, the language use that has evolved by convention, and/or judge's writ, to perform the requirements of the *best mode*, in the recitation of the invention, takes the form of "escalating preferences". Whether the recitation of the *preferred, more preferred, even more preferred,* and *most preferred* modes, refers generally to the embodiments of the invention, or more specifically to significant aspects of the embodiments, such as temperatures, ingredients, steps or other components, operations or processes, such language uses are only found in patents. As a result, such language uses as escalating preferences, are *characteristic of the language of patents.*

The following are three examples, extracted from different patents, to show variation in the way language is used to perform the statutory *best mode requirement.*

(1) [...] for example, a 1-month period or more, over which a weight loss of about 0.5 lb. to up to about 5 lb. or more per month can occur, *preferably* about 1 lb. to up to about 10 lb. or more per month, *preferably* about 3 lb. to about 15 lb. per month, and up to about 20 lb. over a 6-month period, *preferably* up to about 25 lb., *preferably* up to about 35 lb. over a 6-month period. [italics mine]
US 2009123380—*Method for assaying satiety-enhancing tastants.*

(2) While multiple needle gauges can work, *preferred* needle gauges range from 16 to 22 gauge, with an *optimal* needle gauge in some embodiments being between 17 and 20 gauge. [italics mine]
US20170361999A1—*Beverage container cap for use with beverage extractor.*

(3) The body *preferably* comprises *at least one* wall, *more preferably a plurality* of walls, at least partially delimiting the noise suppression cavity, with the inlet of the cavity being located in said at least one wall of the body. [italics mine]
US2017108011A1—*Fan.*

Implications for translation

At the end of the day, understanding the *best mode requirement* prevents translators from fixing, or re-writing, the recitation of escalating preferences, performing the requirement of the *best mode* in the ST. However difficult it is to resist the temptation to re-write what might appear stylistically obtuse in any other context, understanding of this requirement, and its conventional expression, also fosters *reconciliation* with *the language of patents*. A language which many translators often truly see as *contrary* to the beauty and conciseness of the English language.

Understanding the rules for the *best mode requirement*, then clarifies or, at the very least, *lessens* the oddity of the expression, while assisting translators in their efforts to provide "literal" translation of patents. *Literal* translation, in compliance with the provisions of the *MPEP Section 608.01 Part V*, and *despite* the translator's linguistic knowledge of the often-quasi-impossible task of translating literally.

Finally, once aware of these patterns of language use, patent translators are also able to compile such language uses into their term bases and translation memories, for translation purposes. A compilation which will ultimately greatly facilitate the translation process. Otherwise, such compilation of language uses also generously serves the didactic purposes of learning and teaching.

References

35 USC Article 112—Specification. https://www.uspto.gov/web/offices/pac/mpep/mpep-9015-appx-l.html#d0e302824

MPEP Section 2165—The Best Mode Requirement. [R-08.2017]. https://www.uspto.gov/web/offices/pac/mpep/s2165.html

Cited patents

Briend, A. and M. Lescanne (2004). High energy complete food or nutritional supplement, method for preparing same and uses thereof (Patent Application No. US2004 0052918A1). United States Patent and Trademark Office (USPTO). https://image-ppubs.uspto.gov/dirsearch-public/print/downloadPdf/20040052918

Hirsch, A.R. (2009). Method for assaying satiety-enhancing tastants (Patent Application No. US2009123380). United States Patent and Trademark Office (USPTO). https://image-ppubs.uspto.gov/dirsearch-public/print/downloadPdf/20090123380

Johnson, J. et al J. Sir. (2017). *Fan* (Patent Application No. US2017108011A1). United States Patent and Trademark Office (USPTO). https://image-ppubs.uspto.gov/dirsearch-public/print/downloadPdf/20170108011

Lambrecht, G. et al. (2017). *Beverage container cap for use with beverage extractor (*Patent Application *No.* US20170361999A1). United States Patent and Trademark Office (USPTO). https://image-ppubs.uspto.gov/dirsearch-public/print/downloadPdf/2017 0361999

19 The Claims section

Once an invention has been disclosed, according to the regulations mentioned previously, without limitation, the inventor must also draft and file a Claims section, per the following provisions of *Title 37 CFR Section 1.75*:

(a) The specification must conclude with a claim particularly pointing out and distinctly claiming the subject matter which the applicant regards as his invention or discovery.
(b) More than one claim may be presented provided they differ substantially from each other and are not unduly multiplied.

In other words, in the Claims section of the patent application, inventors specify exactly the parts of their inventions that shall be protected, after the patent is granted. Thus, the Claims section is the most important legal aspect of a patent. Indeed, if for one reason, or another, patenting rights were subsequently infringed, the focus of the litigation, even prosecution, would first be on the Claims section.

Implications for translation

For translation, the implications are severalfold. First, the Claims section is a sufficiently separate section, both in terms of form and purpose within the patent application, to become for various reasons a *claims-only* translation, *outside* of the patent application process, and many such requests exist on the patent translation market. Whereas the disclosure of the invention is required to specify the invention in detail, such that those skilled in the art become enabled to reproduce the invention without undue experimentation, the Claims section specifies those aspects of the invention that shall be subject to the right to exclude others from using, marketing, producing, or selling the invention, without inventor or assignee authorization.

Separate *claims-only* translation requests (to French, English and/or German) exist *within* the context of filing for *European Patent Convention* (EPC) patents. Indeed, per the provisions of the *2000 London Agreement*, regarding *Article 65* of the *European Patent Convention* (EPC), inventors are required to

DOI: 10.4324/9781003423003-19

file their applications in just one of the three official languages of the European Patent Office (French, English or German), with *claims-only* sections translated into all three official EPO languages, to cover protection of the invention in those designated member states where the official language is different from English, French and German, and the state signatory to the agreement has a *prescribed* EPO language. As a result, this is the reason why some European patents have bilingual, or even trilingual French, English, German, *claims-only* sections, depending on the member states designated for patent protection. An Agreement which creates a market for *claims-only* translations connected to the application process, while reducing the burden of complete patent application translations that used to be required, for patent protection in designated states, where English, French and German are not official languages.

Secondly, because the Claims section forms the basis of patent litigation and even prosecution, it is crucially important for translators to avoid adding any translation errors that might become legal errors. The Claims section of a patent is replete with formal rules, both for the *drafting* and *recitation* of each of the claims, all of which must be understood and applied in translation, in addition to those rules that govern the patent application as a whole, and the specification of its parts. This is the reason selected claims recitation rules are examined in detail, further into the dedicated sections of this book.

Thirdly, despite the formal and functional separation of the Claims section within a patent application, the Claims section is still connected *legally* to the rest of the application. Indeed, the legal connection between the Claims section and the rest of the description of the invention is even *explicitly* specified on a semantic level, via the requirements of *ascertainability* and *antecedence* that govern the choice of terminology, in the Claims section. Such requirements, discussed in greater detail in a dedicated section further into this book, ensure that both linguistic and legal coherence exist between the claims to the invention and its description.

Thus, translators will also have to fully comply with the two requirements of *ascertainability* and *antecedence*, making sure that the translated terminology of the Claims section finds antecedence in the description. In particular, for a *claims-only* translation, such a verification means searching for the ST description of the invention, in the ST patent or patent application to *ascertain* the meaning of the terms found in the Claims section, and to make sure that there are no specially defined meanings in the description, per the provision of the corollary *Lexicographer Rule*. A search also designed to determine whether any translations might exist for the patent, in the form of any associated patent family member, in the interest of also keeping the claims terminology consistent. At the end of the day, the *claims-only* translation might be a stand-alone source text, and job, but legally it is connected on more than just the formal section-levels of a patent application.

Finally, if there were a canonical form in *the language of patents*, the formulation of the claims to an invention would be the canonical form. The formulation of a patent claim is found *nowhere else* but in reference to an invention.

A patent claim is formally different from any other type of claim, whether for insurance, argumentation, or in other legal domains. In other words, the claims to an invention are different from civil law claims (e.g., for personal injury and tort), business law claims (e.g., for contract disputes), labor law claims (e.g., for class action suits), divorce and family law claims (e.g., for alimony or custody), or real estate law claims (e.g., for property or damages), etc.

Thus, the rules and regulations governing the drafting of patent claims have the most *significant* linguistic impact on translation, requiring the most *prescriptive* language uses to perform the requirements of patent rules and regulations. The explicit constraints that patent claim recitation rules place on punctuation, syntax, and semantics in *drafting a patent application*, simply *cannot be ignored* in the corresponding translation. As a result, the following sections offer an examination of how such rules and regulations must inform the translation process, in an effort to produce *compliant* translations. In other words, translations that avoid any potentially costly error, even if translators, in some instances, might need to seriously re-condition their translation reflexes.

References

37 CFR 1.75e—Claim(s). https://www.uspto.gov/web/offices/pac/mpep/mpep-9020-appx-r.html#d0e320269

Agreement on the application of Article 65 of the Convention on the Grant of European Patents. (PDF full-text version in French, German, and English). https://documents.epo.org/projects/babylon/eponet.nsf/0/7FD20618D28E9FBFC125743900678657/$File/London_Agreement.pdf

MPEP Section 608.1(i)—Claims. [R-08.2012]. https://www.uspto.gov/web/offices/pac/mpep/s608.html#d0e44872

20 The Single-Sentence Rule (SSR)

One of the better-known rules for drafting claims, the *Single-Sentence Rule* (SSR), is a syntactic rule. In contrast to any other linguistic definition of a sentence, involving the required presence of a verb, or analyzed in terms of noun phrases (NP) and verb phrases (VP), the provisions of the patent claim SSR invoke a combination of punctuation and orthography. The provisions of this rule are specified in Section 608.01 (m) of the *MPEP* on the *Form of claims*, as follows.

> Each claim begins with a capital letter and ends with a period. Periods may not be used elsewhere in the claims except for abbreviations.

In practice, this means that some claims might be recited in very long sentences that may run a whole page. In those cases, the provisions of the *MPEP* rule further specify that:

> Where a claim sets forth a plurality of elements or steps, each element or step of the claim should be separated by a line indentation.

For example, in the following patent for the Australian Blue Lizard® sunscreen, where the invention concerns a special UV-sensitive packaging container, which changes color to alert the user in the presence of ultra-violet (UV) radiation, the first claim is a very long sentence. The claim recites all the parts of the packaging container. The claim begins with the base of the packaging container, moving up the sidewalls, which contain the special UV-sensitive dye for alerting the user to apply sunscreen, up to the opening of the container and the cap, which is roughly the same blue color as the rest of the packaging, when actively in the presence of UV radiation.

1. A package for a suncream including:
   a base;
   at least one sidewall extending upwardly from the base for defining collectively with the base a cavity for containing the suncream, wherein the sidewall includes an integral photochromic dye for causing a colour of the sidewall to change from a first predetermined colour to a

DOI: 10.4324/9781003423003-20

second predetermined colour as the intensity of UV radiation incident upon the sidewall increases, the second colour being discernible from the first colour for providing a user with a visible indication that the UV radiation incident upon the sidewall is sufficiently intense to warrant application of the suncream to the exposed skin of the user;

an opening in the sidewall for allowing the user to dispense the suncream from the package; and

a cap for moving between an open and a closed configuration for allowing and preventing the dispensing of the suncream through the opening, wherein the cap is a colour which is about the same as the second colour.

[US6405867—Package for a suncream.][1]

Thus, no matter how long the claim, *no exceptions* are provided to the Single-Sentence-per-claim Rule. McKeown, a law professional, even refers to this rule as one of the "sacred cows" of claim drafting rules. (McKeown, 2003).

Implications for translation

The inflexibility of the SSR for claims drafting cannot be overstressed for its impact on the translation process. Indeed, according to the SSR, translations will have to retain the same number of claims, each consisting of a single sentence, using indentations for the multiple steps or parts being claimed. For a translated claim to comply, the translator will be obligated to provide a single-sentence translation—however stylistically challenging. Besides, patents comprising very long claims are quite common. Consider the following additional example of a fairly typical SSR claim, extracted from Frank Gehry's concert hall acoustics patent, one of the patents masterminding the curved-metal architectural landmark, in Los Angeles.

1. A system for improving the dispersion of sound toward an audience, said sound being produced by an orchestra on a stage, and for reinforcing low frequencies in the spectrum of said sound during the initial portion of reverberation, comprising vertical tubes on said stage at the sides and rear of said orchestra and horizontal tubes supported above said stage in a direction transverse to said stage and said orchestra, at least some of said vertical tubes having a chamber with one open end formed at the upper end of said tube by a transverse partition, and at least some of said horizontal tubes having a chamber with one open end formed at each end of said tube by transverse partitions, the lengths of said chambers in the different tubes varying in approximately equal steps from about 1/4 of the wave-length of the highest frequency to be reinforced to about 1/4 of the wave-length of the lowest frequency to be reinforced.

[US3672463—*Acoustical system employing tubular resonators.*]

In brief, translators run the risk of *invalidating* a claim when good intentions prompt them to "fix" the *terribly* long sentences. As a result, translators may need to re-condition their good writing reflexes.

Because of the SSR, and the subsumed possibility of long single-sentence claims, it follows perhaps tritely that translators might be required to develop impeccably sharp punctuation skills to handle all the nested phrases of a single-sentence claim. There is *no way out but through* a single-sentence claim that runs several paragraphs. Translation of such complex sentences, as the long and winding Frank Gehry patent claim quoted previously are common fare in patents translation. Such claims translations require the use of comas, semi-colons, and colons, without parsimony. If needed, refreshers on correct punctuation usage, such as those respectively provided by *The New York Times* best-selling authors, Lynn Truss (2003), and Steven Pinker (2014), will make the punctuation review task actually quite pleasurable.

A final word of caution. Asking a client for permission to *fix* the length of specific patent claims will probably result in a dismissal of translation responsibilities, least of all because the patent fee structure is based on the number of claims, their dependent and independent status.

Note

1 The US *utility* patent US6405867 recites the Blue Lizard® invention packaging using the standard Australian English spelling *colour*, which is consistent with the provisions of the US patent regulations (MPEP Section 608.01) which do not require that US patent applications be filed in American English. However, the Australian English term "colour" appears in contrast with the US standard spelling "color", consistently used elsewhere in this book.

Reference

MPEP Section 608.01—Specification. [R-07.2022]. https://www.uspto.gov/web/offices/pac/mpep/s608.html#d0e42440

MPEP Section 608.01 (m)—Form of claims. [R-10.2019]. https://www.uspto.gov/web/offices/pac/mpep/s608.html#d0e45061

McKeown, J.F. (August 2003). Claim drafting strategies revisited: Is the "Single-Sentence Rule" too inflexible? *Intellectual Property Today*.

Pinker, S. (2014). *The sense of style: The Thinking Person's Guide to Writing in the 21st Century*. New York, NY: Penguin Books.

Truss, L. (2003). *Eats, shoots and leaves. The zero tolerance approach to punctuation!* New York, NY: Gotham Books. ISBN 1-592-40203-8.

Cited patents

Moore, P.J. (2002). Package for a suncream (Patent No. US64e05867). United Stated Patent and Trademark Office (USPTO). https://image-ppubs.uspto.gov/dirsearch-public/print/downloadPdf/6405867

Jaffe, C. and F.O. Gehry, F. (1972). *Acoustical system employing tubular resonators* (Patent No. US3672463). United Stated Patent and Trademark Office (USPTO). https://image-ppubs.uspto.gov/dirsearch-public/print/downloadPdf/3672463

21 Direct-object function

Add *fuel to fire*, and consider yet another syntactic twist, governing the form of claims. The provisions of *Section 608.01(m)* of the *MPEP* further specify the following:

> While there is no set statutory form for claims, the present Office practice is to insist that each claim must be the object of a sentence starting with "I (or we) claim," "The invention claimed is" (or the equivalent). If, at the time of allowance, the quoted terminology is not present, it is inserted by the Office of Data Management.

The extra sentence, "I (or we) claim" or equivalent, provided at the top of the claims section of a patent, or added by the United States Patent and Trademark Office (USPTO), when the application is examined, thus appears to provide coherence to the claims recitation. It also explains the use of an indefinite article at the beginning of at least the first claim, if not all of them, depending on the patent. For example, consider the following two claims, extracted from a set of 22 claims, in one of the Nike *flyknit*[1] patents, US8631589B2:

> The invention claimed is:
>
> 1. An article of footwear having an upper and a sole structure secured to the upper, the upper comprising: a lace region defining a plurality of lace-receiving elements;
>   a lower region where the sole structure is secured to the upper, and
>   a plurality of strands extending from the lace region to the lower region, the Strands being secured to the upper in the lace region and the lower region, and the Strands being unsecured for a distance of at least five centimeters in an area between the lace region and the lower region;
>   the upper further includes a first layer and a second layer that each extend from the lace region to the lower region, the first layer and the second layer are unsecured to each other for said distance of at least five centimeters in the area between the lace region and the lower region;
>   wherein the strands are located between the first layer and the second layer through at least said distance of at least five centimeters; and

DOI: 10.4324/9781003423003-21

wherein the strands include a first strand and a second strand, ends of the first strand and the second strand being proximal to each other in the lace region, and opposite ends of the first strand and the second strand being distally spaced from each other in the lower region.

2. The article of footwear recited in claim 1, wherein the first layer and the second layer are secured to each other in one or more of the lace region and the lower region.

[US8631589B2—*Article of footwear incorporating floating tensile strands*.]

The claims section of the patent begins with the phrase "The invention claimed is", followed by the use of an indefinite article at the beginning of the first claim, whereas the rest of the claims begin with a definite article. Notice also that all the nested phrases of the long single sentence first claim are slightly indented per the additional provisions of *Section 608.1 (m)* of the *MPEP*.

Implications for translation

The *direct-object function* of claims, together with the *Single Sentence Rule* (SSR) governing claim drafting, according to the definition of a sentence exclusively based on orthography and punctuation, have astounded more than one patent translator. My favorite patent translator quote, in this regard, extracted from the *ATA Japanese Patent Translator's Handbook*, is the following:

> It is not against the law to write claims so that they are easy to understand, but it appears of fairly low priority.
>
> (Gooding, p. 14, 1997)

Note

1 *Flyknit* is a portemanteau term, combining "flyfishing and knitting" because the Nike *flyknit* invention technology, designed to make Nike sport shoe uppers, invokes knitted high strength fibers, similar to flyfishing line fibers. Knitting such fibers then creates zero waste, compared to cutting out templates from a sheet made of traditional shoe upper material, such as leather, fabric, plastic or other.

References

Gooding, G. (1997). Translating oppositions and official actions. Chapt. 8 in *The ATA Japanese Patent Translator's Handbook*, pp. 150–166.

MPEP Section 608.01(m)—Form of claims. [R-10.2019]. https://www.uspto.gov/web/offices/pac/mpep/s608.html#d0e45061

Cited patent

Dojan, F.J. (2014). Article of footwear incorporating floating tensile strands (US Patent No. US8631589B2). United States Patent and Trademark Office (USPTO). https://image-ppubs.uspto.gov/dirsearch-public/print/downloadPdf/8631589

22 Claim structure

Beyond the formal Single-Sentence Rule (SSR), and the direct-object rule, each claim also consists of three parts: *preamble*, *transitional phrase*, and *body* or *characterizing part*, per the provisions of *Section 1.75(e)* of the *Code of Federal Regulations Title 37*, cited below.

(1) A preamble comprising a general description of all the elements or steps of the claimed combination which are conventional or known.
(2) A phrase such as "wherein the improvement comprises".
(3) Those elements, steps, and/or relationships which constitute that portion of the claimed combination which the applicant considers as the new or improved portion.

Thus, part (2), the *transitional phrase* 'wherein', also called a *coordinating phrase*, functions as a fulcrum to connect part (1), *the preamble* (what belongs to the prior art) to part (3), the body or characterizing part (what is *new and non-obvious* that is being claimed as the invention).

Consider, for example, the British Anywayup cup™ invention, known as the "sippy cup" in the United States. This invention was filed in Great Britain by the award-winning female industrial designer, Mandy Haberman, who was granted the British patent GB2266045 for this invention. The Anywayup cup™ has many applications for the elderly, for people with disabilities, and for children, considering that the cup is spill-proof. However, the core purpose of the invention was to gently coach a child, away from the breast, towards more feeding independence.

Applied to the Anywayup cup™ invention, the three-part structure of a claim: *preamble* + *transitional phrase* + *what is new and non-obvious*, enables the inventor to claim exactly those characteristic aspects of the invention that are *new and non-obvious*. For example, the *new and non-obvious* inventive features of *this* particular drinking vessel are recited relative to all previously existing drinking vessels. Indeed, Haberman claims that it is the container cap, equipped

DOI: 10.4324/9781003423003-22

with a mouthpiece, containing a one-way valve, actuated via a child's suction that comprise the invention of her drinking vessel.

The first two claims of the Anywayup cup™ patent are cited below:

1. A drinking vessel suitable for use as a trainer cup or the like, comprising: an open-mouthed generally cup-shaped container; and a lid for the open mouth of said container, the lid having a mouthpiece associated therewith; the vessel being provided with valve means adapted to prevent flow of liquid from the interior of the container through the mouthpiece unless a predetermined level of lip pressure and suction is applied to the mouthpiece.
2. A drinking vessel according to Claim 1, wherein said valve means is a separate valve member located in use between the container and the lid. [underlining mine]

(GB2266045—Drinking vessel suitable for use as a trainer cup.)

Notice how the *preamble*, that which is already generally known in the prior art, in both patent claims for this invention, concerns "*a drinking vessel*". The underlined *transitional phrase*, coordinating the *drinking vessel* to what is *new and non-obvious*, is expressed in the first claim with the verb "*comprising*"[1], whereas, in the second claim, the coordinating function is expressed, using the underlined *transitional phrase*, "*wherein*".

The claimed invention, that which is considered *new and non-obvious*, is thus recited as a *subset* of the drinking vessels of the prior art. In other words, paraphrasing the claims, the invention claimed is "a drinking vessel *wherein* the invention drinking vessel has a lid and a mouthpiece, in which a specially designed one-way valve prevents any of the liquid from spilling, unless a child applies suction". An invention, whose various specific aspects, such as the position of the valve relative to the mouthpiece, the particular configuration of the mouthpiece, and the means to prevent flow, from the interior to the outside of the cup, are each further recited in the remaining 12 claims, in view of obtaining the rights to exclude others from using, manufacturing or selling the invention, without license, or other legal form of authorization.

Implications for translation

For translation, the question that arises is how to best use the target language to express the regulated three-part structure of a claim, and in particular, which target language terms to use for the terms *wherein* or *comprising*, and variations, functioning as *transitional phrases*, coordinating the *prior art* with what is *new and non-obvious*. After all, *transitional phrases* in patent claims are very important terms. Such phrases serve to introduce the specifics of the invention

Table 22.1 PCT and EPC claims structure rules (English version)

Regulations under the PCT Rule 6	*European Patent Convention—Rule 43*
(b) Whenever appropriate, claims shall contain: (i) a statement indicating those technical features of the invention which are necessary for the definition of the claimed subject matter but which, in combination, are part of the prior art, (ii) a characterizing portion—preceded by the words "characterized in that,", "characterized by", "wherein the improvement comprises", or any other words to the same effect—stating concisely the technical features which, in combination with the features stated under (i), it is desired to protect. **[English version]**	(1) The claims shall define the matter for which protection is sought in terms of the technical features of the invention. Wherever appropriate, claims shall contain: (a) a statement indicating the designation of the subject-matter of the invention and those technical features which are necessary for the definition of the claimed subject-matter but which, in combination, form part of the prior art; (b) a characterizing portion, beginning with the expression "characterized in that" or "characterized by" and specifying the technical features for which, in combination with the features stated under sub-paragraph (a), protection is sought. **[English version]**

proper, in particular, the *new and non-obvious* aspects of the invention. *New and non-obvious* aspects, which are precisely being claimed, in view of soliciting protection, and excluding others from using, reproducing, or marketing such an invention.

Fortunately, the almost exact same rules exist for European (EP) and World Intellectual Property Organization (WO) patents. This means that standardized translations also exist, in the three official languages of the European Patent Organization (French, English and German), and/or in all the official publication languages of the UN World Intellectual Property Organization (WIPO) (including English, French and Spanish), for the terms performing this particular coordinating function and its variations. The *European Patent Convention* (EPC) and WIPO *Patent Cooperation Treaty* (PCT) rules, cited in English in Table 22.1, correspond *directly* to the United States *Code of Federal Regulations* [*37 CFR 1.75(e)*] cited previously, in regards claim structure, and specifically the claim's *transitional phrases*. Note that the *transitional phrase* "*wherein*" is preferred in United States patents, whereas the English transitional phrases "*characterized in that*" or "*characterized by*" are preferred in EPC and PCT patents.

Thus, the structure of claims, and in particular the expressions such as: *wherein*, *comprises*, *characterized in that* or *characterized by*, each functioning as *transitional phrases* between the *prior art* and those specifically *new and non-obvious* features of the invention being claimed, also have very clear dedicated expressions in the other official languages of the EPO and WIPO, per the explicit provisions of the corresponding rules and regulations. This is also the case where the national IP laws of the contracting states might have corresponding regulations. For example, this is certainly the case for France, and Canada, respectively.

For reference purposes, the corresponding French version of the *WIPO PCT Regulation 6* and *European Patent Convention Rule 43* are cited below, in Table 22.2. The corresponding EPC German and WIPO PCT Spanish versions are cited in Table 22.3.

Table 22.2 PCT and EPC claims structure rules (French version)

Règlement d'exécution du PCT—Règle 6	*Convention sur le brevet européen (CBE)—Règle 43*
(b) Chaque fois que cela est approprié, les revendications doivent contenir: (i) un préambule indiquant les caractéristiques techniques de l'invention qui sont nécessaires à la définition de l'objet revendiqué mais qui, en étant combinées, font partie de l'état de la technique; (ii) une partie caractérisante—précédée des mots "caractérisé en", "caractérisé par", "où l'amélioration comprend", ou tous autres mots tendant au même effet—exposant d'une manière concise les caractéristiques techniques que, conjointement avec les caractéristiques techniques mentionnées au point i), l'on désire protéger. **[OMPI PCT Règle 6—French version]**	(1). Les revendications doivent définir, en indiquant les caractéristiques techniques de l'invention, l'objet de la demande pour lequel la protection est recherchée. S'il y a lieu, les revendications doivent contenir: (a) un préambule mentionnant la désignation de l'objet de l'invention et les caractéristiques techniques qui sont nécessaires à la définition de l'objet revendiqué mais qui, combinées entre elles, font partie de l'état de la technique; (b) une partie caractérisante introduite par l'expression "caractérisé en" ou "caractérisé par" et exposant les caractéristiques techniques pour lesquelles, en liaison avec les caractéristiques indiquées à la lettre a), la protection est recherchée. **[CBE Règle 43—French version]**

Table 22.3 PCT claims structure rules (Spanish version) and EPC claims structure rules (German version)

Reglamento del PCT—Regla 6 Reivindicaciones	*Regel 43 Form und Inhalt der Patentansprüche*
(b) Cuando proceda, las reivindicaciones deberán contener: (i) un preámbulo que indique las características técnicas de la invención que sean necesarias para la definición del objeto reivindicado, pero que, en combinación, formen parte del estado de la técnica; (ii) una parte característica—precedida de las palabras "caracterizado en que", "caracterizado por", "en el que la mejora comprende", o cualesquiera otras palabras con el mismo efecto—que exponga concisamente las características técnicas que se desea proteger, en combinación con las características mencionadas en el apartado i).	(1) Der Gegenstand des Schutzbegehrens ist in den Patentansprüchen durch Angabe der technischen Merkmale der Erfindung anzugeben. Wo es zweckdienlich ist, haben die Patentansprüche zu enthalten: (a) die Bezeichnung des Gegenstands der Erfindung und die technischen Merkmale, die zur Festlegung des beanspruchten Gegenstands der Erfindung notwendig sind, jedoch in Verbindung miteinander zum Stand der Technik gehören; (b) einen kennzeichnenden Teil, der mit den Worten "dadurch gekennzeichnet" oder "gekennzeichnet durch" beginnt und die technischen Merkmale bezeichnet, für die in Verbindung mit den unter Buchstabe a angegebenen Merkmalen Schutz begehrt wird.
[OMPI PCT Regla 6—Spanish version]	**[EPC Regel 43—German version]**

Note

1 The transitional verb "comprising" is the object of special provisions of the *Patent Cooperation Treaty*, the *European Patent Convention* and United States regulations, which are examined and discussed in detail, in the following, dedicated Section 23 of this book.

References

37 CFR 1.75(e)—Claims. https://www.uspto.gov/web/offices/pac/mpep/mpep-9020-appx-r.html#d0e320269

Convention sur le brevet européen—Troisième Partie. Chapt. II. Règle 43 Forme et contenu des revendications. [French]. https://www.epo.org/law-practice/legal-texts/html/epc/2020/f/r43.html

Europäisches Patentübereinkommen—Dritter Teil. Kapitel II. Regel 43 Form und Inhalt der Patentansprüche. [German]. https://www.epo.org/law-practice/legal-texts/html/epc/2020/d/r43.html

European Patent Convention—Part III. Chapt. II. Rule 43 Form and content of claims. https://www.epo.org/law-practice/legal-texts/html/epc/2020/e/r43.html

Regulations under the PCT—Rule 6—Form and content of claims. https://www.wipo.int/pct/en/texts/rules/r6.html#_6

Règlement d'exécution du PCT—Règle 6 Forme et contenu des revendications. [French]. https://www.wipo.int/pct/fr/texts/rules/r6.html
Reglamento del PCT—Regla 6 Reivindicaciones. [Spanish]. https://www.wipo.int/pct/es/texts/rules/r6.html

Cited patent

Haberman, M.N. (1993). Drinking vessel suitable for use as a trainer cup (Patent No. GB2266045). Intellectual Property Office of the United Kingdom. https://worldwide.espacenet.com/patent/search/family/010713718/publication/GB2266045A?q=GB2266045

23 Transitional verbs *comprising* vs. *consisting of* (EN), *comprenant* vs. *constituer de* (FR), *umfassen* gegenüber *bestehen aus* (DE), *que comprende* vs. *consistente en* (ES)

Regulations for the recitation of United States, European and World *Patent Cooperation Treaty* (PCT) patent claims introduce a semantic distinction between the verbs *comprising* and *consisting of*, functioning as *transitional phrases*, which coordinate the *prior art* and the *new* and *non-obvious* features of an invention-at-hand. The verb *comprise* is understood in the *open-ended sense* of "includes but not limited to", whereas the verb *consists of* is understood in the *closed-ended sense* of "includes exclusively" [*EPO Guidelines Part F., Chapt. IV. 4.20, MPEP 2111.03, PCT Guidelines 5.24*].

Thus, for example, if a shampoo is claimed to include a list of ingredients *consisting of* versus *comprising*, this means that in the case of *consisting of*, no other unrecited ingredients fall within the scope of the claimed invention, whereas in the case of *comprising*, the presence of other non-recited ingredients might also fall within the scope of the claimed shampoo invention. In the case of *consisting of* the list of shampoo ingredients is *closed*, whereas in the case of *comprising*, the list of shampoo ingredients is *open*.

Although experts in the legal profession will point to many differences between the rules and regulations governing European, *Patent Cooperation Treaty*, and US patents, the matter of the difference in meaning between the *transitional verbs comprising* and *consisting of* is <u>not</u> one of them. A true consensus exists in the provision of the rules and regulations, across international patent treaties and United States patent rules on the differences between the meaning of the verbs *comprising* versus *consisting of*, functioning as *transitional phrases*.

The following example, provided at the European Patent Office, concerns a chemical patent where, for a compound *consisting of* the components A, B, and C, the sum total of the components **must equal 100%**. In contrast, for a compound, *comprising* the components A, B, and C, the sum total of the components A, B, and C do <u>not</u> exclude the presence of other components. Thus, the components A, B, and C do **<u>not</u> necessarily equal 100%**. Other unrecited components, such as fragrances for example, might exist in the 100% total, which would not affect the essential characteristics of the composition.

- The term ***consists of*** <u>excludes</u> other components of the composition, thus creating a **<u>closed</u>** composition.

DOI: 10.4324/9781003423003-23

- The term ***comprising*** implies that other components might be included in the composition, although they are unrecited. Other components, which might be included, such as pharmaceutically acceptable ingredients, thus create an **open** composition.

As a result, in case of litigation, the semantic difference between *consisting of* and *comprising* is critical. A claim constructed with the *transitional* verb *consisting of* would *exclude* other components. In contrast, for a claim constructed with the verb *comprising*, the fact that other components are not recited does not mean they are excluded, and therefore from protection.

For example, the distinction between *comprising* and *consisting of* was precisely the issue at stake in the case: Gillette Co. v. Energizer Holdings Inc. A case involving Gillette's wet shave safety razors *comprising* "a group of first, second and third blades", where Energizer Holdings could not successfully argue that their four-bladed QUATTRO® wet shave safety razor was not infringing Gillette's multiple blade wet shave safety razors, on the grounds that the Energizer Holdings razors had more blades. An adjudicated case, cited in the provisions of the *MPEP Section 2111.03, as follows*:

> In *Gillette Co. v. Energizer Holdings Inc.*, 405 F.3d 1367, 1371–73, 74 USPQ2d 1586, 1589–91 (Fed. Cir. 2005), the court held that a claim to "a safety razor blade unit comprising a guard, a cap, and a group of first, second, and third blades" encompasses razors with more than three blades because the transitional phrase "comprising" in the preamble and the phrase "group of" are presumptively open-ended. "The word 'comprising' transitioning from the preamble to the body signals that the entire claim is presumptively open-ended."

Implications for translation

A fortiori, the distinction between *comprising* and *consisting of* is also critical in translation, where the choice of terms must reflect the *open ended* versus *closed ended* adjudicated notions of inclusion or exclusion. Thus, a single verb in the translation of a claim might *completely* change the scope of the claim, and the resulting protection that is conferred, potentially resulting in litigation, or even before this possibility, the rejection of the patent application.

It follows that the differences in the meaning of the terms *comprising* and *consisting of* must be understood in the ways in which they are examined at the patent offices and adjudicated in Case Law. A dictionary definition is not enough to properly translate the terms, which have implications in terms of what is *included* or *excluded* in a claim, and therefore what might become the object of litigation.

In sum, the terms *comprising* and *consisting of* are *not* legally interchangeable in the context of patents, even if official synonyms are listed respectively for *comprising* and *consisting of*. Indeed, the provisions of the *MPEP Section 2111.03* list the transitional phrases "*including*, *containing*, or *characterized by*" as synonyms for *comprising*; and "*containing*" as synonym for *consisting of*. However, the provisions of the *MPEP Section 2111.03* also *clearly* specify, on the basis of adjudication, that, for other transitional phrases, such as "*having*", or even "*consisting essentially of*", a determination will have to be made, on a case-by-case basis, whether they are to be *construed* as *open-ended transitional phrases*, functioning like *comprising*, or *closed-end transitional phrases*, functioning like *consisting of*, depending on the specification of the invention.

In particular, for the case of *consisting essentially of*, the MPEP even states that this transitional phrase occupies a *middle ground*, alternatively used to

Table 23.1 European Patent Convention Guidelines 4.20 "Comprising" vs. "consisting of" (including French and German versions)

4.20 "Comprising" *vs.* "consisting of" [English]

This section outlines how the terms "comprising" and "consisting of" are to be interpreted when construing a claim.

A claim directed to an apparatus/method/product "comprising" certain features is interpreted as meaning that it includes those features, but that it does not exclude the presence of other features, as long as they do not render the claim unworkable.

On the other hand, if the wording "consist of" is used, then no further features are present in the apparatus/method/product apart from the ones following said wording. [...]

4.20 Sens des termes "comprenant" et "constitué de" [French]

Cette partie explique quel sens il y a lieu de donner aux termes "comprenant" et "constitué de" lors de l'interprétation d'une revendication.

Une revendication portant sur un dispositif/procédé/produit qui "comprend" certaines caractéristiques est interprétée comme signifiant qu'elle inclut ces caractéristiques, mais qu'elle n'exclut pas la présence d'autres caractéristiques, tant qu'elles ne rendent pas la revendication inopérante. Par contre, si l'expression "constitué de" est employée, aucune autre caractéristique ne figure dans le dispositif/procédé/produit en dehors de celles qui suivent cette expression. [...]

4.20 "umfassen" gegenüber "bestehen aus" [German]

In diesem Abschnitt wird erläutert, wie die Begriffe "umfassen" und "bestehen aus" bei der Anspruchsauslegung zu verstehen sind.

Ein Anspruch, der auf eine Vorrichtung/ein Verfahren/ein Erzeugnis gerichtet ist, die bzw. das bestimmte Merkmale "umfasst", wird so ausgelegt, dass diese Merkmale darin enthalten sind, das Vorhandensein anderer Merkmale aber nicht ausgeschlossen ist, solange diese nicht dazu führen, dass der Anspruch nicht ausführbar ist.

Wird hingegen die Formulierung "bestehend aus" verwendet, können in der Vorrichtung/dem Verfahren/dem Erzeugnis neben den im Anschluss an diese Formulierung genannten keine weiteren Merkmale vorhanden sein. [...]

Table 23.2 WIPO PCT International Search and Preliminary Examination Guidelines, Pt. II International Application. Chapt. 5.24 for open and closed claims

5.24 In evaluating novelty or inventive step, the examiner should consider which type of transition phrase, such as "consisting of," "comprising," "characterized by," or "consisting essentially of" is used in the claims. The subject matter to be searched depends on the type of transition phrase used.
(a) Where a claim is drafted using a "closed" type of transition phrase, the claim cannot be construed as including products or processes that include structural elements or process steps other than those set forth in the claim. [...]
(b) Where a claim is drafted using an "open" type of transition phrase, it can be construed as including products or processes that include non-recited components or process steps, respectively. [...]
(c) Where a claim is drafted using "consisting essentially of" as the transition phrase, the claim occupies a middle ground between closed claims that are written in a closed format and fully open claims. The transitional phrase "consisting essentially of" limits the scope of a claim to the specified materials or steps "and those that do not materially affect the basic and novel characteristic(s)" of the claimed invention. For the purposes of search and examination, absent a clear indication in the description or claims of what the basic and novel characteristics actually are, "consisting essentially of" will be construed as equivalent to open (for example, "comprising") language.
[English Guidelines]

function as one, or the other, of the *open-ended* or *closed-ended* claim constructions, *depending on* the specification of the patent-at-hand. In particular, the *MPEP Section 2111.03* stipulates, in reference to an adjudicated case:

> A 'consisting essentially of' claim occupies a middle ground between closed claims that are written in a 'consisting of' format and fully open claims that are drafted in a 'comprising' format. PPG Industries v. Guardian Industries, 156 F.3d 1351, 1354, 48 USPQ2d 1351, 1353–54 (Fed. Cir. 1998).

A US MPEP provision set forth for the expression *consisting essentially of* that is 100% consistent with the provisions of the World PCT *International Search and Preliminary Examination Guidelines, Pt. II, Chapt. 5.24 (c)* for *open* and *closed* claims, cited in Table 23.2.

Thus, the point cannot be stressed enough that dictionaries are hardly the best sources of terminology for translating patents, claims in particular. The specification of the patent-at-hand, same family patents, or cited prior art patents, are far more reliable resources for terminology, exemplification, and background information, especially when it comes to construing *open-ended* versus *closed-ended* claims, using *comprising* versus *consisting of* -type *transitional phrases*.

Finally, considering that provisions for distinguishing *comprising* and *consisting of* are found not only in the United States *Manual for Patent Examination Procedure*, but also in the European Patent Organization, *European Patent Convention* (EPC) *Guidelines for Examination*, and in the World Intellectual

Table 23.3 OMPI Directives concernant la recherche internationale et l'examen préliminaire international selon le PCT. Deuxième partie. La demande internationale. Chapitre 5.24 Revendications de type ouvert ou fermé

5.24 Lorsqu'il évalue la nouveauté ou l'activité inventive, l'examinateur doit tenir compte du type d'expression de transition (par exemple: "consistant en", "comprenant", "caractérisé par" ou "consistant essentiellement en") qui est utilisé dans les revendications. L'objet de la recherche dépend en effet du type d'expression de transition utilisé.

(a) Lorsqu'une revendication comprend une expression de transition de type "fermé", elle ne peut pas être interprétée comme comprenant des produits ou des procédés incluant eux-mêmes des éléments structurels ou des phases de procédé autres que ceux qui sont exposés dans la revendication. [...]

(b) Lorsqu'une revendication comprend une expression de transition de type "ouvert", elle peut être interprétée comme comprenant des produits ou des procédés incluant eux-mêmes des éléments structurels ou des phases de procédé non cités. [...]

(c) Lorsque l'expression de transition "consistant essentiellement en" est utilisée dans une revendication, celle-ci se trouve dans une position intermédiaire entre les revendications du type fermé comprenant une expression de transition du type fermé et les revendications du type entièrement ouvert. L'expression de transition "consistant essentiellement en" limite la portée d'une revendication aux matières ou étapes spécifiées "et à celles qui n'affectent pas matériellement la ou les caractéristique(s) de base et nouvelle(s)" de l'invention revendiquée. Aux fins de la recherche et de l'examen, l'expression "consistant essentiellement en" sera interprétée comme équivalant à une expression de type ouvert (telle que "comprenant"), sauf si la description ou les revendications contiennent une indication précise de ce que sont effectivement les caractéristiques de base et nouvelles.

[French Guidelines]

Property Organization (WIPO), *Patent Cooperation Treaty* (PCT) *International Search and Preliminary Examination Guidelines*, this means that official translations exist, in French and German, the two other official languages of the EPO, besides English; as well as in Spanish, besides English and French, for PCT patents. Thus, the English distinction between *comprising* and *consisting of* officially translates in French as *comprenant* versus *constituer de*, in German as "*umfassen*" gegenüber "*bestehen aus*", and in Spanish as "*consistente en*" versus "*que comprende*".

In fact, official translations exist not only for the legally distinguished verbs, but also for the complete provisions of the EPC and PCT rules governing the distinctions. Complete multilingual provisions, supplying regulatory explanations, just in case further clarification is required, to support target language uses that correctly perform the distinguished differences in meaning.

For reference purposes, the *EPC Guidelines 4.20* for the distinction between *comprising* versus *consisting of* are cited below, in Table 23.1, in French, German and English. Whereas Tables 23.2 (English), 23.3 (French), and 23.4 (Spanish) each respectively specify, in three official WIPO languages, the provisions of the *PCT International Search and Preliminary Examination Guidelines, Pt. II, Chapt. 5.24* for *open* and *closed* claims, including the "in-between" case of *essentially consisting in*.

Table 23.4 OMPI Directrices de búsqueda internacional y de examen preliminar internacional del PCT. Parte II Solicitud internacional. Capítulo 5.24 Reivindicaciones de tipo abierto y cerrado

5.24 Cuando evalúe la novedad o la actividad inventiva, el examinador deberá tener en cuenta el tipo de expresión de transición (por ejemplo: "consistente en", "que comprende", "caracterizado por" o "consistente esencialmente en") que se utilice en las reivindicaciones. En efecto, el objeto de la búsqueda depende del tipo de expresión utilizada.

(a) Cuando una reivindicación comprenda una expresión de transición de tipo "cerrado", no podrá interpretarse como que comprende productos o procedimientos que a su vez incluyen elementos estructurales o fases de procedimiento distintos de los expuestos en la reivindicación. [...]

(b) Cuando una reivindicación comprenda una expresión de transición de tipo "abierto", podrá interpretarse en el sentido de que comprende productos o procedimientos que a su vez incluyen componentes o fases de procedimiento no citados, respectivamente. [...]

(c) Cuando se utiliza en una reivindicación la expresión de transición "consistente esencialmente en", se encuentra en una posición intermedia entre las reivindicaciones de tipo cerrado que contienen una expresión de transición de tipo cerrado y las reivindicaciones de tipo totalmente abierto. La expresión de transición "consistente esencialmente en" limita el alcance de una reivindicación a las materias o etapas especificadas "y a las que no afectan materialmente a la característica o características de base y nueva(s)" de la invención reivindicada. A los efectos de la búsqueda y del examen, la expresión "consistente esencialmente en" se interpretará que equivale a una expresión de tipo abierto (como "comprendiendo"), salvo si la descripción o las reivindicaciones contienen una indicación precisa de en qué consisten efectivamente las características de base y nuevas.

[Spanish guidelines]

References

EPO Guidelines for examination—Part F. Chapt IV. 4.20 "Comprising" *vs.* "consisting of". https://www.epo.org/law-practice/legal-texts/html/guidelines/e/f_iv_4_20.htm

Directives relatives à l'examen pratiqué—Partie F. Chapt. IV. 4.20 Sens des termes "comprenant" et "constitué de". [French]. https://www.epo.org/law-practice/legal-texts/html/guidelines/f/f_iv_4_20.htm

Gillette Co. v. Energizer Holdings Inc., 405 F.3d 1367, 1371-73, 74 USPQ2d 1586, 1589–91 (Fed. Cir. 2005). https://casetext.com/case/gillette-co-v-energizer-holdings-inc

Richtlinien für die Prüfung—Teil F. Kapitel IV. 4.20 "umfassen" gegenüber "bestehen aus". [German]. https://www.epo.org/law-practice/legal-texts/html/guidelines/d/f_iv_4_20.htm

MPEP 2111.03—Transitional Phrases. [R-08.2017]. https://www.uspto.gov/web/offices/pac/mpep/s2111.html#d0e200824

OMPI Directives concernant la recherche internationale et l'examen préliminaire international selon le PCT. Deuxième partie. La demande internationale—Partie II. Chapitre 5.24 Revendications de type ouvert ou fermé. https://www.wipo.int/export/sites/www/pct/fr/docs/texts/ispe-11.pdf

OMPI Directrices de búsqueda internacional y de examen preliminar internacional del PCT—Parte II Solicitud internacional. Capítulo 5.24 Reivindicaciones de tipo abierto y cerrado. https://www.wipo.int/export/sites/www/pct/es/docs/texts/ispe.pdf

PCT International Search and Preliminary Examination Guidelines—Part II International Application. Chapter 5.24 Open and closed claims. https://www.wipo.int/pct/en/texts/ispe/5_20_28.html

PPG Industries v. Guardian Industries, 156 F.3d 1351, 1354, 48 USPQ2d 1351, 1353–54 (Fed. Cir. 1998). https://casetext.com/case/ppg-industries-v-guardian-industries

24 Claims recitation rules

Backward only and in the alternative

As mentioned previously, according to US Patent Law, the specification of a patent must conclude with at least one or more claims. Further to this provision, when there is more than one claim, the claims might be *independent*, *dependent*, or *multiple dependent*, per the following statutory provisions of the United States Code, *Title 35*, *Article 112 (b)* and *(c)*:

- (b) CONCLUSION—The specification shall conclude with one or more claims particularly pointing out and distinctly claiming the subject matter which the inventor or a joint inventor regards as the invention.
- (c) FORM—A claim may be written in independent or, if the nature of the case admits, in dependent or multiple dependent form.

Still further, when there is a plurality of claims, *independent*, *dependent*, *multiple dependent*, the statute specifies the following recitation rules, respectively for *dependent* claims and *multiple dependent* claims, per the following statutory provisions of *Title 35 USC Section 112 (d) and (e)*:

- (d) REFERENCE IN DEPENDENT FORMS—Subject to subsection (e), a claim in dependent form shall contain a reference to a claim previously set forth and then specify a further limitation of the subject matter claimed. A claim in dependent form shall be construed to incorporate by reference all the limitations of the claim to which it refers.
- (e) REFERENCE IN MULTIPLE DEPENDENT FORM—A claim in multiple dependent form shall contain a reference, in the alternative only, to more than one claim previously set forth and then specify a further limitation of the subject matter claimed. A multiple dependent claim shall not serve as a basis for any other multiple dependent claim. A multiple dependent claim shall be construed to incorporate by reference all the limitations of the particular claim in relation to which it is being considered. [Underline mine].

The corresponding *MPEP Section 608* regarding *Disclosure* is helpful for understanding the above provisions of patent law, pertaining to the recitation

DOI: 10.4324/9781003423003-24

of claims, and the resulting language uses that are invoked to perform the requirements. Succinctly, the *dependent* or *multiple dependent* claims to an invention may refer respectively to one or several recited claims separately. In this case, the reference is always *backward* to previously recited claims, *never forwards*. For example, where there are *dependent* and *multiple dependent* claims, a hypothetical Claim 3 may never refer *forward* to Claim 4. Claim 3 may refer *backward only* to Claim 1 or Claim 2. When the claim refers *backward* to a single claim it is called a *dependent claim*. When the claim refers *backward* to *several* previously recited claims, the claim is called a *multiple dependent claim*. However, in the case of a *multiple dependent claim*, the claim may *refer backward only* <u>*in the alternative*</u> to any <u>one</u> of several previously recited claims (not all or several of them *cumulatively*).

Typically, the *backward only and in the alternative* rule for *multiple dependent* claims is performed using the terms "*according to* <u>*any one*</u> *of the* preceding claims", and variations. In other words, if Claim 3 is hypothetically a *multiple dependent* claim, the *preamble* will be recited as: *Claim 3, according to any one of Claims 1 and 2*. An expression that translates to French as: "*selon l'une quelconque des revendications 1 et 2…*". Table 24.1 lists varying language uses performing the requirements of "*backward only and in the alternative*" in both English and French.

Specifically, the *MPEP Section 608.01(n)* on *Dependent Claims*, provides the following examples of <u>proper and acceptable wording</u> for *multiple dependent* claims:

Claim 5. A gadget as in any one of Claims 1, 2, and 3, in which …
Claim 3. A gadget as in either Claim 1 or Claim 2, further comprising …
Claim 4. A gadget as in Claim 2 or 3, further comprising …
Claim 16. A gadget as in Claims 1, 7, 12, or 15, further comprising …
Claim 5. A gadget as in any of the preceding claims, in which …
Claim 8. A gadget as in one of Claims 4–7, in which …
Claim 5. A gadget as in any preceding Claim, in which …
Claim 10. A gadget as in any of Claims 1–3 or 7–9, in which …
Claim 11. A gadget as in any one of Claims 1, 2, or 7–10 inclusive, in which …

In each of the above cited examples of *multiple dependent* claims, the *multiple dependent* claim refers *backward only* and *in the alternative*, meaning that the

Table 24.1 Expressions for referring backward in the alternative in English and French

… according to any one of Claims 1, 2 and 3 …	*… selon l'une quelconque des revendications 1, 2, et 3.*
… according to any preceding Claim …	*… selon l'une des revendications précédentes …*
… according to either Claim 1 or Claim 2 ….	*… selon soit la revendication 1 soit la revendication 2 …*

multiple dependent claim refers to *any one or the other*, and not *to both, or all*, of previously cited or recited claims.

In contrast, the provisions of the previously cited *MPEP Section 608.01(n)* also specify the following improper and unacceptable wording for *multiple dependent* claims, where the *multiple dependent* claims are erroneously referring backward *cumulatively*, instead of *in the alternative* to previously recited claims:

> Claim 9. A gadget according to Claims 1–3, in which ...
> Claim 9. A gadget as in Claims 1 or 2 and 7 or 8, which ...
> Claim 6. A gadget as in the preceding claims in which ...
> Claim 6. A gadget as in Claims 1, 2, 3, 4, and/or 5, in which ...
> Claim 10. A gadget as in Claims 1–3 or 7–9, in which ...

According to the same provisions of the *MPEP Section 608.01(n)*, the reason for the rule on reference *in the alternative* for *multiple dependent claims* is to "avoid undue confusion in determining how many prior claims are actually referred to in a multiple dependent claim". This rule also simplifies the calculation of fees, which must be paid every year to maintain patent protection. It is for the same reason that "a multiple dependent claim cannot form the basis of another multiple dependent claim". In other words, a *multiple dependent* claim cannot refer back to another *multiple dependent* claim. A *multiple dependent* claim can refer back only to another *independent* or *dependent* claim (or several of them *in the alternative*).

However, another important linguistic reason might also be invoked to explain the provisions for recitation *in the alternative*. Such a reason concerns the *known* ambiguity of plural Noun Phrases (NPs), whether functioning as subject or direct object in a sentence. An ambiguity whereby nothing in a plural Noun Phrase suggests whether the elements of the plural Noun Phrase are taken as *a whole* or *separately*. For example, according to Adams and Kaye (2006), in the sentence: "*The Stockbrokers shall inform Acme*", nothing in the sentence suggests whether it is *each individual Stockbroker* that is required to inform Acme, or *all the Stockbrokers taken collectively* that are required to inform Acme. An ambiguity with consequences unlimited to the flow of information and decision making. Most importantly, an ambiguity that would *also* exist for the plural Noun Phrases of a patent claims section, containing *dependent* and/or *multiple dependent* claims, *without* the provisions of an explicitly stated *in the alternative* rule, as further detailed below.

Implications for translation

An understanding of the way in which claims are thus *nested* as *independent*, *dependent*, and *multiple dependent* claims, and of how *reference* functions *backward only* and *in the alternative*, per the previously cited statutory provisions, and those of the MPEP *Section 608*, is crucial for the translation process. Crucial because translations must also comply with the requirement of *backward only* and *in the alternative* reference, whenever such a requirement applies, or else run the risk of invalidating the translated claim. The examples of acceptable

Table 24.2 Regulations under the PCT Rule 6.4(a) on dependent claims, in English, French, and Spanish

a) Any claim which includes all the features of one or more other claims (claim in dependent form, hereinafter referred to as "dependent claim") shall do so by a reference, if possible at the beginning, to the other claim or claims and shall then state the additional features claimed. Any dependent claim which refers to more than one other claim ("multiple dependent claim") shall refer to such claims *in the alternative only*. Multiple dependent claims shall not serve as a basis for any other multiple dependent claim. Where the national law of the national Office acting as International Searching Authority does not allow multiple dependent claims to be drafted in a manner different from that provided for in the preceding two sentences, failure to use that manner of claiming may result in an indication under Article 17.2(b) in the international search report. Failure to use the said manner of claiming shall have no effect in a designated State if the manner of claiming actually used satisfies the national law of that State. **[English version, italics mine]**
a) Toute revendication qui inclut toutes les caractéristiques d'une ou de plusieurs autres revendications (revendication de forme dépendante, ci-après appelée "revendication dépendante") doit le faire par une référence, si possible au commencement, à cette ou à ces autres revendications, et doit préciser les caractéristiques additionnelles revendiquées. Toute revendication dépendante qui se réfère à plus d'une autre revendication ("revendication dépendante multiple") ne doit se référer à ces autres revendications *que dans le cadre d'une alternative*. Les revendications dépendantes multiples ne doivent servir de base à aucune autre revendication dépendante multiple. Lorsque la législation nationale de l'office national qui agit en qualité d'administration chargée de la recherche internationale ne permet pas que les revendications dépendantes multiples soient rédigées d'une manière différente de celle qui est prévue dans les deux phrases précédentes, le fait de ne pas rédiger les revendications de cette manière peut donner lieu à une indication selon l'article 17.2(b) dans le rapport de recherche internationale. Le fait de ne pas rédiger les revendications de ladite manière n'a pas d'effet dans un État désigné si les revendications ont été rédigées d'une manière conforme à la législation nationale de cet État. **[French version, italics mine]**
a) Toda reivindicación que comprenda todas las características de una o más reivindicaciones (reivindicación en forma dependiente, denominada en adelante "reivindicación dependiente"), deberá comenzar, a ser posible, mediante una referencia a esa o a esas otras reivindicaciones, y deberá precisar las características adicionales reivindicadas. Toda reivindicación dependiente que se refiera a más de una reivindicación ("reivindicación dependiente múltiple") *solo deberá referirse a dichas reivindicaciones en forma alternativa*. Las reivindicaciones dependientes múltiples no podrán servir de base a ninguna otra reivindicación dependiente múltiple. Cuando la legislación nacional de la Oficina nacional que actúe en calidad de Administración encargada de la búsqueda internacional no permita que las reivindicaciones dependientes múltiples se redacten en forma diferente de la prevista en las dos frases precedentes, el hecho de no redactar las reivindicaciones de esa forma podrá dar lugar a una indicación en el informe de búsqueda internacional conforme al Artículo 17.2(b). El hecho de no redactar las reivindicaciones de esa forma no surtirá efectos en un Estado designado, si las reivindicaciones se han redactado de tal forma que estén en conformidad con la legislación nacional de ese Estado. **[Spanish version, italics mine]**

and unacceptable claims recitation forms provided in the above cited *MPEP Section 608.01(n)*, in this regard, are crystal clear. And such provisions should also directly inform the translation process. The examples might also serve to clarify the wording of official patent translations, serving as models or background texts.

Interestingly, the *backward only* and *in the alternative rule*, for the recitation of US patent claims, also explicitly corresponds to WIPO *Patent Cooperation Treaty* (PCT) WO patents, according to the provisions of the WIPO *Regulations under the PCT, Rule 6.4(a) on Dependent Claims*. As a result, this means that language uses to perform the requirements of such rules also exist in French and Spanish. Thus, the provisions of the *Regulations under the PCT Rule 6.4(a)*, for the recitation of dependent claims in WO patents, are cited below, in English, French and Spanish, for anyone seeking explanation in source or target languages, in addition to English.

Turning to the *European Patent Convention* (EPC), quoted in English, French and German, the provisions of *Rule 43(4)* pursuant to *Dependent Claims* are more ambiguous, because they do not explicitly specify an *in the alternative* requirement. Specifically, the relevant *EPC Rule 43(4)* stipulates:

> (4) Any claim which includes all the features of any other claim (dependent claim) shall contain, if possible at the beginning, a reference to the other claim and then state the additional features. A dependent claim directly referring to another dependent claim shall also be admissible. All dependent claims referring back to a single previous claim, *and all dependent claims referring back to several previous claims*, shall be grouped together to the extent and in the most appropriate way possible.
>
> [English version, italics mine]

> (4) Toute revendication qui contient l'ensemble des caractéristiques d'une autre revendication (revendication dépendante) doit comporter une référence à cette autre revendication, si possible dans le préambule, et préciser les caractéristiques additionnelles. Une revendication dépendante peut également se référer directement à une autre revendication dépendante. *Toutes les revendications dépendantes qui se réfèrent à une ou plusieurs revendications antérieures* doivent, dans toute la mesure du possible, être groupées de la façon la plus appropriée.
>
> [French Version, italics mine]

> (4) Jeder Patentanspruch, der alle Merkmale eines anderen Patentanspruchs enthält (abhängiger Patentanspruch), hat, wenn möglich in seiner Einleitung, eine Bezugnahme auf den anderen Patentanspruch zu enthalten und nachfolgend die zusätzlichen Merkmale anzugeben. Ein abhängiger Patentanspruch, der sich unmittelbar auf einen anderen abhängigen Patentanspruch bezieht, ist ebenfalls zulässig. *Alle abhängigen Patentansprüche, die sich auf einen oder mehrere vorangehende Patentansprüche beziehen*, sind soweit wie möglich und auf die zweckmäßigste Weise zusammenzufassen.
>
> [German version, italics mine]

Table 24.3 Examples of European Patent dependent claims referring backward ambiguously

EP2450453—*Method for the replication, amplification, or sequencing of a DNA template.*
Claim 40. Kit according to Claims 37 to 39 wherein at least one nucleoside triphosphate or one primer is labelled
EP2450436—*Phage phi 29 DNA polymerase chimera.*
Claim 51. Kit according to Claims 48 to 50, wherein at least one nucleoside triphosphate or one primer is labelled
EP2282203A1- *Method of measuring the photocatalytic activity of cementitious materials.*
Claim 3. Method according to Claims 1–2, wherein the photocatalyst is dispersed in bulk in the material or is layered on its surface
[...]
Claim 14. Method according to Claims 1–11, wherein the measured level of photocatalytic activity is used as an indicator for selecting/screening/researching new cementitious materials having a predetermined level of photocatalytic activity

However, the fact that no explicit mention of the terms "*in the alternative*" appears in the relevant EPC *Rule 43(4)*, need not necessarily be construed as dependent claims referring backward *cumulatively* to "*several previous claims*", instead of backward *alternatively* to *any one of* "*several previous claims*". The plural of nouns, as in "*several previous claims*", is an example of the well-documented, and already *known*, "and/or" ambiguity of plural Noun Phrases in legal texts. An ambiguity, precisely because nothing in the surface structure of the sentence specifies whether the reference is to "*several previous claims*" taken as a *whole* (i.e., cumulatively), or to "*several previous claims*" taken *individually* (i.e., separately, and *in the alternative*).

A cursory examination of the dependent claims in 69 European patents (see Appendix III), competing for a European Inventor Award in 2014, uncovers only three patents with multiple dependent claims, referring backward ambiguously to a plurality of claims. In other words, multiple dependent claims referring backward *without* a specifically acceptable *in the alternative* surface structure marker, per the provisions of the MPEP *Section 608.01(n)*, previously cited. For all three examples (listed in Table 24.3), the preamble depends on a plurality of claims ("according to Claims 37 to 39" for EP2450453; "according to Claims 48 to 50" for EP2450436; "according to Claims 1–2" and "according to Claims 1–11" for EP2282203A1). Recitations dependent on *multiple* claims, which might be taken individually (i.e., separately, *in the alternative, <u>to any one or the other</u> of the claims*), or as a whole (i.e., cumulatively to *all of them together*). The three patents found with multiple dependent claims recited without explicit *in the alternative* makers, such as "any one", "either", or "or", are quoted in Table 24.3.

It is beyond the scope of translation to change European patent multiple dependent claims, so that they are recited with an explicit *in the alternative* marker, in view of making the multiple dependent claims unambiguously compliant with US Patent Law. In such cases however, translators informed of the

US *backward only* and *in the alternative* statute are likely to endear themselves to their clients, by pointing out a source of potential examination conflict, using the provisions of the MPEP *Section 608.01(n)*.

References

Adams, K.A. & A.S. Kaye (2006). Revisiting the ambiguity of "and" and "or" in legal drafting. In *St. John's Law Review*, 80(4) Fall 2006. https://scholarship.law.stjohns.edu/cgi/viewcontent.cgi?article=1215&context=lawreview

35 USC 112—Specification. https://www.uspto.gov/web/offices/pac/mpep/mpep-9015-appx-l.html#d0e302824912

MPEP Section 608—Disclosure. [R-11.2013]. https://www.uspto.gov/web/offices/pac/mpep/s608.html

MPEP Section 608.01 (n)—Dependent claims. [R-10.2019]. https://www.uspto.gov/web/offices/pac/mpep/s608.html#d0e45256

Regulations under the PCT—Rule 6.4 (a) Dependent claims. https://www.wipo.int/pct/en/texts/rules/r6.html#_6

Reglamento del PCT—Regla 6.4 (a) Reivindicaciones dependientes. https://www.wipo.int/pct/es/texts/rules/r6.html

Règlement d'exécution du PCT—Règle 6.4(a) Revendications dépendantes. https://www.wipo.int/pct/fr/texts/rules/r6.html

European Patent Convention—Part III. Chapt. II. Rule 43(4) Form and content of claims. https://www.epo.org/law-practice/legal-texts/html/epc/2020/e/r43.html

Convention sur le brevet européen—Troisième Partie. Chapt. II. Règle 43(4) Forme et contenu des revendications. https://www.epo.org/law-practice/legal-texts/html/epc/2020/f/r43.html

Europäisches Patentübereinkommen—Dritter Teil. Kapitel II. Regel 43(4) Form und Inhalt der Patentansprüche. https://www.epo.org/law-practice/legal-texts/html/epc/2020/d/r43.html

Guidelines for Examination—Part F. Chapt. IV. 3.4 Independent and dependent claims. https://www.epo.org/law-practice/legal-texts/html/guidelines/e/f_iv_3_4.htm

Directives relatives à l'examen pratiqué—Partie F. Chapt. IV. 3.4 Revendications indépendantes et revendications dépendantes. https://www.epo.org/law-practice/legal-texts/html/guidelines/f/f_iv_3_4.htm

Richtlinien für die Prüfung—Teil F. Kapitel IV. 3.4 Unabhängige und abhängige Patentansprüche. https://www.epo.org/law-practice/legal-texts/html/guidelines/d/f_iv_3_4.htm

Cited patents

Borzetti, F. et al. (2011). Method of measuring the photocatalytic activity of cementitious materials (Patent No. EU2282203A1). European Patent Office (EPO). https://worldwide.espacenet.com/patent/search/family/041571073/publication/EP2282203A1?q=EP2282203A1

Vega, J. de et al. (2011a). Phage phi 29 DNA polymerase chimera (Patent No. EU 2450436). European Patent Office (EPO). https://worldwide.espacenet.com/patent/search/family/043410525/publication/EP2450436A1?q=EP2450436

Vega, J. de et al. (2011b). Method for the replication, amplification, or sequencing of a DNA template (Patent No. EU2450453). European Patent Office (EPO). https://worldwide.espacenet.com/patent/search/family/043411512/publication/EP2450453A2?q=EP2450453

25 *Antecedence* and *ascertainability* for claims terminology

One of the most important rules for the drafting of claims is a semantic rule, also functioning as a safeguard for the interpretation of claims. This semantic rule, often cited as the *antercedence / ascertainability* requirement, is defined as follows, according to the provisions of *Section 1.75 (d)* of the *CFR Title 37*:

> The claim or claims must conform to the invention as set forth in the remainder of the specification and the terms and phrases used in the claims must find *clear support or antecedent* basis in the description so that the meaning of the terms in the claims may be *ascertainable* by reference to the description. [italics mine]

Thus, according to the provisions of *Title 37 CFR Section 1.75(d)*, the terminology arising in the claims section is required, not only to exist (to have *antecedence*) in the description of the invention. Claims terminology is *also* required to find meaning or clarification (*to be ascertainable*) in the description of the invention. The *MPEP Section 608.01(o)* further clarifies this point, as follows:

> The meaning of every term used in any of the claims should be apparent from the descriptive portion of the specification with clear disclosure as to its import; and in mechanical cases, it should be identified in the descriptive portion of the specification by reference to the drawing, designating the part or parts therein to which the term applies [...]

The *MPEP Section 608.01(g)* goes even as far as stating that the description of an invention is a "dictionary for the claims" per the following terms:

> The description is a *dictionary for the claims* and should provide clear support or antecedent basis for all terms used in the claims. [italics mine]

Implications for translation

The immediate consequence of this rule is that translators are not free to select claims terminology among competing synonyms. For a *claims-only* translation,

DOI: 10.4324/9781003423003-25

translators are required to go back to any existing translation of the description of the invention, to find translation for terms occurring in the claims section. In the absence of such a translated description, the translator might search patent family members for a target language version of the patent description, and/or *claims* section. If no translation precedence exists, and the translation includes the description of the invention as part of the job, then the translator will have to take extra care to ensure consistency in the choice and use of terminology across both the description and the claims section.

Interestingly, such important provisions of patent regulations as *antecedence* and *ascertainability* of the meaning of claims terminology have conventionally resulted in the drafting of claims, where the author actually copies, often *verbatim* the terms and phrases found in the description. For example, French patent law makes this particular interpretation of *antecedence* and *ascertainability* absolutely clear in the provisions of the French Industrial Property Office (*Institut National de la Propriété Industrielle*—INPI) regulations (*Directives brevets et certificats d'utilité*—Section C. Chapt. 4—1.4), in connection with the provisions of the French IP Code 612.6, 612.11, which specify "*mot à mot*" (i.e., *verbatim*) use of the terms and phrases of the description, as a foundation for claims.

In United States applications, this is the *de facto* case for the first claim, which sometimes appears with close to almost 99% match with the Abstract of the invention, and/or with the brief description of the invention, or parts thereof. For example (and there are countless), in the patent application US20130323184, titled *Method of providing fast relief to a user of a nicotine chewing gum*, consider the degree of *verbatim* repetition between the Abstract, paragraph 0023 of the brief description of the invention, and the first claim, as extracted from the patent application, and quoted in Table 25.1.

In sum, for the translation process, the *antecedence / ascertainability* requirement has two significant implications. First, where the selection of synonyms in the *claims-only* section might be "possible", such a possibility is actually contrary to regulatory provisions. Terms and phrases used in the claims section are required both to find *antecedence* and to be *ascertainable* (i.e., strictly cross-referenced) in the description of the invention.

Secondly, any stylistic inclination to avoid repetitions is also contrary to the conventional drafting of a patent application. In particular, any avoidance of repetitions is contrary to the interpretation of the regulation on *antecedence* and *ascertainability*, as set forth the provisions of *Title 37 CFR Section 1.75(d)* cited above. An interpretation which usually results in *de facto verbatim* repetition (for example, per the quoted examples in Table 25.1). Thus, the fact of the matter is that, in patents translation, the *antecedence / ascertainability* requirement also *overrides* any stylistic considerations supporting the avoidance of verbatim repetitions.

Table 25.1 Example of verbatim repetition of terms and phrases in the abstract, description, and first claim in US20130323184

US20130323184—Method of providing fast relief to a user of a nicotine chewing gum.		
Abstract	*Brief description [Parag. 0023]*	*First claim*
The invention relates to a method of relieving nicotine craving comprising the steps of providing at least one chewing gum comprising tobacco alkaloid to a user, providing relief of nicotine craving to said user by transferring of tobacco alkaloid from the chewing gum to the human body of said user by chewing of said chewing gum, said chewing of said chewing gum comprising a chewing process involving a transfer of tobacco alkaloid from said chewing gum above a threshold transfer rate in the period of about 1/2 minute to about 2 1/2 minutes from initiation of said chewing process.	[0023] The invention relates to a method of relieving nicotine craving comprising the steps of providing at least one chewing gum comprising tobacco alkaloid to a user, providing relief of nicotine craving to said user by transferring of tobacco alkaloid from the chewing gum to the human body of said user by chewing of said chewing gum, said chewing of said chewing gum comprising a chewing process involving a transfer of tobacco alkaloid from said chewing gum above a threshold transfer rate in the period of about 1/2 minute to about 21/2 minutes from initiation of said chewing process.	1. Method of relieving nicotine craving comprising the steps of providing at least one chewing gum comprising tobacco alkaloid to a user, providing relief of nicotine craving to said user by transferring of tobacco alkaloid from the chewing gum to the human body of said user by chewing of said chewing gum, said chewing of said chewing gum comprising a chewing process involving a transfer of tobacco alkaloid from said chewing gum above a threshold transfer rate in the period of about 1/2 minute to about 21/2 minutes from initiation of said chewing process.

References

37 CFR 1.75 (d)—Claim(s). https://www.uspto.gov/web/offices/pac/mpep/mpep-9020-appx-r.html#d0e320269

INPI—*La délivrance des brevets et certificats d'utilité*. Section C. Chapt. 4—1.4—La description, fondement de la revendication. https://www.inpi.fr/sites/default/files/directives_brevets_livre1_instruction_des_demandes_07_01_21.pdf

MPEP Section 608.01 (g)—Detailed description of invention. [R-10.2019]. https://www.uspto.gov/web/offices/pac/mpep/s608.html#d0e44731

MPEP Section 608.01 (o)—Basis for claim terminology in description. [R-07.2015]. https://www.uspto.gov/web/offices/pac/mpep/s608.html#d0e46173

Cited patent

Carsten Andersen, V. (2013). Method of providing fast relief to a user of a nicotine chewing gum (Patent No. US20130323184). United States Patent and Trademark Office (USPTO). https://image-ppubs.uspto.gov/dirsearch-public/print/downloadPdf/20130323184

26 Plain meaning

According to the *MPEP Section 2111.01*:

> The plain meaning of a term means the ordinary and customary meaning given to the term by those of ordinary skill in the art at the time of the invention. The ordinary and customary meaning of a term may be evidenced by a variety of sources, including the words of the claims themselves, the specification, drawings, and prior art. However, the best source for determining the meaning of a claim term is the specification—the greatest clarity is obtained when the specification serves as a glossary for the claim terms.

For linguists used to the surface and deep structures of a sentence, the notion of *meaning* is anything but *plain*. At the very least, an assumption exists concerning the fact that more than one ordinary meaning sometimes co-exists for any given term, and that such multiplicity of *meaning*, in certain cases, gives rise to *ambiguity*. For example, the French term *trombone*, referring to the musical instrument, and by extension pictographically to a "paperclip", is one case of *homonymic* meaning, among countless. However, as the next section of this book on the *Lexicographer Rule* will demonstrate, *plain meaning*, according to the provisions of the MPEP, does not necessarily exclude *complexity*.

Implications for translation

The *Plain meaning* rule is directly connected to the notions of *ascertainability* and *antecedence*. For *claims-only* translations, terminology has to be verified in the description of the invention. As a result, the meaning of a term in the claims section might not be "plain or ordinary", <u>if such a term was redefined</u> in the description of the invention. This might be the case, for example, when the applicant has taken the potential role of "lexicographer", introducing a glossary in the disclosure. Otherwise, "plain or ordinary" meaning might be different conceptually, when the invention hinges on new or revised concepts, expressed in new ways. Consequently, this is another reason why translators

DOI: 10.4324/9781003423003-26

commissioned for *claims-only* translations, MUST secure a copy of the specification (and any translations thereof) to make sure that terminology in the claims section is as "plain" or "special" as in the description, where meanings might have been glossed or otherwise redefined.

Consider the following example, involving the prepositions "**at**" *versus* "**to**" in a case involving *Chef America, Inc.*, (Plaintiff-Appellant) *v. Lamb-Weston, Inc.,* (Defendant-Appellee), brought before the Court of Appeals of the Federal Circuit, 358 F.3d 1371, 1372, 69 USPQ2d 1857 (Fed. Cir. 2004).

The issue was to determine whether the following claim segment:

> [...] heating the resulting batter-coated dough to a temperature in the range of about 400 to 850° F
>
> [Extracted from US4761290, titled *Process for making dough products*, owned by Chef America Inc.]

has the meaning:

1. "heating *the dough* **to** a temperature of 400 to 850° F" (as the District Court had previously held).
   or
2. "heating *the oven* **at** a temperature of 400 to 850° F" (as the Appellant contended).

The reason put forward for the difference in meaning was that: if the dough is heated "**<u>to</u> a temperature between 400 and 850°F**", it would mean that the dough would be burnt to a "*charcoal briquette*" crisp, and therefore, that the claim means "**heating the oven <u>at</u> 400 to 850 ° F**". The infringement case was hinging on the fact that the defendant Lamb–Weston was using the patented process at a lower temperature.

The Court of Appeals judge ruled *against* Chef America, Inc., *arguing for the plain meaning of the claim*, and ultimately because of the faulty writing of the claim, if indeed it was to be understood other than in "plain terms". The judge's ruling reads as follows:

> These are ordinary, simple English words whose meaning is clear and unquestionable. There is no indication that their use in this particular conjunction changes their meaning. They mean exactly what they say. The dough is to be heated to the specified temperature. Nothing even remotely suggests that what is to be heated is not the dough but the air inside the oven in which the heating takes place. Indeed, the claim does not even refer to an oven.

The judge further added that the Court could not re-write patent claims:

> Plaintiff's patent could have easily been written to reflect the construction plaintiff attempts to give it today. It is the job of the patentee, and not the court, to write patents carefully and consistently.

Beyond the outcome of the appeal, this is also an example that might be construed to perfectly highlight the risks of uninformed patents translation. In fact, the appellate judge's ruling might be construed as a clear message to translators about heeding what the courts call "literal" translation, another problematic issue for translators, but nonetheless clarified by Martin Cross (2007) further into this book. In other words, should translators have tried to "pad" (*étoffer* in French) their French translation of this patent, using one of the well-known, best-practice strategies put forward by Vinay and Darbelnet (1977, 1995), to handle the "power" of English prepositions, the resulting French translation might have read: *en chauffant la pâte préalablement enrobée dans un four à température comprise entre 400 et 850°F*. As a result, the padded translation would have introduced the term "oven" into the Claim translation (as the Appellant suggests), thereby contradicting the judge's ruling, and ultimately the merits of the case, in the patent's French version, or in a French patent, had the translation been used to file for a French patent.

Even if there is no deep structure specified, or implied, in the "plain meaning" rule, or in the court's presentation of the rule, *translators still need to take great care to avoid ambiguity*, which might nevertheless exist, especially syntactic ambiguity, and even more specifically for the case of dangling prepositional phrases. The use of the preposition "to" in the original patent claim: "heating the resulting batter-coated dough *to a temperature in the range of about 400 to 850°F* is a prime example of ambiguity, with two deep structure meanings:

1. *heating the dough to a temperature in the range of about 400 to 850°F*, and
2. *heating the dough to (*a presupposed *oven) temperature in the range of about 400 to 850°F.*

Two deep structures, generating surface structure ambiguity, which Chef America Inc., actually used in their defense against Lamb-Westin, Inc. Surface structure ambiguity which might also generate a perfectly legitimate *padded* French translation, inclusive of just one of the deep structure meanings, for example the deep structure meaning with the presupposed *oven* temperature. A *padded* translation which would have resolved the source ambiguity in the French version of the patent, and thereby produced a French version of the patent less vulnerable to infringement. Although admittedly, the translation would have been seen as violating the *literal* translation requirement, according to the Appellate judge's ruling. A ruling which in fact upheld the deep structure meaning *without* a presupposed oven.

References

Chef America, Inc. v. Lamb–Weston, Inc. 358 F.3d 1371, 1372, 69 USPQ2d 1857] (Fed. Cir. 2004).

MPEP Section 2111.01—Plain meaning. [R-07.2022]. https://www.uspto.gov/web/offices/pac/mpep/s2111.html#d0e200409

Vinay, J.P. and J. Darbelnet (1977). *Stylistique comparée du français et de l'anglais*. Didier, Paris, France.

Vinay, J.P. and J. Darbelnet (1995). *Comparative stylistics of French and English: A methodology for translation*. Translated by Juan C. Sager and Marie Josee Hamel. John Benjamins, Amsterdam, The Netherlands.

Cited patent

Meraj, P. and T. Nagle (1988). Process for making dough products (Patent No. US4761290). United States Patent and Trademark Office (USPTO). https://image-ppubs.uspto.gov/dirsearch-public/print/downloadPdf/4761290

27 The Lexicographer Rule

In certain instances, the applicant is allowed to 'disavow' the 'plain and customary' meaning of a claim term, in the specification of the invention. According to the provisions of the *MPEP Section 2111.01 (IV)*:

> To act as their own lexicographer, the applicant must clearly set forth a special definition of a claim term in the specification that differs from the plain and ordinary meaning it would otherwise possess. The specification may also include an intentional disclaimer, or disavowal, of claim scope.

The *Lexicographer Rule* requires that the *applicant-acting-as-lexicographer* specify the definition of a new meaning in the description of the invention, as well as how this meaning might differ from the *plain meaning* of a term. As a result, the *acting-lexicographer* might explicitly *disclaim* the scope of a claim, or otherwise *disavow* the *plain meaning* of a term.

The following example is cited in Rosenblatt et. al., (2013), in regard to the case of *Martek Biosciences Corp. v. Nutrinova Inc.,* 579 F.3d 1363 (Fed. Cir. 2009). For background information on the case, Omega-3 fats are essential nutrients to help build and maintain health. They are a key part of every cell, and a source of energy. Omega-3 fats are obtained from foods and dietary supplements. Martek Biosciences produces *docosahexaenoic acid* (DHA) products, one of the essential Omega-3 fatty acids.

The Martek Biosciences Corp's claims, in US patent No. 5698244, are understood to be directed towards:

> […] methods for achieving high concentrations of Omega-3 fats in an <u>animal</u> […] (underlining mine)

The District Court understood the term "animal" to mean "<u>excluding humans</u>", and therefore ruled that the defendant, Nutrinova Inc., was <u>not</u> infringing Martek, because the Nutrinova method applied <u>only to humans</u>.

However, the Federal Circuit Court *reversed the decision*, because Martek explicitly defined "animal" as "any organism belonging to the kingdom *Animalia*," which i<u>ncludes humans</u>. The Federal Circuit Court completely

DOI: 10.4324/9781003423003-27

dismissed the *ordinary* meaning of "animal" which excludes "human", because Martek had explicitly defined the terms in the specification (had acted as *lexicographer*). As a result, the definition *including* humans controlled the *ordinary and customary* definition of the term "animal" (which otherwise might *exclude humans)*. Thus, the definition of the term "animal", set forth in the specification of the invention, governed the meaning of "animal" in the claims, *redefining the ordinary and customary* meaning that might have been construed in the claims.

What this means is that applicants, *acting-as-lexicographers*, can override the '*plain and customary*' meaning of claim terms by ascribing special meaning, or when there is polysemy, by selecting and defining such meaning in the specification of the invention. Thus, the *Lexicographer Rule* consolidates the regulation on *antecedence* and *ascertainability*, which already requires that the meaning of claims be set forth in the description of the invention.

Implications for translation

For translators working on *claims-only* translations, the possibility of the applicant having *acted-as-lexicographer* means, once again, that a copy of the specification (and its translation, if any) will have to be secured. Once secured, the specification will have to be carefully reviewed for any provisions setting forth explicit definitions. Then, any new definitions found in the specification will have to be kept in mind, or entered into a term base, in order to retain, in the claims section, the same terminology and/or any other specific *lexicographer*-defined meanings of the specification.

Otherwise, it should be quite reassuring to linguists that the possibility of the *applicant-acting-as-lexicographer* in fact demonstrates that the courts recognize complex meaning. Complex meaning that can be re-defined and selectively understood, rather than fixed, and set forth as the *only* meaning. Even if *the plain and customary meaning* of claims shall prevail in all instances—unless otherwise defined, or disavowed, by the *applicant-acting-as-lexicographer*.

Implications of the *Lexicographer Rule* also exist regarding the use of dictionaries, glossaries, and *Linguee*-type tools, even concordances, since so much of the meaning in patents is self-contained in the patent specification. Indeed, this is one of the reasons no doubt that prompted Bruce Popp (2009) to state that patents are *the best source of patent terminology*. External terminology resources will sometimes even be at odds with the definitions that an *applicant–lexicographer* has incorporated in a patent. This was the essence of the previously cited Federal Circuit Appeals case, involving *Martek Biosciences Corp. v. Nutrinova Inc.* A case that concerned the definition of the term "animals" *excluding versus including* "humans". Likewise, caution also makes sense concerning the use of conventional sources of terminology for patents terminology, to the extent that patents are all about inventions. Inventions, by definition, that are mapping new territory and new frontiers of knowledge, for which new words are also needed, not necessarily yet incorporated in dictionaries.

The previously mentioned *ascertainability* and *antecedence* requirements are thus two requirements that *cooperate* with the actions of an applicant, taking on the role of *lexicographer*. For translators, such requirements, together with the ways in which they play out in a patent application, must inform the translation process. Information that should result in taking the translation principle of *"consistency"* to the higher level of legal significance. *Consistency* to a higher level of legal significance, because on the one hand, a claim might be invalidated when it is not *ascertainable* in the description, and on the other hand, the *"ordinary and customary"* meaning of words might have been re-ascribed in a patent specification. As a result, such possibilities as the re-definition of terms in the patent drafting process are going to control the use of terminology throughout the patent, *a fortiori* in translation.

References

Martek Biosciences v. Nutrinova, 579 F.3d 1363 (Fed. Cir. 2009). https://casetext.com/case/martek-biosciences-v-nutrinova

MPEP Section 2111.01—Plain meaning. [R-07.2022] IV. Applicant may be own lexicographer and/or may disavow claim scope. https://www.uspto.gov/web/offices/pac/mpep/s2111.html#d0e200409

Popp, B. (May 2009). Using patents to find the terminology you need. *ATA Chronicle*, 38(5), 16–23.

Rosenblatt et al (2013). Patent lexicography: a double-edged sword. *Westlaw Journal Intellectual Property*, 19(26). https://www.jenner.com/a/web/joHm727cYejEwbT1apG4D8/4HRMZQ/rozenblat_et_al_article.PDF?1367305885

Cited patent

Barclay, W.R. (1997). Method for raising animals having high concentrations of Omega-3 highly unsaturated fatty acids (Patent No. US5698244). United States Patent and Trademark Office (USPTO). https://image-ppubs.uspto.gov/dirsearch-public/print/downloadPdf/5698244

28 Format, numbering, spacing, and fonts

The presentation of the claims section in a patent application is also regulated. For example, the following regulatory provisions *(f)*, *(h)* and *(i)* of *Title 37 CFR Section 1.75* apply specifically to the presentation of the claims section of a patent application:

> *(f)* If there are several claims, they shall be numbered consecutively in Arabic numerals.
> [...]
> *(h)* The claim or claims must commence on a separate physical sheet or electronic page. Any sheet including a claim or portion of a claim may not contain any other parts of the application or other material.
> *(i)* Where a claim sets forth a plurality of elements or steps, each element or step of the claim should be separated by a line indentation.

Similarly, the following regulatory provisions of *Title 37 CFR Section 1.52* apply to all documents filed at the USPTO, for permanent record, whether for patent application, re-examination, or supplemental examination. Specifically, the provisions of subparagraphs (b)(2) stipulate that the specification (including abstract and claims) shall have:

> (i) lines that are 1 1/2 or double spaced;
> (ii) text written in a nonscript type font (e.g., Arial, Times Roman, or Courier, preferably a font size of 12) lettering style having capital letters which should be at least 0.3175 cm. (0.125 inch) high, but may be no smaller than 0.21 cm. (0.08 inch) high (e.g., a font size of 6); and
> (iii) only a single column of text.

Implications for translation

The above formatting rules for the claims section, and more generally for patent applications, apply to all US applications, *and* to all translations to English for US filing, considering the provisions of *Title 37 CFR Section 152 (b)(1)(ii)* that a US patent application must:

DOI: 10.4324/9781003423003-28

> (ii) be in the English language or be accompanied by a translation of the application and a translation of any corrections or amendments into the English language together with a statement that the translation is accurate.

Consequently, translators might have to recondition any reflexes which would lead them, for example, to use a combination of Roman numbers and letters for claims with various steps, instead of Arabic numerals and indents; or who would endeavor to keep the two-column format of any original two-column ST provided.

The above cited rules come as close as possible to a style guide for patents translation, except that the consequences of not following the rules of claims presentation, or more generally for filing a patent application, are far more serious than those resulting from formatting errors in the submission of an article for publication. An article for publication that deviates from the specification of a style guide is likely to be edited before publication, without further ado. An incorrectly formatted claims section is a non-compliant document, which is likely to result in a penalty, an objection, or at worse a denial of the application.

Otherwise, in the absence of exhaustive citation, the above-cited extracts are illustrative of the stylistic guidance, also set forth in patent-related rules and regulations. As a result, translators might consider consulting the complete provisions of the rules cited for more information, or the USPTO website directly, in case of an unanswered query. For example, the provisions on paper size might be consulted, considering the differences between US and European paper size.

References

37 CFR 1.52 (b)(1) (ii)—Language, paper, writing, margins, read-only optical disc specifications. https://www.uspto.gov/web/offices/pac/mpep/mpep-9020-appx-r.html#d0e318327

37 CFR 1.75 (a) to (i)—Claim(s). https://www.uspto.gov/web/offices/pac/mpep/mpep-9020-appx-r.html#d0e320269

29 Representation of recited claims

The Claims Tree function at Espacenet

The *Espacenet* patent database at the European Patent Office (EPO) portal, includes a useful Claims Tree function, which can be applied, with a single click, to the claims section of any patent retrieved, whether US, EP, WO, or national. With this function, the hierarchical order of claims independence, dependence and multiple dependence can be graphically generated for visualization in tree-structure format. Once the tree structure is generated, it then becomes possible to see the relationships among claims, both to verify understanding of such relationships, and to ensure that the correct expression of *in the alternative* is used, in the translation for US patents, as previously discussed.

The claims tree structure shown in Table 29.1 was generated based on the claims section of the West Paw, Inc., US *utility* patent, US20130087104, titled *Pet toy with interlocking arms and recess for treat*.

On the left side, the list of claims recited, with expand buttons on two levels. On a first level, the independent Claim 1 expands to Claim 2, which is dependent on Claim 1. On a second level, Claim 2 expands to Claims 3, 4, and 5, each separately dependent on Claim 2. On the right side, the generated Claims structure tree displays, at a glance, the dependency of each of the Claims (i.e., Claims 3, 4, and 5, each on Claim 2, and Claim 2 on Claim 1.)

Implications for translation

Short of being able to input a *claims-only* translation into the EPO Claims Tree function, to verify that the target text (TT) claims tree *matches* the ST claims tree, the Claims Tree function nonetheless supplies unique visualization of the *cohesive* relationship between the claims of a patent ST. *Cohesion* governed by statutory requirements. Statutory requirements, outlined previously, per the provisions of *Title 35 USC Sections 112 (c), (d) and (e)*, requiring that dependent and multiple dependent claims refer *backward only* (not forward), and *in the alternative* (not cumulatively) to *any one* of previously recited claims. Requirements that apply *a fortiori* to translation of the claims section. Whether as an aid to pre-translation understanding of the ST, or as checklist for post-translation review, the claims tree anchors the ST claims section in a visual manner that is useful to the translation process.

DOI: 10.4324/9781003423003-29

Table 29.1 Claims tree generated for the claims section of US20130087104

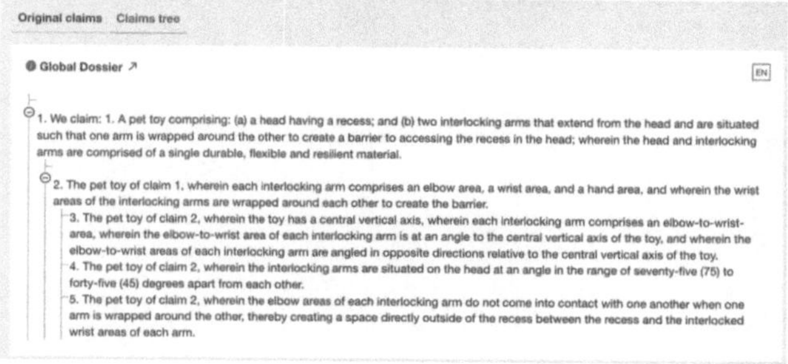

Original claims Claims tree

Global Dossier ↗

EN

1. We claim: 1. A pet toy comprising: (a) a head having a recess; and (b) two interlocking arms that extend from the head and are situated such that one arm is wrapped around the other to create a barrier to accessing the recess in the head; wherein the head and interlocking arms are comprised of a single durable, flexible and resilient material.

2. The pet toy of claim 1, wherein each interlocking arm comprises an elbow area, a wrist area, and a hand area, and wherein the wrist areas of the interlocking arms are wrapped around each other to create the barrier.

3. The pet toy of claim 2, wherein the toy has a central vertical axis, wherein each interlocking arm comprises an elbow-to-wrist-area, wherein the elbow-to-wrist area of each interlocking arm is at an angle to the central vertical axis of the toy, and wherein the elbow-to-wrist areas of each interlocking arm are angled in opposite directions relative to the central vertical axis of the toy.

4. The pet toy of claim 2, wherein the interlocking arms are situated on the head at an angle in the range of seventy-five (75) to forty-five (45) degrees apart from each other.

5. The pet toy of claim 2, wherein the elbow areas of each interlocking arm do not come into contact with one another when one arm is wrapped around the other, thereby creating a space directly outside of the recess between the recess and the interlocked wrist areas of each arm.

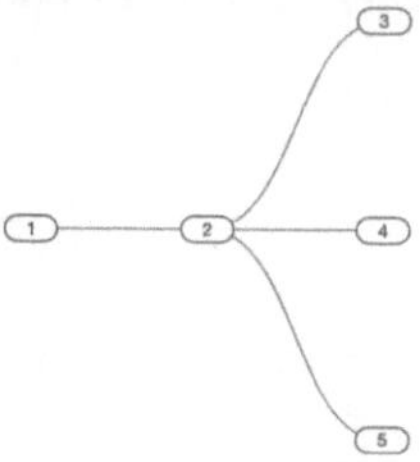

References

European Patent Office (EPO)—Espacenet. https://worldwide.espacenet.com/

35 USC 112—Specification (c), (d) and (e). https://www.uspto.gov/web/offices/pac/mpep/mpep-9015-appx-l.html#d0e302824912

Cited patent

Williams, S. et al. (2013). Pet toy with interlocking arms and recess for treat (Patent Application No. US20130087104). United States Patent and Trademark Office (USPTO). https://image-ppubs.uspto.gov/dirsearch-public/print/downloadPdf/20130087104

30 Abstract of the invention

The provisions of *Title 37 CFR Section 1.72(b)* supply the following guidance regarding the *Abstract* of an invention:

> A brief abstract of the technical disclosure in the specification must commence on a separate sheet, preferably following the claims, under the heading "Abstract" or "Abstract of the Disclosure." The sheet or sheets presenting the abstract may not include other parts of the application or other material. The abstract must be as concise as the disclosure permits, preferably not exceeding 150 words in length. The purpose of the abstract is to enable the Office and the public generally to determine quickly from a cursory inspection the nature and gist of the technical disclosure.

As a result, for anyone hesitating between the terms *summary*, *synopsis*, *digest* or *abstract*, the provisions of *Title 37 CFR Section 1.72(b)* should reduce the possibilities to naught. This is one example among many. Patent rules and regulations supply key structural terminology, whether it is for use of the term *embodiment* versus *example*, the *transitional phrase* options for the internal coordination of claims, or for the differences in interpretation arising from the uses of the verb *comprise* versus *consisting of*. Terms such as *abstract* (with no exceptions) are regulatory, which means they are different from any semantically competing synonyms.

As previously mentioned within the context of the *antecedence / ascertainability* requirement, the content of the *Abstract* has evolved conventionally, and/or by judge's writ, in cross-reference to the *first patent claim* and to the *brief summary of the invention*, within the specification of the invention.

Consider the following additional example (among countless), extracted from the patent application **US20130302777A1**, titled **Systems and methods of object recognition within a simulation**, reciting the children's augmented reality (AR) game Tiggly®. A 100% match exists between the *Abstract* and the *Brief summary of the invention*, and a 90% match exists with the *first claim* of the patent.

DOI: 10.4324/9781003423003-30

Table 30.1 Comparison of language used in the abstract, first claim, and brief summary, for disclosing the Tiggly® invention, in the patent application US20130302777Al

US20130302777A1 Systems and methods of object recognition within a simulation		
Abstract	*Brief summary of the invention*	*First Claim*
According to another embodiment, a system configured to execute at least one simulation is provided. The system includes a memory, a touch screen, at least one processor coupled to the memory and the touch screen, and a simulation component executed by the at least one processor. The simulation component is configured to detect a manipulation of at least one object disposed on the touch screen, determine adegree of compliance of the manipulation to rules of the at least one simulation, and communicate a characterization of the degree of compliance to an external entity	According to another embodiment, a system configured to execute at least one simulation is provided. The system includes a memory, a touch screen, at least one processor coupled to the memory and the touch screen, and a simulation component executed by the at least one processor. The simulation component is configured to detect a manipulation of at least one object disposed on the touch screen, determine a degree of compliance of the manipulation to rules of the at least one simulation, and communicate a characterization of the degree of compliance to an external entity.	1. A system configured to execute at least one simulation, the system comprising:a memory; a touch screen; at least one processor coupled to the memory and the touch screen; and a simulation component executed by the at least one processor and configured to: detect a manipulation of at least one object disposed on the touch screen; determine a degree of compliance of the manipulation to rules of the at least one simulation; and communicate a characterization of the degree of compliance to an external entity.
100%	100%	90%

Thus, as previously explained, conventional repetitions preserve meaning across both the description of the invention and the claims section, preventing the introduction of new terminology. In turn, such repetitions facilitate compliance with the *antecedence* and *ascertainability* requirement for interpreting the meaning of claims.

Implications for translation

On another note, conventional repetitions in the drafting of patents are especially relevant to translation, essentially because the target text must also comply with the requirements of *antecedence* and *ascertainability*. Thus, where repetitions in the source text are grounded in requirements intended to safeguard both the integrity of the disclosure, and the rules for interpreting the meaning of the claims to an invention, such repetitions must be present in the target text in view of performing the same degree of *antecedence* and *ascertainability* as in the ST. Again, in patents translation, stylistic considerations in favor of avoiding repetitions are overruled.

For *Abstract-only* translations, a copy of the complete ST patent is once again required, and if it exists, a copy also of the translated disclosure of the invention, and/or of the claims section. A copy of the complete ST patent is required to verify the extent of ST repetitions between the first claim, the brief description and the *Abstract*. Whereas a copy of any existing translation of the disclosure and claims section would be required to import *verbatim* those sections that are repeated, in view of ensuring that no new terminology is introduced.

Such pre-translation steps are necessary for *Abstract-only* translations, considering that a potential introduction of new *abstract*-specific terms might be at odds with the terms of the description, and consequently the interpretation of the claims section. Securing the complete source text and any translations of the claims section, and/or the specification, is also important, because published patent. *Abstracts* appear on the bibliographic cover sheet of patents or patent applications. A strategic position in the publication of the patent, which makes the *Abstract* directly accessible via patent search function and engines, *before* consultation of the larger patent specification. Direct access to *Abstracts* that informs search reports, forming the basis of a decision on *patentability*. Direct access that otherwise informs the translator's background research on patents.

Otherwise, the *World Intellectual Property Organization* (WIPO) also publishes *General guidelines for the preparation of abstracts of patent documents* (Standard ST. 12/A, referenced in English, French and Spanish), the provisions of which might be leveraged, for further understanding of patent *Abstracts*, and informing the translation process. The WIPO Standard is intended to provide uniformity to the *drafting* of all patent *Abstracts*, contingent upon requirements specific to any relevant patent-granting authority. Supplemental requirements specific to relevant patent-granting authorities, to which such conventional language uses, as *repetition* and *cross-referencing* described above, might also be considered.

Finally, for bidding or billing purposes of *Abstract-only* translations, the number of full-rate words is going to be reduced commensurate with the possibility of conventional *verbatim* repetitions between the ST *Abstract*, the corresponding *brief description of the invention* and/or the *first claim*. However, this does not mean that *Abstract-only* translations should be provided *pro-bono*, or even pro-rated per the number of repetitions. Quite the contrary, considering that stacks of *Abstract-only* translations are seldom provided with the corresponding patent specifications. The research tasks consisting in time spent searching for and retrieving patents, to determine whether the source *Abstracts* contain repetitions, or not; as well as time spent searching for any existing translations of the specifications, corresponding to the target patent *Abstracts*, will largely justify a full-rate word fee, or equivalent hourly rate.

References

37 CFR 1.72 (b)—Title and abstract. https://www.uspto.gov/web/offices/pac/mpep/mpep-9020-appx-r.html#d0e320224

OMPI Norma ST. 12/A—Directrices generales para la preparación de resúmenes de documentos de patentes. [Spanish]. https://www.wipo.int/standards/es/pdf/03-12-a.pdf

OMPI Norme ST.12/A—Principes directeurs de caractère général relatifs à la préparation des abrégés de documents de brevet. [French]. https://www.wipo.int/standards/fr/pdf/03-12-a.pdf

WIPO Standard ST. 12/A—General guidelines for the preparation of abstracts of patent documents. https://www.wipo.int/standards/en/pdf/03-12-a.pdf

Cited patent

Tomkins, M. et al. (2013). Systems and methods of object recognition within a simulation (Patent Application No. US20130302777A1). United States Patent and Trademark Office (USPTO). https://image-ppubs.uspto.gov/dirsearch-public/print/downloadPdf/20130302777

31 Patent drawings

The statutory provisions of *Title 35 USC Section 113* specify that:

> The applicant shall furnish a drawing where necessary for the understanding of the subject matter sought to be patented.

Thus, the India ink figure drawings of a patented invention are not only beautiful blueprints of the inventions recited in patents. Required when necessary for illustration purposes, as a consequence of the *Enablement* requirement (*Title 35 USC Section 112*), and according to the provisions of *Title 35 USC Section 113*, patent drawings are also essential tools for translation.

Implications for translation

Indeed, if a picture is worth one thousand words, a keyed patent drawing is also an invaluable patent translation method and tool. Expert patent translators (e.g., Popp, 2009) not only recommend using the illustrations to inform understanding in the choice of translations. They also recommend systematically finding all the indexed terms in the detailed description of the invention, and keying them on the drawing (as performed for the Biro fountain pen Figures 6 and 7 in Table 31.1), so as to name the numbered parts of the drawing, and as a way of ensuring both consistency and accuracy of translations throughout the patent document.

Such a recommendation becomes especially relevant, when translating an invention like the Biro fountain pen (US2258841). An invention where *semantically contiguous* terms, such as *hollow barrel* (1), *tube* (3), *central bore* (4), and *narrow passage* (6); or *opening* (36) and *cavity* (38), once keyed to the numbers indexing the patent drawing, become anchored and clearly differentiated. In turn, each of these unmistakably different parts of the biro might be separately, and consistently translated, throughout the text, in view of avoiding any possible confusion. Potential confusion of terms, which could otherwise interfere with *ascertainability* and *antecedence* requirements for the meaning of

DOI: 10.4324/9781003423003-31

Table 31.1 Key to Figures 6 and 7 extracted from the Biro fountain pen patent US2258841

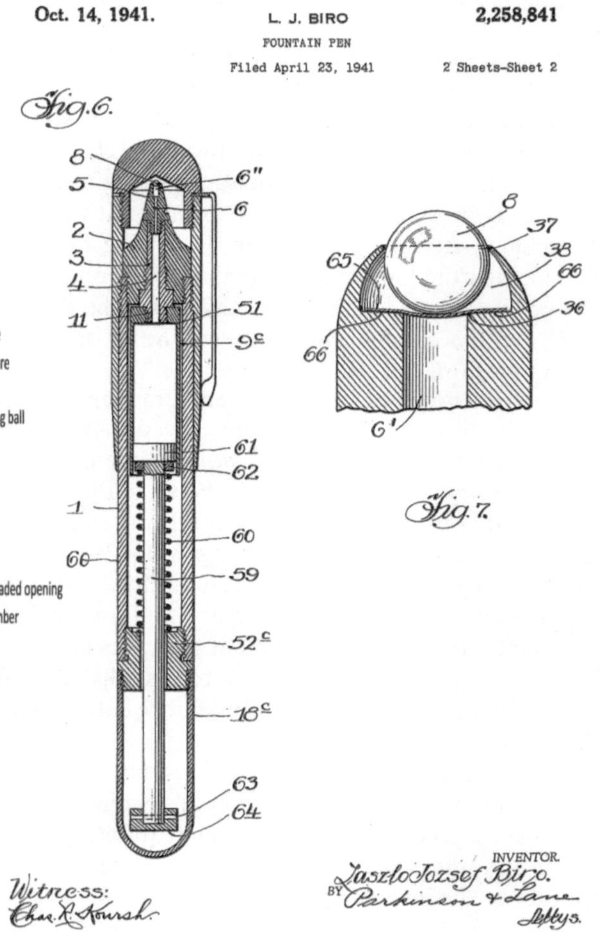

1. hollow barrel
2. feeder
3. tube
4. central bore
5. writing head
6. narrow passage
6'. longitudinal bore
6". outlet
8. rotatable writing ball
9c. container
18c. end cap
36. opening
37. contact edge
38. cavity
51. internally threaded opening
52c. coupling member
59. rod
60. feeding spring
61. piston
62. annular ring
63. pin
64. knob
65. leaf spring
66. shoulder

claims terminology in the description. Potential confusion that needs to be avoided, *a fortiori* in translation.

Otherwise, hypothetically for the now expired Biro fountain pen patent, any one of the parts of the invention, and especially the hollow barrel (1), tube (3), central bore (4), or narrow passage (6), could have been subject to infringement. A case compounded by a layer of translation error, had the terms not been consistently and separately translated in both the description and the claims. Indeed, no small error, considering the potential consequences of "biros lost", both to infringement, and British English. The eponymous term "biro" entered British English use as a common noun as early as 1958, and the transitive verb form "to biro" as early as 1962, per the *Oxford English Dictionary*.

After all, the fact of the matter is that, in the 1941 patent, US2258841, Laszlo Joszef Biro was precisely addressing, from the dual perspective of chemistry *and* mechanical engineering, the problematic situation of pasty ink that caked the prior art of roller ball pens. From the chemistry perspective, the ink formula was changed. From the mechanical engineering perspective, the amount of space collecting the pasty ink formula, at the tip of the pen, was narrowed. No small steps in the domain of writing tools, since to date the name *biro* endures in the United Kingdom, as the eponymous designation for all ballpoint pens, while it is fair to say that both the design and chemistry, preventing drying and caking of the ink, endure in one form or another, in ballpoint pens *worldwide*.

The bottom line, however, is that patent drawings are *also enabling for translators*, albeit differently than within the disclosure of an invention, where they serve to *enable the reproducibility* of the invention. Patent drawings are *enabling* resources in translation, because they may be used to prevent patent translations from becoming the source of legal issues. Per the provisions of the *MPEP Section 2164* regarding the *Enablement Requirement*, patent drawings contribute to the full disclosure of the invention, *enabling* those skilled in the art, in turn, to make and use the invention, without undue experimentation. In contrast, patent drawings are *enabling for translators*, because they may be used not only to visually identify the invention parts that are referenced in the description, but equally important *to separate semantically contiguous terms*.

Finally, systematically keyed patent drawings may also be used as a method of organizing terminology. An organization of terminology that might in turn contribute to ensuring the level of consistency required for achieving *translated ascertainability* and *antecedence* of the meaning of claim terms, in the translated description of the invention.

References

35 USC 113—Drawings. https://www.uspto.gov/web/offices/pac/mpep/mpep-9015-appx-l.html#d0e302850

37 CFR 1.81—Drawing required in patent application. https://www.uspto.gov/web/offices/pac/mpep/mpep-9020-appx-r.html#aia_d0e320940

37 CFR 1.83—Content of drawing. https://www.uspto.gov/web/offices/pac/mpep/mpep-9020-appx-r.html#d0e320967

37 CFR 1.84—Standards for drawings. https://www.uspto.gov/web/offices/pac/mpep/mpep-9020-appx-r.html#d0e320999

MPEP Section 2164—The enablement requirement. [R-11.2013]. https://www.uspto.gov/web/offices/pac/mpep/s2164.html

Popp, B. (May 2009). Using patents to find the terminology you need. *ATA Chronicle*, 38(5), 16–23.

Cited patent

Biro, L.J. (1941). Fountain pen (Patent No. US2258841). United States Patent and Trademark Office. https://image-ppubs.uspto.gov/dirsearch-public/print/downloadPdf/2258841

32 Design *vs.* utility patents

The USPTO (United States Patent and Trademark Office) grants three sorts of patents: *plant*, *design*, and *utility* patents. Although the differences in content and form are significant between all three, the differences between US *design* and *utility* patents call for specific conceptual clarification.

Differences between US *design* and *utility* patents are immediately recognizable, as their identifying codes are different. US *utility* patents, numbered continuously since the *dawn of US patent time*, during the eighteenth century, are prefixed with the United States country code "US". In contrast, *design* patents are prefixed with the letters "USD", the United States country code, plus the letter "D", which designates a *design* patent.

However, more substantial differences exist between US *design* and *utility* patents. According to the provisions of *Section 1502.01* of the *MPEP*, US *utility* and *design* patents are different, in that:

> a "utility patent" protects the way an article is used and works (35 USC 101), while a "design patent" protects the way an article looks (35 USC 171)

In other words, a *design* patent protects the *ornamental properties* of an invention, whereas a *utility* patent protects the *functional properties* of an invention. *Functional properties* that may include manufacturing processes, when such processes are patentable.

Thus, for example, the architect Frank Gehry's wood lattice furniture (e.g., as recited in USD344191S, titled *Dining chair*; USD334098S, titled *Chair*, and USD341263S, titled *Club chair*) was granted US *design* patents. In contrast, the manufacturing processes of the bended lattice wood, used to make the chairs, were awarded two US *utility* patents (e.g., US5284380A and US5154486A, both titled: *Furniture comprising laminated slats and methods of manufacturing such furniture*).

Conversely, the electronic engineering subsumed in the multiple parts of the Softbank humanoid robot, Nao, was granted multiple *utility* patents (e.g., US2015122073, titled *Spine for a humanoid robot*, and US2016325437, titled *Actuation of a hand intended for being provided on a humanoid robot*). Whereas

DOI: 10.4324/9781003423003-32

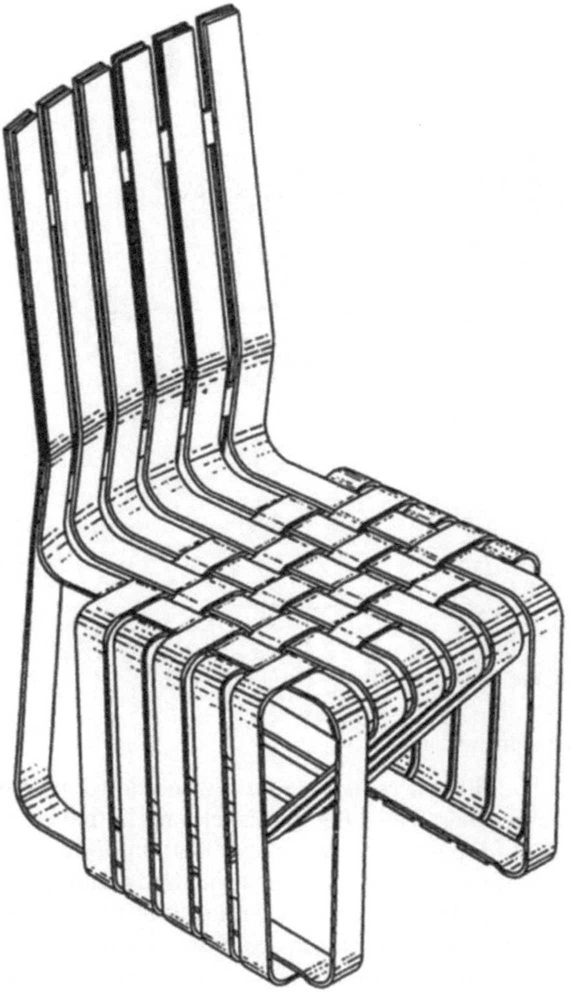

Figure 32.1 Gehry dining chair (USD344191S)

Nao's particular appearance was granted just one US *design* patent, USD774148S1, titled *Humanoid Robot*.

Additionally, from a legal perspective, *design* patents are granted for a period of 15 years, for applications filed on or after May 13th 2015, per the provisions of *Title 35 USC Section 173*, regarding the *Term of a design patent*. In contrast, the protection period granted for a US *utility* patent is 20 years, per the provisions of *Title 35 USC Section 154 a(2)*, regarding the *Contents and term of a patent*.

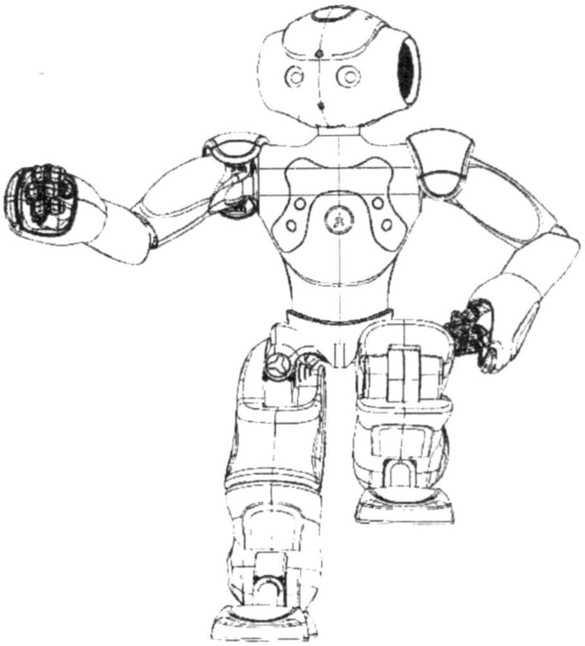

Figure 32.2 Nao, the humanoid robot (USD774148S1)

Implications for translation

For translators, the differences between *utility* and *design* patents matter also, albeit for distinct reasons. The difference is relevant in that only United States *utility* patents contain the full narrative specification of an invention, according to all the relevant regulations for disclosing and claiming an invention. In contrast, according to the provisions of United States patent rules and regulations, generally applicable to inventions, and the specifics applicable to United States *design* patents (e.g., *Title 37 CFR 1.154b*), *design* patent applications include just a single claim, supported by drawings, together with brief descriptions of the drawings. Therefore, United States *utility* patents are usually commissioned for translation, whereas United States *design* patents require very little translation, since they essentially consist of drawings together with a single claim.

References

35 USC 101—Invention patentable. https://www.uspto.gov/web/offices/pac/mpep/mpep-9015-appx-l.html#d0e302376

35 USC 154 (a) (2)—Contents and term of a patent: provisional rights. https://www.uspto.gov/web/offices/pac/mpep/mpep-9015-appx-l.html#d0e303482

35 USC 171—Patents for designs. https://www.uspto.gov/web/offices/pac/mpep/mpep-9015-appx-l.html#d0e304480
35 USC 173—Term of a design patent. https://www.uspto.gov/web/offices/pac/mpep/mpep-9015-appx-l.html#d0e304510
37 CFR 1.154—Arrangement of application elements in a design application. https://www.uspto.gov/web/offices/pac/mpep/mpep-9020-appx-r.html#d0e324243
MPEP Section 1502.01—Distinction between design and utility patents. [R-07.2015]. https://www.uspto.gov/web/offices/pac/mpep/s1502.html#d0e150263

Cited patents

Gehry, F.O. (1992). Furniture comprising laminated slats and methods of manufacturing such furniture (Patent No. US5154486A). United States and Trademark Office (USPTO). https://image-ppubs.uspto.gov/dirsearch-public/print/downloadPdf/5154486
Gehry, F.O. (1993). Chair (Patent No. USD334098S). United States and Trademark Office (USPTO). https://image-ppubs.uspto.gov/dirsearch-public/print/downloadPdf/D334098
Gehry, F.O. (1993). Club chair (Patent No. USD341263S). United States and Trademark Office (USPTO). https://image-ppubs.uspto.gov/dirsearch-public/print/downloadPdf/D341263
Gehry, F.O. (1994). Dining chair (Patent No. USD344191S). United States and Trademark Office (USPTO). https://image-ppubs.uspto.gov/dirsearch-public/print/downloadPdf/D344191
Gehry, F.O. (1994). Furniture comprising laminated slats and methods of manufacturing such furniture (Patent No. US5284380A). United States and Trademark Office (USPTO). https://image-ppubs.uspto.gov/dirsearch-public/print/downloadPdf/5284380
Hong, R. (2016). Humanoid Robot (Patent No. USD774148S1). United States and Trademark Office (USPTO). https://image-ppubs.uspto.gov/dirsearch-public/print/downloadPdf/D774148
Laville, J. et al (2016). Actuation of a hand intended for being provided on a humanoid robot (Patent No. US2016325437). United States and Trademark Office (USPTO). https://image-ppubs.uspto.gov/dirsearch-public/print/downloadPdf/20160325437
Maisonnier, B. (2015). Spine for a humanoid robot (Patent No. US2015122073). United States and Trademark Office (USPTO). https://image-ppubs.uspto.gov/dirsearch-public/print/downloadPdf/20150122073

33 Plant patents

Prior to passage of the 1930 US *Plant Act*, a law extending patents to horticulture, plants were *excluded* from patents for two reasons. First, because plants were considered products of nature, and therefore that horticulturists could not *invent* them. Secondly, because it was believed that plants would not be amenable to the sort of written description set forth in the provisions of US Patent Law *Title 35 Article 112*. As a result, the US *Plant Act* introduced the distinction of *asexual reproduction*, to capture the hybridizing work of horticulturist inventors, "aiding nature". Additionally, the requirements for describing inventions, effective for *utility* patents, were "relaxed" for *plant* patents, to include descriptions that were "as complete as reasonably possible".

Consequently, to date, in addition to US *design* and *utility* patents, the United States Patent and Trademark Office (USPTO) grants patents for plants, designated with the four-letter code USPP—*United States Plant Patent*. According to US Patent Law, *Title 35 USC Section 161*, the USPTO grants *plant* patents to:

> Whoever invents or discovers and asexually reproduces any distinct and new variety of plant, including cultivated sports, mutants, hybrids, and newly found seedlings, other than a tuber propagated plant or a plant found in an uncultivated state [...].

The provisions of the *MPEP Section 1601* shed further light on the patent statute, in particular on what is understood by *asexually reproduced* plants, specifying that:

> Asexually propagated plants are those that are reproduced by means other than from seeds, such as by the rooting of cuttings, by layering, budding, grafting, inarching, etc. [..]

Likewise, regarding the exception of *tubers*, the provisions of the *MPEP Section 1601* further specify:

> This exception is made because this group alone, among asexually reproduced plants, is propagated by the same part of the plant that is sold as food.

DOI: 10.4324/9781003423003-33

Thus, for example, tubers such as the Irish potato and Jerusalem artichoke are *excluded* from patenting, because the tuber (short thick portion underground) that *could* be propagated (i.e., asexually reproduced)—*and therefore, patented as a US plant patent*—is also used for food, which is only patentable as a US *utility patent.*

On average, during the past 25 years, the USPTO has granted approximately 1000 *plant* patents per year, combining applications originating in the United States, and from other countries (*USPTO Report*).

Implications for translation

Although US *plant* patent descriptions are different from US *utility* patent descriptions, considering they are purported to have resulted from a "relaxation" of the rules, governing the description of *utility* patents, *plant* patent descriptions are *no less technical.* Indeed, *plant* patent descriptions have evolved by convention, into detailed *botanical* descriptions of the new *plant* varietal. Thus, translators taking on *plant* patent translations should be well prepared to understand the categories of a *botanical* description. *Botanical* categories of description, according to the USPTO (General Information about US *plant* patents), which cover such items as:

- Genus and species
- Habit of growth
- Cultivar name
- Precocity (if applicable)
- Botanical characteristics of plant structures (i.e., buds, bark, foliage, flowers, fruit, etc.)
- Fertility (fecundity)
- Other characteristics which distinguish the plant such as resistance(s) to disease, drought, cold, dampness, etc., fragrance, coloration, regularity and time of bearing, quantity or quality of extracts, rooting ability, timing or duration of flowering season, etc.

Botanical categories of description invoking language uses, such as any combination of the following descriptors:

Flower: Blooming habit, Bud, Sepals (size, color, peduncle, bracts); Bloom (size, borne, petalage, general tonality from a distance, base of petals—point of attachment); color (outer petals, inner petals, petal texture, appearance, and petal form).

Reproductive organs: Stamens, filaments, and anthers, Arrangement (color, pollen), Stigmas (color), Hips (shape and size).

Plant: Form, Growth, Foliage, Size, Quantity, Color, Shape, Texture, Petiole, Stipules, Auricle, Rachis, and resistance to Disease.

Wood: New shoots (bark, wood); Old Wood (bark), flower stem, Thorns (quantity, form, prickles), Winter hardiness, Uniqueness.

Specifically, for example, in the description of the *Hybrid Tea Rose named Ruivonk*, recited in USPP14663 P3, the extracted section on *Reproductive organs* alone is described in the following terms:

> REPRODUCTIVE ORGANS
>
> Stamens, filaments, and anthers: Stamens are approximately 90 in number; filaments are about 0.8 to 1 cm in length, not all possess an anther; anthers are about 0.2 to 0.3 cm in length, all open at approximately the same time.
>
> Arrangement: Regularly arranged around styles.
>
> *Color*—Stamens near 9C, filaments near 9C, anthers near 9A.
>
> *Pollen*—Color near 161D.
>
> Styles: Bunched, medium length, about 0.8 cm, color near 51A.
>
> Stigmas: Color near 155B.
>
> Hips:
>
> *Shape*—Funnel shaped.
>
> *Size*—Length about 1 cm, width at top about 1 cm [...]

A fortiori, botanical *plant* patent descriptions are also *incomparable* to US *design* patents, which do not require narrative descriptions of the ornamental aspects of an invention, relying instead on drawings, per the provisions of *Title 37 CFR Section 1.154*.

References

35 USC 161—Patents for plants. https://www.uspto.gov/web/offices/pac/mpep/mpep-9015-appx-l.html#d0e304416

37 CFR 1.154—Arrangement of application elements in a design application. https://www.uspto.gov/web/offices/pac/mpep/mpep-9020-appx-r.html#d0e324243

Hoover, H. (May 13, 1930). Plant patent Act of 1930. https://history.house.gov/Historical-Highlights/1901-1950/1930_05_13_Plant_Patent/

MPEP—Section 1601 Introduction: The act, scope, type of plants covered. [R-11.2013]. https://www.uspto.gov/web/offices/pac/mpep/s1601.html

USPTO—General Information About 35 U.S.C. 161 Plant Patents. https://tinyurl.com/mv4f9vj7

USPTO—Plant Patents Report—Granted: 01/01/1996—12/31/2020—Number of Patents Granted as Distributed by Year of Patent Grant, Breakout by Country of Origin (Table A1-1a) and by Ownership Category (Table A1-1b). https://www.uspto.gov/web/offices/ac/ido/oeip/taf/plant.htm#PartA1_1

Cited patent

Pouw, A. (2004). Hybrid Tea Rose named 'Ruivonk' (Plant Patent No. USPP14663). United States Patent and Trademark Office (USPTO). https://image-ppubs.uspto.gov/dirsearch-public/print/downloadPdf/PP14663

34 Units of measurement

One of the questions that invariably arises in patents translation (and elsewhere in technical, scientific, and medical translation also), is whether, or not, to convert the measurements provided into local units. For example, if the ST measurements are all metric, should the translator localize to American units of measurement or to the British Imperial System, and *vice versa*?

US regulations

The United States Patent and Trademark Office (USPTO) regulations, regarding the matter of converting units of measurement in patents, are clearly specified in the *MPEP Section 608.01, Subsection IV*, as follows:

> In order to minimize the necessity in the future for converting dimensions given in the English system of measurements to the metric system of measurements when using printed patents as research and prior art search documents, all patent applicants should use the metric (S.I.) units followed by the equivalent English units when describing their inventions in the specifications of patent applications.
>
> The initials S.I. stand for "Le Système International d'Unités," the French name for the International System of Units, a modernized metric system adopted in 1960 by the International General Conference of Weights and Measures based on precise unit measurements made possible by modern technology.

European regulations

Per the provisions of the *Guidelines for Examination at the European Patent Office (EPO), Part F., Chapt II, 4.13 on Physical values and units*, the rules requiring the use of the S.I. system are also applicable to the 39 European countries party to the European Patent Convention (EPC). Countries party to the EPC, which include the current 27 members of the European Union (EU), plus more, such as the United Kingdom, Norway, and Turkey, which are not members of the EU.

DOI: 10.4324/9781003423003-34

Specifically, the provisions of the *EPO Guidelines for Examination., Part F., Chapt II, 4.13*, specify that:

> Physical values must be expressed in the units recognised in international practice, which is generally in the metric system, using SI units and the other units referred to in Chapter I of the Annex to EEC Directive 80/181/EEC of 20 December 1979, as amended [...]. Any values not meeting this requirement must also be expressed in the units recognised in international practice. Values expressed in the system of imperial units (e.g., inches/pounds) or in units having local character (e.g., pint), in general, do not meet the criterion "recognised in international practice".

The list of all units recognized in international practice are published in *Annex II* of the European Patent Office (EPO) *Guidelines for Examination*. In particular, the list includes those units permitted in specialized fields only, such as the vergency of optical systems measured in *dioptres*, the mass of precious stones measured in *metric carats*, or blood pressure and pressure of other body fluids measured in *millimeters of mercury*.

WIPO international regulations

Finally, the provisions of Rule 10 of the *Regulations under the Patent Cooperation Treaty (PCT)* for international WO patents are consistent with the provisions of both USPTO and EPC rules cited above, specifically as follows:

10.1 Terminology and Signs

- (a) Units of weights and measures shall be expressed in terms of the metric system, or also expressed in such terms if first expressed in terms of a different system.
- (b) Temperatures shall be expressed in degrees Celsius, or also expressed in degrees Celsius, if first expressed in a different manner.
- (c) [Deleted]
- (d) For indications of heat, energy, light, sound, and magnetism, as well as for mathematical formulae and electrical units, the rules of international practice shall be observed; for chemical formulae, the symbols, atomic weights, and molecular formulae, in general use, shall be employed.
- (e) In general, only such technical terms, signs and symbols should be used as are generally accepted in the art.
- (f) When the international application or its translation is in Chinese, English or Japanese, the beginning of any decimal fraction shall be marked by a period, whereas, when the international application or its translation is in a language other than Chinese, English or Japanese, it shall be marked by a comma. [...]

Implications for translation

Fortunately for patents translation, specific regulations pertaining to the expression of units of measurement exist to inform the drafting process of patent applications. Regulations, which translators might, in turn, also leverage to inform the translation process. In this case also, the rules are crystal clear, as specified above for US, European, and International WO patents. The International System of metric units, designated with the French abbreviation SI, for *Système international d'unités*, governs drafting, with other units, if any, also retained *a fortiori* in translation.

References

European Patent Office (EPO) Guidelines for Examination—Part F. Chapter II. Annex 2—4. Units and names of units permitted in specialized fields only. https://new.epo.org/en/legal/guidelines-epc/2023/f_iia2_4.html#GLF_CIIA2_4

European Patent Office (EPO) Guidelines for Examination—Part F. Chapt. II. 4.13 Physical values, units. https://new.epo.org/en/legal/guidelines-epc/2023/f_ii_4_13.html

MPEP Section 608.01—Specification. [R-10.2019] IV. Use of metric system of measurements in patent applications. https://www.uspto.gov/web/offices/pac/mpep/s608.html#d0e42440

Regulations under the PCT—Rule 10 Terminology and signs. https://www.wipo.int/pct/en/texts/rules/r10.html

35 The literal translation requirement

Contrary to both linguistic and translation theory, US Courts and Government Agencies require submission of a *literal translation*. The provisions of the MPEP *Section 608.01 Part V* clearly specify:

> The translation must be a literal translation and must be accompanied by a statement that the translation is accurate. [underlining mine]

The conflict that the *literal translation* requirement might create for translators in terms of *accuracy*, was fortunately resolved by Martin Cross, an expert patent translator. In a chapter, titled *Literal translation of patents*, published in the *American Translators Association (ATA) Patent Translator's Handbook*, Cross (2007) provides guidelines for translators to follow, which reconcile the notion of *literal translation* required by the United States courts with what translators do to ensure both accuracy and readability of their translations. For example, Cross offers *six rules of literal patent translation* **1>** Reproduce meaning. **2>** Reproduce register. **3>** Respect sentence breaks and carriage returns. **4>** Be consistent in the use of vocabulary and phrasing. **5>** Maintain one-to-one correspondence between source and target. **6>** Provide appropriate annotation. Each of which rules also function to perform the Court's definition of *literal translation* as "*an exact and accurate reproduction of the entire content of the source text without embellishment or modification.*"

Clearly then, despite choice of the controversial term "*literal*", the intent of the Court is one shared with translators for *accurate* and *appropriate* translation of meaning. In any event, none of the Court's specifications advocate the kind of surface-level ridicule (e.g., "It's raining *strings*" literally meaning *Il pleut des cordes*), derived from word-for-word translation. Word-for-word translations usually *construed* by linguists, to demonstrate the inappropriateness of *literal translation*, as a method of achieving the transfer of source text meaning to another language. Indeed, the same *Section* of the *MPEP* further

DOI: 10.4324/9781003423003-35

allows for translations to be amended, when they are not formulated with *idiomatic English*, per the following terms:

> If the English translation does not conform to idiomatic English and United States practice, it should be accompanied by a preliminary amendment making the necessary changes without the introduction of new matter prohibited by 35 U.S.C. 132.

Nonetheless, what is perhaps regrettable is that professional translation should not really need a *literal legal translation requirement* as a safeguard for both *accuracy* and *appropriateness*, as well as *consistency*, and *compliance* in the application of the relevant provisions of the rules and regulations governing patents. Professional translation services are normally accredited, according to expert, internationally agreed upon, quality management standards for translation. International Standards, such as ISO 17100:2015 *Requirements for translation services*, ISO 20771:2020 *Requirements for Legal Translation*, and ISO 18587:*2017 Requirements for Post-editing of machine translation output*, to list just a few of such international translation industry standards. Standards that guarantee the delivery of error-free translations. Quality control standards that this book will no doubt further inform for patents translation.

Indeed, the implementation of such quality control standards are verified and inspected—*not only for translations with complex legal ramifications, but also for translations with immediate life or death consequences*—all of which have certainly stood the test of time, *and volume*, with flying colors. Consider, for example, the translation of warnings appended to the handling of hazardous materials, warnings indicating presence of mine fields, labels on medical equipment used in surgery rooms and for intensive care, instructions for the use of implanted prosthetic devices, or pharmaceutical inserts containing critical posology and ingredient information for medications, where just one small undetected translation error could jeopardize lives.

In any event, beyond rekindling the *literal translation* controversy, legal precedence in patent case law undeniably exists for construing very close correlations between the patent source text and the target text. For example, the case for literal translation might certainly be invoked, considering the important requirements of the *ascertainability* and *antecedence* of claims terminology, or regarding the *Lexicographer Rule*, discussed previously. Rules and requirements where attention to the consistency of terminology in patent translation becomes paramount to preventing the layering of translation errors. Translation errors which might become an issue, during examination of a patent application, or in case of litigation. At worse, translation errors which might become impossible to fix.

As discussed previously, the requirement of *antecedence* and *ascertainability* of claims terminology, as well as the possibility of applicants defining their own terms, while disavowing the common (dictionary) meaning of terms, raise the translation principle of consistency to a higher level of legal significance. A higher level of legal significance, in turn requiring that translators follow the same patent and claim recitation rules *in translation*, or risk rendering the application invalid, or the patent permeable to infringement. A level of consistency that *verbatim* repetitions serve to guarantee, and literal translation seeks to preserve.

Indeed, the *literal translation* requirement might also be understood to serve as a defense against the introduction of new or inconsistent terminology, which could in turn inject new meanings into the claims section or the description. The fact of the matter, regarding what literal translation might seek to avoid (e.g., the introduction of new terms, or synonyms which might render claims *unascertainable*), is that the *Lexicographer Rule* even prevents translators from using their dictionaries for patent translation. A rule that requires translators to *stick to* any applicant-defined definitions found in a patent, *and none other*, at the risk of changing the scope of a claim, or rendering the claim *undefendable*.

Thus, the matter of *literal* patent translation rests, enmeshed in a legal web of connected rules and requirements, the understanding of which makes it easier to accept.

References

37 CFR 1.52 (b) (ii)—Language, paper, writing, margins, read-only optical disc specifications. https://www.uspto.gov/web/offices/pac/mpep/mpep-9020-appx-r.html#d0e318327

Cross, M. (2007). Literal translation of patents. *The Patent Translator's Handbook*. Alexandria, VA: ATA—American Translators Association, pp. 19–28.

International Organization for Standardization (ISO). https://www.iso.org/standards.html

ISO 17100:2015 *Requirements for translation services*. https://www.iso.org/standard/59149.html

ISO 20771:2020 *Requirements for Legal Translation*. https://www.iso.org/standard/69032.html

ISO 18587:*2017 Requirements for Post-editing of machine translation output*. https://www.iso.org/standard/62970.html

MPEP Section 608.01 - Specification. [10-209] V. Filing of non-English applications. https://www.uspto.gov/web/offices/pac/mpep/s608.html#d0e42440

36 Translations filed at the United States Patent and Trademark Office

According to the provisions of *Title 37 CFR Section 1.52 (b) (ii)*, patent applications must be filed in English at the USPTO. When applications are filed in a language other than English, under specific conditions, the application must include a translation, together with an appended certificate of accuracy. Specifically, the provisions of *Title 37 CFR Section 1.52 (b) (ii)*, stipulate that the patent application, any amendments, or corrections must:

> (ii) Be in the English language or be accompanied by a translation of the application and a translation of any corrections or amendments into the English language together with a statement that the translation is accurate.

Implications for translation

Considering that approximately half of US *utility* patent applications, filed at the USPTO, are foreign (see source cited below), and that a total of approximately half a million *utility* patents combined are filed *each year* at the USPTO, the above requirement, that a patent application "be in English or be translated or accompanied by a translation", guarantees a specialized patent translation market. Consequently, as this book endeavors to demonstrate, such a specialized translation market should also include training venues for patent translation, considering the complexity of patent documents. A complexity that is too often, exclusively measured, in terms of subject matter. Clearly, however, the provisions of statutory, regulatory, and precedent law, governing the recitation of inventions, together with their linguistic impact on translation, also require explication, precisely *to turn the tide* of some of the complexity.

References

37 CFR 1.52 (b) (ii)Language, paper, writing, margins, compact disc specifications. https://www.uspto.gov/web/offices/pac/mpep/mpep-9020-appx-r.html#d0e318327

USPTOUS patent statistic chartCalendar Years 1963–2020. https://www.uspto.gov/web/offices/ac/ido/oeip/taf/us_stat.htm

DOI: 10.4324/9781003423003-36

37 Translations filed at the European Patent Office

Translation requirements into one of the three official languages (French, German, and English) of the *European Patent Office* (EPO), per the provisions of the *European Patent Convention* (EPC) *Article 65* are different from those for filing English patent application translations, at the USPTO. The rules for filing translations at the EPO are inherently more complicated, considering that so many additional languages are involved, among the now 39 contracting states of the *European Patent Convention* (EPC). However, in the interest of limiting the number of translations, connected to a patent application, and the enforcement of patents in several or all of the different designated states, each with different official languages, this situation was greatly simplified.

The most recent simplification occurred in June 2023, when the *Unitary Patent System* became effective in 17 current European Union signatory states (EPO Press release). A system in the interest of a borderless Europe that requires *Unitary Patent* applications to be filed simply in one of the three official languages of the EPO.

However, prior to the *Unitary Patent System*, simplification of translation requirements for European patents occurred via the *London Agreement* (also called the *London Protocol*), which remains effective for *European Patent Organization* members, who are not members of the European Union. An agreement ratified in 2000, specifically addressing translation requirements, in regard to *Article 65* of the EPC. The essential provisions of the *London Agreement* are the following:

- A state which has an official language in common with one of the official languages of the EPO shall dispense entirely with the translation requirements provided for in Article 65(1) EPC.
- A state which does not have an official language in common with one of the official languages of the EPO shall dispense with the translation requirements provided for in Article 65(1) EPC if the European patent has been granted in the official language of the EPO prescribed by that State, or translated into that language and supplied under the conditions provided for in Article 65(1) EPC. These states may however require that a translation of the claims into one of their official languages be supplied.

DOI: 10.4324/9781003423003-37

In practice, this means that for filing purposes at the EPO, the *claims-only* section often appears translated in two or three official languages of the EPO, simply because the member states with different official languages that are designated in a patent application for enforcement of the patent, have a prescribed official EPO language, different from the official language in which the patent is filed. The *London Agreement* also dispenses with filing a patent translation in each of the official languages of the designated states, that are different from the three EPO official languages, except for the claims section which might still be required in certain designated states.

Implications for translation

For the process of translation anywhere, the publication of many European patents, with trilingual *claims-only* sections, offers *unprecedented* official background and parallel material, whether in the three official languages of the EPO, French, English, and German, or even a combination of two, depending on the designated states. Thus, for example when European (EP) patents are same family members with national or US patents, any trilingual or bilingual *claims-only* section might offer a rich source of parallel information, which might be leveraged, or consulted, specifically in support of pre-translation, translation, and even post-translation tasks. Indeed, for example, the request for an *Abstract-only* translation, where the ST abstract was drafted using the first claim of the patent, might be largely done before even started, when there is a European family member patent, with the right trilingual, or bilingual claims-only section.

References

Agreement on the application of Article 65 EPC—London Agreement (Oct. 17, 2000). https://www.epo.org/law-practice/legal-texts/london-agreement.html

Agreement on the application of Article 65 of the Convention on the Grant of European Patents (pdf full text version in French, German, and English). https://documents.epo.org/projects/babylon/eponet.nsf/0/7FD20618D28E9FBFC125743900678657/$File/London_Agreement.pdf

European Patent Convention—Part II., Chapt. III., Article 65 Translation of the European patent. https://www.epo.org/en/legal/epc/2020/a65.html

EPO Press release (Jan. 6, 2023). Start of the Unitary Patent: A historic step for innovating businesses in Europe. https://new.epo.org/en/news-events/press-centre/press-release/2023/535927

38 Translations filed at the World Intellectual Property Organization

Regulations for the languages accepted in the filing of an international patent application, at the *World Intellectual Property Organization* (WIPO), as well as those for translations, are specified in the provisions of the *Regulations under the Patent Cooperation Treaty* (PCT) *Rule 12*, as follows:

(a) An international application shall be filed in any language which the receiving Office accepts for that purpose.
(b) Each receiving Office shall, for the filing of international applications, accept at least one language which is both:
  (i) a language accepted by the International Searching Authority, or, if applicable, by at least one of the International Searching Authorities, competent for the international searching of international applications filed with that receiving Office, and
  (ii) a language of publication

Considering WIPO's 157 member states, the organization distinguishes ten acceptable official languages for patent publication (Arabic, Chinese, English, French, German, Japanese, Korean, Portuguese, Russian and Spanish). Ten languages which might also be acceptable to the International Searching Authority, receiving the application, and in charge of examining the prior art, for the purposes of determining the patentability of an invention. When the filing language is both an official WIPO language of publication and a language acceptable to the International Searching Authority, no translation of the application (specification and claims section) is required. When the language in which the application is filed is not acceptable to the International Searching Authority, a translation is required into a language that is both acceptable for publication and to the International Searching Authority. Conversely, if the language of the application is acceptable to the International Searching Authority, and *not* one of the 10 currently acceptable WIPO official languages of patent publication (e.g., Dutch) then a translation is required, that is both suitable for WIPO publication *and* acceptable to the International Searching Authority. In this case, the patent would be published in the language of the translation.

DOI: 10.4324/9781003423003-38

Regarding the official languages of publication and those of translations filed for World Intellectual Property Organization (WO patents), *when English is not the language of publication*, the following *Rule 48.3 (c)* further stipulates:

(a) If the international application is filed in Arabic, Chinese, English, French, German, Japanese, Korean, Portuguese, Russian or Spanish ("languages of publication"), that application shall be published in the language in which it was filed.
(b) If the international application is not filed in a language of publication and a translation into a language of publication has been furnished under Rule 12.3 or 12.4, that application shall be published in the language of that translation.
(c) If the international application is published in a language other than English, the international search report to the extent that it is published under Rule 48.2(a)(v), or the declaration referred to in Article 17(2)(a), the title of the invention, the abstract and any text matter pertaining to the figure or figures accompanying the abstract shall be published both in that language and in English. The translations, if not furnished by the applicant under Rule 12.3, shall be prepared under the responsibility of the International Bureau.

Thus, regardless of the language of publication, WO patents are also required to display—*in English*—a copy of the International Search Report, included at the conclusion of the patent application, as well as the information of the bibliographic data sheet, pertaining to the title of the invention, the abstract, and any text associated with the abstract drawing (e.g., see Table 38.1).

Implications for translation

For the translation process, the provisions of the above-cited PCT regulations, particularly *Rule 48.3 (c)*, offer a rich source of officially translated bilingual English terminology, background, or parallel information. A rich source of bilingual English information, found in both the International Search Report and on the bibliographic data sheet, for published WO patent applications, in any one of nine official languages other than English. Official languages other than English that include Arabic, Chinese, French, German, Japanese, Korean, Portuguese, Russian and Spanish.

In fact, when searching a list of same family patents, or any other hit list of patents returned, which might include one or several WO patents, it is *always* worth consulting the published WO documents. The consultation is rewarding, precisely because the patent bibliographic (cover) sheet, comprising the patent title [INID code (54)] abstract [INID code (57)] and any text associated with an abstract drawing, will always be bilingual to English, when English is not the publication language used in the application, in compliance with the PCT *Rule 48.3 (c)* in question. For the same reason, one of the Search Reports

Table 38.1 Bilingual Korean/English bibliographic data sheet (WO2012176949)

(12) 특허협력조약에 의하여 공개된 국제출원

(19) 세계지식재산권기구
국제사무국

(43) 국제공개일
2012 년 12 월 27 일 (27.12.2012)

WIPO | PCT

(10) 국제공개번호
WO 2012/176949 A1

(51) **국제특허분류**:
G06Q 50/00 (2006.01)

(21) **국제출원번호**: PCT/KR2011/004780

(22) **국제출원일**: 2011 년 6 월 30 일 (30.06.2011)

(25) **출원언어**: 한국어

(26) **공개언어**: 한국어

(30) **우선권정보**:
10-2011-0060014 2011 년 6 월 21 일 (21.06.2011) KR

(71) **출원인** (US 을(를) 제외한 모든 지정국에 대하여): **글로벌에스엠테크 리미티드 (GLOBAL SM TECH LIMITED)** [GB/KR]; 인천광역시 서구 당하동 743-6 번지, 404-819 Inchoen (KR).

(72) **발명자; 겸**
(71) **출원인** : **나태인 (NA, Tae In)** [KR/KR]; 인천광역시 서구 심곡동 285 대동아파트 106 동 1404 호, 404-792 Incheon (KR). **서종혁 (SEO, Jong Hyuk)** [KR/KR]; 경기도 고양시 일산동구 백석동 1330 브라운스톤 101 동 811 호, 410-360 Gyeonggido (KR).

(72) **발명자; 겸**
(75) **발명자/출원인** (US 에 한하여): **나윤복 (NA, Yun Bok)** [KR/KR]; 인천광역시 서구 심곡동 285 대동아파트 106 동 1404 호, 404-792 Incheon (KR). **서용기 (SEO, Yong Gi)** [KR/KR]; 경기도 고양시 일산동구 백석동 1330 브라운스톤 101 동 811 호, 410-360 Gyeonggido (KR).

(74) **대리인**: **이은철 (LEE, Un Cheol)**; 서울특별시 강남구 역삼동 648-23 여삼빌딩 11 층 5T 국제특허법률사무소, 135-080 Seoul (KR).

(81) **지정국** (별도의 표시가 없는 한, 가능한 모든 종류의 국내 권리의 보호를 위하여): AE, AG, AL, AM, AO, AT, AU, AZ, BA, BB, BG, BH, BR, BW, BY, BZ, CA, CH, CL, CN, CO, CR, CU, CZ, DE, DK, DM, DO, DZ, EC, EE, EG, ES, FI, GB, GD, GE, GH, GM, GT, HN, HR, HU, ID, IL, IN, IS, JP, KE, KG, KM, KN, KP, KZ, LA, LC, LK, LR, LS, LT, LU, LY, MA, MD, ME, MG, MK, MN, MW, MX, MY, MZ, NA, NG, NI, NO, NZ, OM, PE,

[다음 쪽 계속]

WO 2012/176949 A1

(54) **Title**: SYSTEM FOR CONVERTING GREENHOUSE GAS EMISSIONS TO CARBON CREDIT AND METHOD FOR SAME

(54) **발명의 명칭** : 온실가스 배출량의 탄소배출권 변환 시스템 및 그 방법

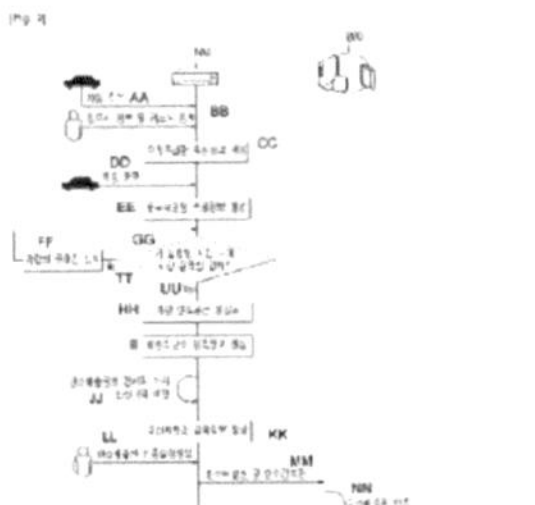

AA Vehicle refueling
BB Oil refueling company information and card company information
CC Generation of measurement information on the amount of fuel filled
DD Driving of the vehicle
EE Generation of measurement information on the amount of fuel usage
FF Vehicle idling prevention
GG Is vehicle movement detected within a preset time?
HH Vehicle fuel supply normalization
II Generation of carbon dioxide reduction information
JJ Economic value of carbon credit
Conversion history index
KK Generation of carbon dioxide reduction information
LL Carbon credit certification requirement information
MM Carbon credit and carbon reduction amount
NN Carbon credit certification
OO Generation of carbon credit certification information
PP Product payment completion information
QQ Carbon credit selling requirement information
RR Carbon credit selling
SS SMS transmission
TT No
UU Yes

(57) **Abstract**: The present invention relates to a system for converting greenhouse gas emissions to carbon credit and a method for same. The system for converting the greenhouse gas emissions to carbon credit includes a carbon emission reduction device which detects an amount of fuel filled in a vehicle and an amount of fuel used by the vehicle, minimizes the supply of fuel to the engine of the vehicle to prevent excessive fuel consumption and limit carbon emissions when the vehicle does not move within a preset time, supplies fuel to the engine of the vehicle in a normal manner when the vehicle is moved according to detection of the acceleration pedal of the vehicle, generates carbon dioxide reduction information by adding or subtracting an emitted amount of carbon dioxide that is limited during an idling prevention time to or from the emitted amount of carbon dioxide of the vehicle, and converts the carbon dioxide reduction information to carbon credit which includes a generated economic value upon reduction of a ton of carbon emissions. According to the present invention, a greenhouse gas reference emission amount for the vehicle may be reduced, and the greenhouse gas reduction amount for the vehicle may be converted into carbon credit that includes an economic value through the carbon emission reduction device so as to induce active participation by individuals for the reduction of greenhouse gas. Thus, the country, companies, and also individuals may play a role in resolving the problem of global warming, and the economic value of carbon credit generated by reducing the greenhouse gas from the vehicle may be sold or transferred to or acquired from the country or companies to provide economic benefit to the individual and stable growth for the companies.

(57) **요약서**:

[다음 쪽 계속]

본 발명은 온실가스 배출량의 탄소배출권 변환 시스템 및 그 방법에 관한 것으로서, 차량의 유류주입량과 차량의 유류 사용량을 감지하고, 기 설정된 시간 내에 차량의 움직임이 없는 경우, 차량 엔진으로의 연료공급을 최소화하여 공회전에 따른 연료소모를 방지하여 탄소배출을 억제하며, 차량의 엑셀 페달 감지에 따라 차량이 움직이는 경우, 차량 엔진으로의 연료공급을 정상화시키며, 차량이 방출하는 이산화탄소 배출량에서 공회전 방지 시간에 방출이 억제된 이산화탄소 배출량을 가감하여 이산화탄소 감축정보를 생성하고, 이산화탄소 감축정보를 1톤의 탄소배출 감축시 발생하는 경제적 가치를 포함하는 탄소배출권으로 변환하는 탄소배출 감축장치를 포함한다. 상기와 같은 본 발명에 따르면, 탄소배출 감축장치를 통해 차량의 온실가스 기준 배출량을 감축시키고, 차량의 온실가스 감축량을 경제적 가치를 포함하는 탄소배출권으로 변환함으로써, 온실가스 감축에 개인의 적극적인 참여를 유도하고, 국가나 기업뿐만 아니라 개인이 지구온난화 문제를 해결하는데 일조하게 하며, 차량의 온실가스 감축을 통해 생성된 탄소배출권의 경제적 가치를 국가 또는 기업에게 매매, 양도 및 양수를 할 수 있도록 함으로써, 개인의 경제적 이익과 기업의 안정적인 성장을 제공하는 효과가 있다.

comprising references to the prior art, related to the patent-at-hand, will also be in English. Thus, for the translation process, the provisions of the PCT *Rule 48.3 (c)* offer official bilingual English information, found on each end of the patent application, that greatly expands both the scope and availability of translated terminology to English, and of access to English bilingual background information.

Table 38.1, for example, captures a sample bilingual Korean to English WO patent bibliographic datasheet for the WIPO PCT patent WO2012176949, titled *System for converting greenhouse gas emissions to carbon credit and method for same*. The language of publication is Korean. Thus, according to the provisions of *PCT Rule 48.3 (c)*, the title of the invention, the abstract, and any text matter pertaining to the figure or figures, accompanying the abstract, are also required to appear in English, precisely as shown on the bibliographic datasheet. Bilingual Korean to English information that might be further amplified by consulting the English copy of the International Search Report, appended at the conclusion of the patent application, consistent with the same provisions of *PCT Rule 48.3 (c)*.

References

Administrative Instructions under the Patent Cooperation Treaty, Section 103—Languages of the forms used by the international authorities. https://www.wipo.int/pct/en/texts/ai/s103.html

Regulations under the PCT Rule 12—Language of the international application and translations for the purposes of international search and international publication. https://www.wipo.int/pct/en/texts/rules/r12.html#_12

Regulations under the PCT Rule 48.3—Languages of publication. https://www.wipo.int/pct/en/texts/rules/r48.html#_48_3_a

Cited patent

Na, T.I. et al. (2012). System for converting greenhouse gas emissions to carbon credit and method for same (Patent No. WO2012176949). World Intellectual Property Organization (WIPO). https://patentscope.wipo.int/search/en/detail.jsf?docId=WO2012176949&_cid=P22-LNO1PU-46706-1

39 Patent search tools at the World Intellectual Property Organization

Patent Offices, such as the World Intellectual Property Organization (WIPO), offer patent search tools, enabling visitors to navigate their vast databases of patents. Such tools are primarily designed for various types of professionals, for example: examiners seeking to determine the patentability of an invention, IP attorneys seeking to find specific documents, inventors who want to check if their idea is already patented, researchers interested in seeing which technologies are developed in their fields, and entrepreneurs seeking to find out who the competition might be. However, this hardly means that patent search tools have no dedicated role in translation. In fact, nothing could be farther from the truth, especially considering the multilingualism of the WIPO patent database and of the WIPO tools design, intended to facilitate exploration and analysis of IP data.

Implications for translation

If patent translation experts, such as Popp (2009), are right when they assert that patents are the richest source of terminology, background information, and parallel texts for patents translation; and if patent databases contain millions of patents, then translators definitely need both tools and knowhow to search the mega patent databases, at the Patent Offices. Fortunately, state-of-the-art tools exist to perform searches, enabling to easily retrieve information. Below, a succinct overview is provided of the patent search tools found at the UN World Intellectual Property Office (WIPO). Specifically, information is included for both: 1. *Patentscope*, the WIPO patent database and search engine, and 2. *WIPO Pearl*, a multilingual, patent-based, terminology portal, together with links to tutorials for learning how to use such tools.

Patentscope—The WIPO patent search engine

Number of documents: 108 million patent documents, including 4.5 million published patent applications

Collection: Published *Patent Cooperation Treaty* (PCT) patents and applications, including national collections from PCT member states

DOI: 10.4324/9781003423003-39

Languages: Arabic, German, English, Spanish, French, Japanese, Korean, Portuguese, Russian, and Chinese

Search functions: See *The Patentscope User's Guide* (Last updated Dec. 2023) https://patentscope.wipo.int/search/help/en/users_guide.pdf

Search results: The list of hits may be viewed in a list, or split screen mode with the list of hits on one side and access to a selected patent from the list on the other side. Access to a single patent includes a series of tabs, facilitating direct access to specific patent-relevant sections such as: *Bibliographic data, Description*, *Drawings*, *Claims*, *Patent Family*, and *Documents*, such as pdf copies of the original patent documents. Direct access to patent-relevant sections of a patent bypasses scrolling through a patent document to the relevant information, and thus speeds up the search for information.

Machine translation (MT) engine: *WIPO Translate* with Google neural network technology is the WIPO machine translation engine, from and into 14 languages. For example, see Table 39.1 below. The Table 39.1 MT screenshot captures the title and abstract, to Finnish, of the WIPO patent application, WO2007088279, titled *Cooking appliance with stirring means and associated method*, appearing highlighted on the patent cover sheet, in place of the English version. Notice that the translation comes

Table 39.1 Screenshot of the WIPO Translate MT Finnish output for the English WO2007088279 title and abstract

with a pop-up disclaimer, on the upper right corner, regarding the limits of machine translation.

***Tutorials*:** https://patentscope.wipo.int/search/en/help/tutorial.jsf

Versions: Mobile and desktop.

Cost: free

WIPO Pearl—Multilingual Terminology Portal

WIPO Pearl is a multilingual terminology portal that provides access to terminology and semantic concept maps, derived from patent documents stored in the *Patentscope* database, in the ten official languages of patent publication at WIPO. As a result, when searching for a term using WIPO Pearl, the term retrieved has multiple connections. The hit term is displayed: 1. Indexed according to one or several International Patent Classification (IPC) domains; 2. Linked to patents, images and/or concept maps; *and* 3. Translated in as many as nine languages. Translations listed for the searched term, termed *language equivalences*, are expert-rated for reliability, or otherwise flagged when derived from Machine Translation. Thus, WIPO Pearl offers vetted, multilingual patent-connected terminology, together with expert ratings, provided in partnership with universities, and large international translation organizations, such as the *International Federation of Translators*. As of May 24, 2023, the WIPO Pearl database contained more than 240,000 WIPO–PCT-validated terms.

WIPO Pearl offers two search modes: *linguistic* and *concept map* searches. Each of these modes are illustrated respectively in Tables 39.2 and 39.3.

Table 39.2 is a screenshot showing an extract of the hitlist for a WIPO Pearl *linguistic search* on the term *transgenic*. The extract includes just the first returned term, *transgenic mouse*, in the domain of Science/Genetics, with equivalents in nine WIPO publication languages: Arabic, German, Spanish, French, Portuguese, Chinese, Russian, Japanese, and Korean. The screenshot displays a drop-down *patent definition* for the term *transgenic mouse*, in English, obtained via the expanded left triangle ▼. The screenshot also depicts an expanded view of the right, horizontal three-dot menu (•••) for the English term *transgenic mouse*, enabling users to optionally link the English term to: 1. *Patentscope* for a list of related patents; 2. Google images for illustration of the searched term; and 3. WIPO semantic Concept Maps. Due to space limitations, definitions for the equivalent terms are hidden, as well as further three-dot expansions to the right.

Table 39.3 captures a frozen state extract of the interactive WIPO Pearl English *concept map* for the term "transgenic mouse". *Concept maps* for "transgenic mouse" exist for all nine additional WIPO patent publication languages, designated with the letter codes Arabic (AR), French (FR), German (DE), Spanish (ES), Japanese (JA), Korean (KO), Chinese (ZH), Russian (RU), and Portuguese (PT). The *concept maps* are interactive, enabling users to drag concepts in view of exploring associations. *Concept map searches* might be performed separately from *Linguistic searches* at WIPO Pearl, or they may be explored as linked to a *linguistic search* via the right three-dot (•••) menus shown in Table 39.2.

Table 39.2 Screenshot of the WIPO PEARL hitlist for a linguistic search on the English term 'transgenic', returning 'transgenic mouse' first, including equivalent terms in nine additional WIPO publication languages (Arabic, German, Spanish, French, Portuguese, Chinese, Russian, Japanese, and Korean)

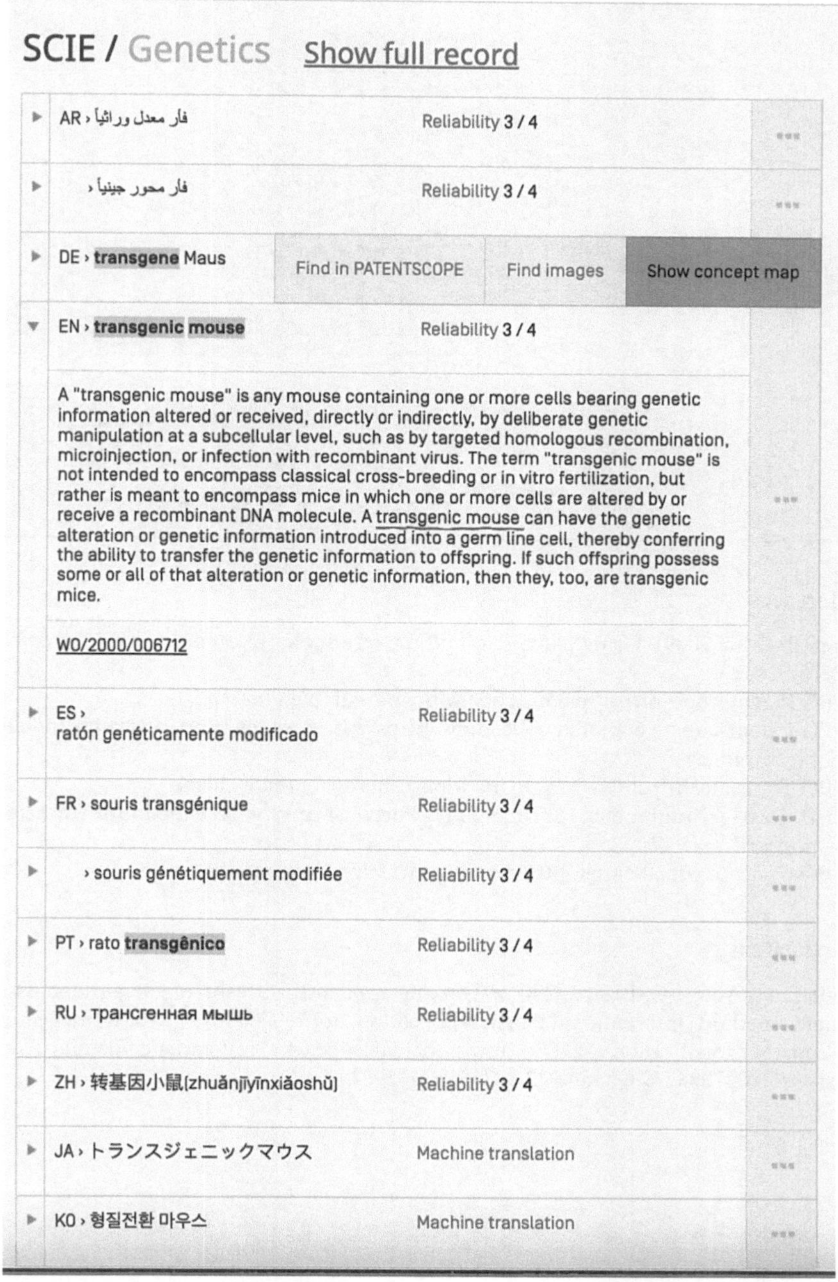

Table 39.3 Screenshot of an extract of the WIPO PEARL interactive English concept map for the term 'transgenic mouse', showing related concepts and domains, and their proximity/distance to the core search term

References

Popp, B. (May 2009). Using patents to find the terminology you need. *ATA Chronicle*, 38(5), 16–23.

WIPO Patentscope. https://patentscope.wipo.int/search/en/search.jsf

WIPO Patentscope—National collections. https://patentscope.wipo.int/search/en/help/data_coverage.jsf

WIPO Translate. https://www.wipo.int/wipo-translate/en/index.html

WIPO Pearl—Multilingual Terminology Portal. https://www.wipo.int/reference/en/wipopearl/

WIPO Concept Map Search. https://wipopearl.wipo.int/en/conceptmap

Cited patent

Goderiaux, A. & J-C. Bizard (2007). Cooking appliance with stirring means and associated method (International Patent Application No. 2007088279). World Intellectual Property Organization (WIPO). https://patentscope.wipo.int/search/en/detail.jsf?docId=WO2007088279&_cid=P22-LNJ5WO-15053-1

40 Patent search tools at the European Patent Office

The European Patent Office (EPO) patent search tools at *Espacenet*, the EPO database that federates all the patent collections of contracting member states, are *indispensable* to the patent translation process, *a fortiori* in the multilingual context of Europe.

Implications for translation

The EPO patent search tools at *Espacenet* are *indispensable*, because once again, if patents are indeed the best sources of terminology, background information, and parallel texts for patents translation, with millions of patents stored as sources of information, then translators need to know both how to navigate the patent databases at major Patent Offices, and most importantly, how to retrieve information from the millions of patents contained within the databases. Specifically, concerning the *European Patent Office* (EPO), the following datasheet outlines some of the essential *Espacenet* features, and enabling tools for translators.

Espacenet

Number of documents: > 120 million documents

Collection: Patents and patent applications from all national databases of the EPO member states, plus more, same family patents from non-members states.

Languages: French, English, German (official languages of the EPO), and a total of 32 languages covering all the member states of the *European Patent Organization*, plus any languages for same family patents from non-member states.

Search functions: See *Espacenet Pocket Guide* https://tinyurl.com/4pcndtek

Search results:

- *Espacenet* search results are presented on a split-screen display, allowing anyone searching for patents to conveniently see different

DOI: 10.4324/9781003423003-40

sections of a patent side-by-side (for example patent drawings side-by-side with the narrative description of the invention).

- Several options exist for presenting the returned list of search results, including *Text only*, *Text and thumbnail*, *Drawings only*, and *Compact list*, enabling for example to differentiate patents with same titles, at-a-glance.
- Interface tabs enable online consultation of a retrieved patent, according to relevant patent sections, such as *Claims*, *Description*, *Bibliographic Datasheet* or *Drawings*.
- A toggle button enables switching from portrait to landscape to view any patent drawings, appearing in contrasting views, thus bypassing the need to print any of the drawing pages.
- The New (and current) *Espacenet* interface is a much-improved edition of the original *Espacenet*, with an easy to navigate display, that also includes mouseover pop-up help, directly on screen, for any of the buttons, functions, and menus available.

Machine translation (MT) engine: *Patent Translate* with Google neural network technology is the EPO machine translation (MT) engine, from and into 32 languages. For example, see below the Tables 40.1 and 40.2 showing machine translations to Dutch and Greek, for the European patent abstract, EP2330255A1, titled *Extensible, transportable habitable cell*. The screenshots also respectively show: mouseover popups of the English version of the abstract, the *Patent Translate* right sidebar panel

Table 40.1 Screenshot of the EPO Patent Translate MT Dutch output for the English EP2330255A1 Abstract

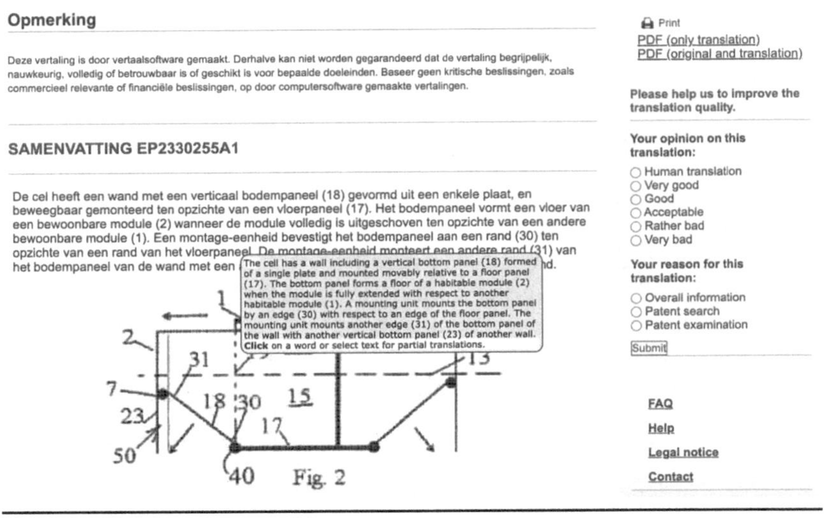
Opmerking

Deze vertaling is door vertaalsoftware gemaakt. Derhalve kan niet worden gegarandeerd dat de vertaling begrijpelijk, nauwkeurig, volledig of betrouwbaar is of geschikt is voor bepaalde doeleinden. Baseer geen kritische beslissingen, zoals commercieel relevante of financiële beslissingen, op door computersoftware gemaakte vertalingen.

SAMENVATTING EP2330255A1

De cel heeft een wand met een verticaal bodempaneel (18) gevormd uit een enkele plaat, en beweegbaar gemonteerd ten opzichte van een vloerpaneel (17). Het bodempaneel vormt een vloer van een bewoonbare module (2) wanneer de module volledig is uitgeschoven ten opzichte van een andere bewoonbare module (1). Een montage-eenheid bevestigt het bodempaneel aan een rand (30) ten opzichte van een rand van het vloerpaneel. De montage-eenheid monteert een andere rand (31) van het bodempaneel van de wand met een … nd.

The cell has a wall including a vertical bottom panel (18) formed of a single plate and mounted movably relative to a floor panel (17). The bottom panel forms a floor of a habitable module (2) when the module is fully extended with respect to another habitable module (1). A mounting unit mounts the bottom panel by an edge (30) with respect to an edge of the floor panel. The mounting unit mounts another edge (31) of the bottom panel of the wall with another vertical bottom panel (23) of another wall. **Click** on a word or select text for partial translations.

Fig. 2

Print
PDF (only translation)
PDF (original and translation)

Please help us to improve the translation quality.

Your opinion on this translation:
- Human translation
- Very good
- Good
- Acceptable
- Rather bad
- Very bad

Your reason for this translation:
- Overall information
- Patent search
- Patent examination

Submit

FAQ
Help
Legal notice
Contact

Table 40.2 Screenshot of the EPO Patent Translate MT Greek output for the English EP2330255A1 Abstract

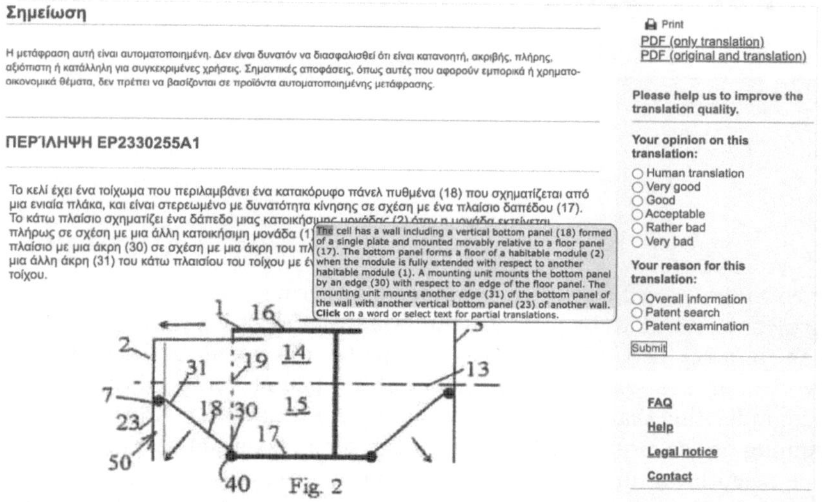

with a user feedback form, and at the top, a disclaimer note, regarding the limits of machine translation.

Tutorials: YouTube video—New *Espacenet* https://youtu.be/KLxnB5dqP70

Versions: mobile and desktop.

Costs: free.

Reference

EPO Espacenet Patent Search. https://www.epo.org/searching-for-patents/technical/espacenet.html

Cited patent

Beau, E. (2011). Extensible, transportable, habitable cell (Patent No. EP2330255A1). European Patent Organization (EPO). https://worldwide.espacenet.com/patent/search/family/042797173/publication/EP2330255A1?q=EP2330255A1

41 *Patent Public Search* at the United States Patent and Trademark Office

United States patents have a continuous numbering system since "the beginning of time", 1790 to be precise. Thus, for any current US *utility* patent number, the number also indicates how many patents are on file at the USPTO. On May 11th 2021, for example, the United States patent number 11,000,000 was issued, indicating that a total of 11 million patents had been granted, since the beginning of the United States patenting system. A system that dates back to the eighteenth century, considering that powers to award *Letters patent* were granted to Congress, in the United States Constitution, at the birth of the nation.

As a result, the USPTO collection of patents is both historical, and on the far edge of discovery. Thanks to the work of archival specialists, the historical handwritten documents were also converted to print, which is now digitized. As a result, the complete 300-year old collection is available to everyone at the click of a button, and even the oldest patents are perfectly legible.

A new USPTO *Public Patent Search* portal became exclusively available on September 30th 2022, replacing the legacy system for searching one of two databases: the *Patent Full-Text and Image Database* (PatFT) and the *Patent Application Full-Text and Image Database* (AppFT). The new *Public Patent Search* portal offers two options: *Basic Search* and *Advanced Search* for searching the databases, and retrieving patents in PDF format. For information on conducting a patent search, see the USPTO references included below.

Implications for translation

The USPTO possesses the most complete record of US patents and patent applications, all patent categories combined (*Utility*, *Design* and *Plant*). Even if various Internet patent search tools, with or without a fee, provide access to US patents, third party search engines negotiate and pay for access to the USPTO patent collections. As a result, such access is usually partial. Thus, for US patents, the most *complete and up-to-date* source is found at the USPTO. Consequently, translators should keep the new *Public Patent Search*

DOI: 10.4324/9781003423003-41

portal URL on file, for searching and retrieving US patents, and especially patent applications. Searching for patents at the USPTO is also 100% free of charge.

References

USPTO—How to conduct a preliminary US Patent search—A step-by-step strategy. https://www.uspto.gov/video/cbt/prelim-patent-search/index.html

USPTO—Patent Public Search. https://ppubs.uspto.gov/pubwebapp/static/pages/landing.html

USPTO—Search for Patents. https://www.uspto.gov/patents/search

42 Patent-related bioethical controversies

Patented medicines

One of the most significant and well-known patent-related bioethical controversy concerns patented medicines. A controversy that is rightly one of the most pressing. First, because the issue of patented medicines is longstanding, dating back to the nineteenth century, when European legislators purposefully *excluded* medicines from patenting. Nineteenth-century European legislators clearly saw the potential conflict of interest between public health and the price monopolies that could result from patenting medicines. Secondly, because this is a conflict that sadly played out more than once, *exactly as originally avoided*, as soon as medicines became patentable in the early 1960s.

Indeed, the most well-known bioethical issue, surrounding patented medicine, is the cause initially taken up by the Nobel Prize-winning humanitarian organization, *Doctors Without Borders/Médecins Sans Frontières*. A cause, which is to date relentlessly championed (e.g., Engelberg et al., 2022). Essentially, a cause that concerns thousands of lives cut short, without access to the completely prohibitive (patented) antiretroviral therapies (ART), used for the treatment of the acquired immunodeficiency syndrome (AIDS), in both Third World *and* developed countries. Also, a cause that set precedence in the ongoing search for solutions, aimed at bringing down the costs of largely unaffordable patented medicines, for example most recently, within the context of the coronavirus pandemic (e.g., *Médecins Sans Frontières*, 2020).

Pirated raw materials

Beyond the most widely documented bioethical controversy, concerning access to patented medicines, the question of the bioethics of patents might also be framed from the perspective of ecology. The bioethics of patents, in an ecological perspective, arises in a context where plant-based patented technologies (pharmaceutical, medicinal and cosmetics) require *mining* the resources of indigenous communities, for their raw materials. The harvesting of a single resource to the point of diminished returns, or extinction in the worst-case scenario. Indeed, extinction happens when the rate of harvest is greater than natural plant mortality, and its capacity for reproduction.

DOI: 10.4324/9781003423003-42

For example, within the context of medicinal plant-based patents, overharvesting creates a double risk: the risk of extinction, and in turn the risk of shortages for the indigenous populations who have relied on the same plant remedies for centuries. According to Shi-Lin Chen et al. (2016), citing the *International Union for Conservation of Nature* and the *World Wildlife Fund*: "*There are between 50,000 and 80,000 flowering plant species used for medicinal purposes worldwide. Among these, about 15,000 species are threatened with extinction from overharvesting and habitat destruction.*" The authors further state that: "*There are over 1300 medicinal plants used in Europe, of which 90 % are harvested from wild resources; in the United States, about 118 of the top 150 prescription drugs are based on natural sources.*" Plants that contribute to biodiversity and that are in some cases actively protected from extinction (Roberson, 2008).

Introduced by the well-known Indian physicist and activist, Vandana Shiva, the term *pirating* is generally used when there is evidence that the depletion of natural resources upsets fragile ecosystems, creating corollary problems of sustainability (Shiva, 1997, 2002). Specifically, Shiva uses the term *pirating*, to denounce the excesses of the response to the demand for raw materials, in the production of patented plant-based medicines.

Misappropriated traditional knowledge (TK)

Under the above-mentioned conditions of *plunder*, *traditional knowledge* (TK) associated with the harvesting of raw materials and resources is deemed *misappropriated*, when it cannot be researched in print, as prior art (Dumesnil, 2012). Essentially, *traditional knowledge* is by definition *unsearchable in print as prior art*, because such knowledge is transmitted in oral traditions, or in languages unknown to the western world. The fact of the matter is that, in certain instances, where enough pressure and evidence of *misappropriation* was presented before the issuing patent offices, *patents were revoked*. This was the case for two patents: EP436257, titled *Method of controlling fungi on plants by the aid of hydrophobic extracted Neem oil*, and US5401504, titled *Use of turmeric in wound healing*. Patents respectively claiming the fungicide properties of *Neem Tree oil* and the anti-inflammatory, anti-microbial properties of *turmeric*. Two plants produced and processed, precisely for these purposes, for centuries, in India. Both revoked patents, comprising two of the better-known cases of redress, in both the United States and Europe, set precedence in the bid for more just, equitable, and sustainable patent-related practices.

Transgenic animals

Still another way of framing the bioethics of patents concerns the controversial issue of genetically engineered animals, such as *knockout* (KO) or *knockin* (KI) transgenic mice. In 1980, the United States Supreme Court ruled that micro-organisms made by humans were patentable, because they are "manufactured" or fall within the scope of "compositions of matter", per the statute

Title 35 USC Section 101, invoked in the case *Diamond v. Chakrabarty*—488 US 303, 1980. According to Sherman (1997), "This [decision] cleared the way for the ability to obtain patents for genetically engineered plants, microorganisms, and animals in the United States." Clearly, according to Thickstun (2007) this was a decision that paved the way for the patenting of: "Anything under the sun that is made by man". Likewise, on the European front, the *oncomouse* would become patentable, precisely because it was argued that the *oncomouse* was *not a species*. Otherwise, the *oncomouse* would have been *included* in the *non-patentable* European category of animal species.

As a consequence of such rulings, the fact of the matter is that, in 1988, the first animal patent was granted, in the United States, for genetically engineered mice, with a gene that caused cancer. Specifically, the United States patent, US4736866, titled *Transgenic non-human mammals*, was awarded to Phillip Leder and Timothy Stewart (and assigned to Harvard University) for: "*...a transgenic nonhuman animal whose germ cells and somatic cells contain an activated oncogene.*" Since then, many such transgenic mice have been engineered and patented, for sale to researchers, not only studying varying types of cancer, but other diseases. For example, other illnesses under study include infectious diseases, diabetes, heart disease, obesity, arthritis, substance abuse, anxiety, Parkinson's disease, etc.

Part genetic-hypothesis testers, part drug-testing animals, patented transgenic mice are now manufactured on demand. For example, at the *InGenius Targeting Laboratory*, in partnership with *Emory University Transgenic and Gene Targeting Core*, advertisements for the production of custom transgenic mice run: "*You think it up, we knock it out ... or in*". Not to mention the manufacture of other types of patented transgenic animals, not all for the same reasons, such as cows, pigs, and pet fish (e.g., GloFish). A production of patented transgenic animals that is unanimously *defended* by scientists, and such regulatory agencies as the *Food and Drug Administration* (FDA). The manufacture of transgenic animals is *defended*, essentially because of the breakthrough genomic evidence such patented, man-made animals provide, together with the promise of cures for both humans, *and* animals.

Genetically modified crops (GMCs)

Considering the abovementioned Supreme Court ruling on the patentability of "man-made" organisms considered "compositions of matter", the bioethics of patents might also be framed in agriculture. The controversy in this domain concerns genetically modified crops (GMCs), or what Michael Polan termed "Playing God in the Garden of Eden" (Polan, 1998). Patented GMCs engineered resistant to pests, such as NewLeaf® potatoes resistant to the *Colorado potato beetle*. Patented GMCs such as YieldGuard® corn, engineered resistant to the *European corn borer*. Patented GMCs also engineered resistant to weather conditions, particularly drought. Alternatively, patented GMCs engineered resistant to herbicides, in particular resistant to the *glyphosate herbicide*

Roundup®. A herbicide, now banned, or under restricted use, in several states of the United States and countries worldwide, due to mounting evidence and repeated verdicts, confirming the carcinogenic effects of the *herbicide glysophate*, affecting gardeners and farmers, who handle treated plants (e.g., Jacobs, 2019).

Patented seed controversies in this domain have been most convincingly and eloquently discussed by Vandana Shiva, physicist and activist, who argues in this case *against* the *reductionism* of life to genes, and of genes to mechanistic parts that function like machines. For Shiva "growing" crops is different from "engineering" them.

Relying on the theoretical work of Chilean scientists Maturana & Varela (1998), Shiva distinguished *nature* from *machine engineering*, in terms of *self-organizing systems*, adaptation, and the unpredictability of change. For empirical support, Shiva turned to research on *super pests* and *super bugs* that become tolerant to transgenic pesticidal and insecticidal crops (e.g., *The Organic Center* 2014). A line of insecticide-resistance research, which to date *confirms* failure to manage super bug adaptation to insecticides (e.g., Gassmann, 2014; Chen, et al., 2023), *exactly* as Shiva anticipated in one of her early books on *Biopiracy* (1997), per the following quote:

> When an organism or system is mechanically manipulated to improve a one-dimensional function, including the increase in one dimensional productivity, either the organism's immunity decreases, and it becomes vulnerable to disease and attack by other organisms, or the organism becomes dominant in an ecosystem, and displaces other species, pushing them to extinction. *Ecological problems arise when applying the engineering paradigm to life.*
>
> (p. 32) [italics mine]

Shiva has also received much criticism for sounding the alarm, concerning high farmer suicide rates in India (e.g., Thomas & de Tavernier, 2017). High suicide rates explained in a context of *negative cultural disruption of ancestral agricultural practices*. In other words, ancestral practices such as *saving and sharing seeds*, adversely disrupted by patented technologies such as *Genetic Use Restriction Technologies*, also known as GURTs. Specifically, T-GURTS, when the technology prevents the use of engineered seeds without another patented activator compound. And V-GURTS, when the second generation of seeds is *engineered sterile*, making it impossible to save seeds for planting the next season.

Implications for translation

As fascinating as the above patent-related bioethical issues might appear, the question of relevance to the translation process arises anew with full force, just as the corpus of laws, rules, regulations, and international agreements, at the very beginning of this book, was questioned for its relevance to translation. Indeed, whereas the initial question driving this book is now clearly answered manifold times, considering how significant the linguistic impact of the selected provisions of laws, rules, regulations, and international agreements, on the translation process, another question arises at the conclusion of this book. The question of whether patent-related bioethical controversies are relevant to the translation process. This time, a question that has to do more specifically with the broader context of *language acts*, or what translation *does* in the world.

Regardless of how "invisible" the role of translators, or how much motivational displacement might be required to "step into other people's shoes" when translating, the fact of the matter is that translations become part of larger *conversations-for-action* in the world. Larger conversations, which are sometimes at the intersection of politics, public health, and economics. Conversations that might encompass any one of the above-mentioned bioethical controversies, concerning access to patented medicines, the mining of natural resources, the potentially misguided use of engineered seeds, or the largely *silent* manufacture and use of transgenic animals. Conversations that include translations, traveling as episodes in side-channel, or at the forefront of discussion in the web of communication.

In defiance of invisibility, it is no small fact that the United Nations General Assembly recognized "*The role of professional translation in connecting nations and fostering peace, understanding and development*", when proclaiming the celebration, each year, of *International Translation Day*, on September 30th, the Day of the Feast of Saint Jerome (UN resolution A/RES/71/288). The celebration of a critical role that the President of the International Federation of Translation, Alison Rodrigues, reframed as one that *prevents linguistics from overshadowing politics* (Rodriguez, 2022).

Thus, however remote the previously mentioned patent controversies might appear from focused linguistic tasks such as, for example, complying with the *single-sentence rule* (SSR) for translating patent claims, the extended meanings and connections of patent source texts simply *cannot be ignored* in translation, or completely dissociated from the source text. Aligned with UN resolution A/RES/71/288, recognizing the role of translation in the political, economic, and cultural arena, this book deliberately objects to concealing the extended meanings of patent source texts, however contentious. Such controversial background or foreground meanings, associated with patent source and target texts, *a fortiori* <u>*must*</u> be made explicit, and understood, so that such information might *also* inform the translation process. Information that may not show up in translator notes, or as intext explications, but rather as an *understanding* of the potential roles of patent translations. Indeed, such information forms the basis of an *awareness* of the scope of full-fledged *participation* and *agency* in the mediation process.

References

35 USC 101 - Invention patentable. https://www.uspto.gov/web/offices/pac/mpep/mpep-9015-appx-l.html#d0e302376

Diamond v. Chakrabarty, 447 U.S. 303 (Supreme Court 1980). https://supreme.justia.com/cases/federal/us/447/303/

Chen et al. (2016). Conservation and sustainable use of medicinal plants: problems, progress, and prospects. *Chinese Medicine*, v. 11, 2016. DOI: 10.1186/s13020-016-0108-7. https://pubmed.ncbi.nlm.nih.gov/27478496/

Chen, Y. H., et al. (2023). Rapid evolution of insecticide resistance in the Colorado potato beetle, *Leptinotarsa decemlineata. Current Opinion in Insect Science*, Feb. 55. 101000. DOI: 10.1016/j.cois.2022.101000. https://pubmed.ncbi.nlm.nih.gov/36521782/

Dumesnil, C. (2012). Les savoirs traditionnels médicinaux pillés par le droit des brevets? *Revue internationale de droit économique* 2012/3 (t. XXVI), pages 321 à 343. DOI: 10.3917/ride.256.0321. https://www.cairn.info/revue-internationale-de-droit-economique-2012-3-page-321.htm

Engelberg, A.B., et al. (2022). A New Way to Contain Unaffordable Medication Costs — Exercising the Government's Existing Rights. *New England Journal of Medicine*, March 24, 2022, (12):1104—1106. DOI: 10.1056/NEJMp2117102. ePub 2022 Feb 9. PMID: 35139270. https://pubmed.ncbi.nlm.nih.gov/35139270/

Gassmann, A., et al. (2014). Field-evolved resistance by western corn rootworm to multiple Bacillus thuringiensis toxins in transgenic maize. *Proceedings of the National Academy of Sciences of the United States of America (PNAS)*, 111(14). DOI: 10.1073/pnas.1317179111. https://pubmed.ncbi.nlm.nih.gov/24639498/

Hanahan, D. et al. (2007). The origins of oncomice: A history of the first transgenic mice genetically engineered to develop cancer. *Genes & Development* 21(18):2258–2270. DOI: 10.1101/gad.1583307. PMID: 17875663. https://pubmed.ncbi.nlm.nih.gov/17875663/

Ingenious Targeting Laboratory. https://www.genetargeting.com/

Jacobs, J. (March 27, 2019). Monsanto Ordered to Pay $80 Million in Roundup Cancer Case. *NY Times*. https://www.nytimes.com/2019/03/27/us/monstanto-roundup-california-verdict.html

Maturana, H.R. and F.J. Varela (1998). *The tree of knowledge: The biological roots of human understanding*. Revised Edition. Boston, MA: Shambhala Press.

Médecins Sans Frontières—Doctors Without Borders (March 27, 2020). MSF to Pharma: No profiteering on coronavirus pandemic. *MSF/DWB*. https://www.doctorswithoutborders.org/latest/msf-pharma-no-profiteering-coronavirus-pandemic

Polan, M. (Oct. 25, 1998). Playing God in the Garden of Eden. *The New York Times*. https://www.nytimes.com/1998/10/25/magazine/playing-god-in-the-garden.html

Roberson, E. (2008). Medicinal plants at risk. Nature's pharmacy, our treasure chest: Why we must conserve our natural heritage: A native plant conservation campaign report. Center for Biodiversity. https://www.biologicaldiversity.org/publications/papers/Medicinal_Plants_042008_lores.pdf

Rodriguez, A. (Sept. 29, 2022). Overcoming babel: Why translation is key to lasting peace and development. *United Nations Chronicle*. https://www.un.org/en/authors-og-936/alison-rodriguez

Sherman, S. (1997). Biomedical, pharmaceutical and biotechnology patents Japanese to English translations. Chapt. 7 in *The ATA Japanese Patent Translator's Handbook*, pp. 140–9.

Shiva, V. (1997). *Biopiracy: The plunder of nature and knowledge*. Cambridge, MA: South End Press.

Shiva, V. (2002). *Protect or plunder: Understanding intellectual property rights (global issues)*. London, UK: Zed Books.

Thickstun, O. (2007). Intellectual property and biotechnology patents. In *The Patent Translator's Handbook*. Alexandria, VA: ATA—American Translators Association, pp. 85–96.
Thomas, G. and J. de Tavernier (2017). Farmer-suicide in India: debating the role of biotechnology. *Lifesciences, Society and Policy*, Dec. 13: 8. DOI: 10.1186/s40504-017-0052-z. https://pubmed.ncbi.nlm.nih.gov/28497354/
The Organic Center (March 2014). GMO crops continue to foster development of super bugs. https://www.organic-center.org/research/gmo-crops-continue-foster-development-super-bugs
UN resolution A/RES/71/288. The role of professional translation in connecting nations and fostering peace, understanding and development. https://digitallibrary.un.org/record/1288376?ln=en#record-files-collapse-header

Cited patents

Das, S.K. and H.P. Cohly (1995). Use of turmeric in wound healing (Patent No. US5401504). United States Patent and Trademark Office (USPTO). https://image-ppubs.uspto.gov/dirsearch-public/print/downloadPdf/5401504
Leder, P. and T.A. Stewart (1988). Transgenic non-human mammals (Patent No. US4736866). United States Patent and Trademark Office (USPTO). https://image-ppubs.uspto.gov/dirsearch-public/print/downloadPdf/4736866
Locke, J.C. et al. (1991). Method of controlling fungi on plants by the aid of hydrophobic extracted Neem oil (Patent No. EP436257). European Patent Office (EPO). https://worldwide.espacenet.com/patent/search/family/023814062/publication/EP0436257A1?q=EP436257

Appendix I

Instructions for obtaining circled INID code numbers

Circled numbers using the Microsoft Word **Symbols** font are only available up to the number 19 (e.g., ⑲). **CombiNumerals** is a free font suitcase by The Fontsite, which provides circled INID code numbers >20, such as (54) for the title of the invention, and (72) for the name(s) of the inventor(s).

1. Go to the FontSpace to download the free **CombiNumerals** font at: http://www.fontspace.com/category/numbers,circles
2. Download the fonts.
3. Open the zipped suitcase with an unzip program.
4. Click on the CNFree.ttf files to open them, and click the Install button on the top left.
5. Once installed, the font will appear as a **CombiNumerals** option in the dropdown font menu of all your applications (MS Word, Excel, etc.), just like the **Calibri**, **Arial**, **Times Roman** font options. (Path: Home>Font>Dropdown fonts menu>**CombiNumerals**)
6. Scroll down the list of fonts after opening the dropdown fonts menu, and click on **CombiNumerals** to select it.
7. To insert a *single digit* circled number, type the regular QWERTY letter keys: Q=θ, W=ω, E=ε, etc. To insert *double-digit* circled numbers, for example the number 7#: type the number 7 using the keyboard numbers, and then shift 3.
8. Repeat steps 6 and 7 for each INID code.
9. Refer to the ***CombiNumerals: User Guide & Character Chart*** pdf, included in the zip suitcase that was downloaded, for more information on using the circled fonts.

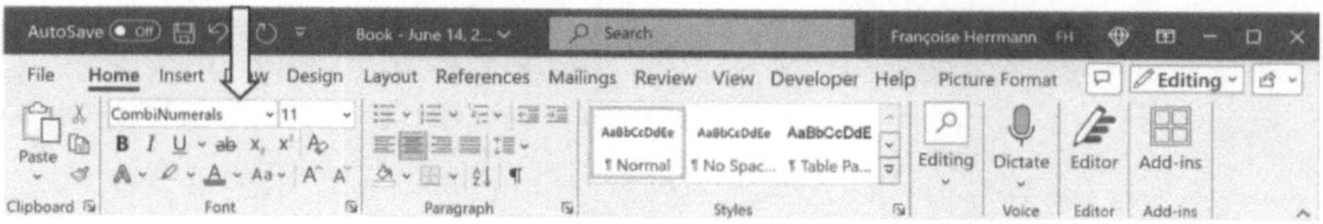

Figure A.1 CombiNumerals font uploaded to MS Word

Troubleshooting: Make sure that the **CombiNumerals** font is always selected when typing a single digit **CombiNumeral** number, or double-digit number sequence, as the font selection will revert back to your default **Calibri**, **Ariel**, **Times Roman**, or other font, after each key stroke.

Appendix II
List of cited patents

Patent /Application number		Title of invention	Inventors	Identifier
1.	**EP0672994**	Method and apparatus for reading an optically two-dimensional code	HARA, Masahiro [JP] WATABE, Motoaki [JP] NOJIRI, Tadao [JP] NAGAYA, Takayuki [JP] UCHIYAMA, Yuji [JP]	QR code
2.	**GB2266045**	Drinking vessel suitable for use as a trainer cup	HABERMAN, Mandy Nicola [GB]	Anywayup cup™
3.	**US6102245**	Drinking vessel with valve	HABERMAN, Mandy Nicola [GB]	sippy cup
4.	**US2258841**	Fountain pen	BIRO, Laszlo Jozsef [AR]	Biro
5.	**US2669152**	Trombone	SHUMAN, Davis [US]	Shuman trombone
6.	**US2717437**	Velvet type fabric and method of producing same	MESTRAL, George de [US]	Velcro®
7.	**US2138385**	Elastic top shoe	MILLER GORDON, Ida [US]	I. Miller & Sons
8.	**EP2330255A1**	Extensible, transportable habitable cell	BEAU, Eric [FR]	Beauer caravan
9.	**EP3242166**	Mechanism for triggering an animation	STALDER, Nicolas [FR] BERNARD, Rainer [CH] MEIER, Willy [CH] MAGNIN-FEYSOT, Eric [FR] STRAUMANN, Kurt [CH]	Van Cleef & Arpels complications

Patent / Application number	*Title of invention*	*Inventors*	*Identifier*
10. **EP3239786**	Mechanism for driving an animation of a clock movement	STALDER, Nicolas [FR] MEIER, Willy [CH] MAGNIN-FEYSOT, Eric [FR] STRAUMANN, Kurt [CH]	Van Cleef & Arpels complications
11. **USD762508**	Watch dial	DUCAS, Sebastian [FR] GEIB, Maxime [FR]	Van Cleef & Arpels
12. **USD778757**	Watch dial	DUCAS, Sebastian [FR] GEIB, Maxime [FR]	Van Cleef & Arpels
13. **US3672463**	Acoustical system employing tubular resonators	JAFFE, Christopher [US] GEHRY, Frank O. [US]	Frank Gehry
14. **US5284380A**	Furniture comprising laminated slats and methods of manufacturing such furniture	GEHRY, Frank O. [US]	Frank Gehry
15. **US5154486A**	Furniture comprising laminated slats and methods of manufacturing such furniture	GEHRY, Frank O. [US]	Frank Gehry
16. **USD344191S**	Dining chair	GEHRY, Frank O. [US]	Frank Gehry
17. **USD334098S**	Chair	GEHRY, Frank O. [US]	Frank Gehry
18. **USD341263S**	Club chair	GEHRY, Frank O. [US]	Frank Gehry
19. **US2015122073**	Spine for a humanoid robot	MAISONNIER, Bruno [FR]	Nao, Softbank
20. **US2016325437**	Actuation of a hand intended for being provided on a humanoid robot	LAVILLE, Jérémy [FR] CLERC, Vincent [FR] MAISONNIER, Bruno [FR]	Nao, Softbank

Patent /Application number	*Title of invention*	*Inventors*	*Identifier*
21. **FR3016542A1**	Actionnement d'une main destinée à équiper un robot à caractère humanoïde	LAVILLE, Jérémy [FR] CLERC, Vincent [FR] MAISONNIER, Bruno [FR]	Nao, Softbank (French version)
22. **ES2685961T3**	Accionamiento de una mano destinada a equipar un robot de carácter humanoide	LAVILLE, Jérémy [FR] CLERC, Vincent [FR] MAISONNIER, Bruno [FR]	Nao, Softbank (Spanish version)
23. **USD774148S1**	Humanoid robot	HONG, Robert [FR]	Nao, Softbank
24. **US2017108011A1**	Fan	JOHNSON, Jack [GB] BLANC, Jean-Baptiste [GB]	Dyson
25. **US20130302777A1**	Systems and methods of object recognition within a simulation	TOMKINS, Michael [US] MILLER, Stephen [US] WILSON-KEY, Janee [US] MITTAL, Gopesh [US] GEORGIOU, Phylaktis [US] DORRANS, Jillian [US]	Tiggly®
26. **US2016287769A1**	Breast pump system and method	MAKOWER, Joshua [US] CHANG, John Y. [US] DONOHOE, Brendan M. [US] WANG, Sharon Lam [US] TOROSIS, Michele [US] BRIGHT II, Earl [US]	wireless breast pump
27. **US20130323184**	Method of providing fast relief to a user of a nicotine chewing gum	ANDERSEN, Carsten [DK]	Nicorette®

Patent / Application number	*Title of invention*	*Inventors*	*Identifier*
28. **US4761290**	Process for making dough products	MERAJ, Paul [US] NAGLE, Teri [US]	Chef America, Inc.
29. **US20170361999A1**	Beverage container cap for use with beverage extractor	LAMBRECHT, Gregory [US] RIDER, Michael [US] DERUNTZ, Otto [US]	Corkscrew
30. **US20040052918A1**	High energy complete food or nutritional supplement, method for preparing same and uses thereof	BRIEND, Andre [FR] LESCANNE, Michel [FR]	Plump'Nut®
31. **US6405867**	Package for a suncream	MOORE, Peter John [AU]	Blue Lizard®
32. **US8631589B2**	Article of footwear incorporating floating tensile strands	DOJAN, Frederick J. [US]	Nike
33. **US20130087104**	Pet toy with interlocking arms and recess for treat	WILLIAMS, Spencer [US] JOHNSON, Kathleen [US] PARTAIN, Seth [US] PIERZINA, Ron [US] SANFORD, Stephen [US] YAKOS, David [US] WALTHALL, Bryan [US] SINGLAUB, Niki [US]	West Paw, Inc.
34. **US2009123380**	Method for assaying satiety-enhancing tastants	HIRSCH, Alan R. [US]	Sensa®
35 **USPP14663P3**	Hybrid Tea Rose named *Ruivonk*	POUW, Anton [NL]	plant patent
36. **WO2017156187**	Disdrometer having acoustic transducer and methods thereof	WOLF, Lawrence Adam [US] SIEGFRIED, Benjamin Joseph [US] SMITH, Adam Lee [US]	example & embodiment

Patent / Application number	*Title of invention*	*Inventors*	*Identifier*
37. **WO2012176949**	System for converting greenhouse gas emission to carbon credit and method for same	NA, TAE IN [KR] SEO, JONG HYUK [KR] NA, YUN BOK [KR] SEO, YONG GI [KR]	green technology
38. **EP436257**	Method of controlling fungi on plants by the aid of hydrophobic extracted Neem oil	LOCKE, James Charles [US] LAREW, Hiram Gordon III [US] WALTER, James Frederic [US]	bioethics, revoked patent
39. **US5401504**	Use of turmeric in wound healing	DAS, Suman K. [US] COHLY, Hari Har P. [US]	bioethics, revoked patent
40. **US4736866**	Transgenic non-human mammals	LEDER, Philip [US] STEWART, Timothy A. [US]	bioethics, transgenic animals
41. **WO2010111189**	Magnetic blocs and method of making magnetic blocks	HAUGHEY, Christopher Harwood [US] HAUGHEY, William Harcourt [US] DELISLE, William Joseph [US]	Tegu®
42. **US9498083B2**	Cooking appliance with stirring means and associated method	GODERIAUX, Arnaud [FR] BIZARD, Jean-Claude [FR]	SEB, T-Fal Actifry (English version)
43. **WO2007088279**	Appareil de cuisson avec moyen de remuage et procédé affèrent	GODERIAUX, Arnaud [FR] BIZARD, Jean-Claude [FR]	SEB, T-Fal Actifry (French version)
44. **ES2362025T3**	Aparato de cocción con medio de removido y procedimiento correspondiente	GODERIAUX, Arnaud [FR] BIZARD, Jean-Claude [FR]	SEB, T-Fal Actifry, (Spanish version)

Patent / Application number	*Title of invention*	*Inventors*	*Identifier*
45. **US1798271**	Shoe closure (1929)	PERUGIA, André [FR]	history, shoe design
46. **FR680710**	Perfectionnements à la fabrication des chaussures (1929)	PERUGIA, André [FR]	history, shoe design
47. **US2015108762A1**	Aerogenerator comprising a trunk and a plurality of branches extending from this trunk	MICHAUD-LARIVIERE, Jérôme [FR]	New World Wind, wind tree
48. **FR2988144A1**	Aérogénérateur comprenant un tronc et une pluralité de branches s'étendant à partir de ce tronc	MICHAUD-LARIVIERE, Jérôme [FR]	New World Wind, wind tree
49. **FR1242870**	Dispositif traceur (1960)	CHAZE, Paul [FR] GRANDJEAN, Arthur [FR]	Etch-a-Sketch®
50. **US3055113A**	Tracing device (1962)	CHAZE, Paul [FR] GRANDJEAN, Arthur [FR]	Etch-a-Sketch®
51. **US2014201026**	Personalized customer shopping experience	ADONI, Siddique M. [IN] DUBY, Scott [US] SCHWARTZ, Robyn R. [US] SHANMUGAM, Dhandapani [IN]	IBM
52. **US2015015475A1**	Multi-function input device	ELY, Colin M. [US] ROTHKOPF, Fletcher R. [US]	Apple, Inc.

Patent / Application number	*Title of invention*	*Inventors*	*Identifier*
53. **EP2450453**	Method for the replication, amplification, or sequencing of a DNA template	SALAS FALGUERAS, Margarita [ES] DE VEGA, Jose Miguel [ES] LAZARO BOLOS, Jose Ma [ES] BLANCO DAVILA, Luis [ES] MENCIA CABALLERO, Mario [ES]	European Inventor Awards
54. **EP2450436**	Phage phi 29 DNA polymerase chimera	SALAS FALGUERAS, Margarita [ES] DE VEGA, Jose Miguel [ES] LAZARO BOLOS, Jose Ma [ES] BLANCO DAVILA, Luis [ES] MENCIA CABALLERO, Mario [ES]	European Inventor Awards
55. **EP2282203A1**	Method of measuring the photocatalytic activity of cementitious materials	BORZETTI, Fabio [IT] GUERRINI, Gian Luca [IT] CASSAR, Luigi [IT] CAMPANELLA, Luigi [IT] VISCO, Giovanni [IT]	European Inventor Awards
56. **US5857351A**	Play ball ice-cream maker	ANGUS, Diana Patricia [US] ANGUS, Robert David [US]	ice-cream, kids, ball
57. **US5698244**	Method for raising animals having high concentrations of Omega-3 highly unsaturated fatty acids	BARCLAY, William Robert [US]	Case law, lexicographer rule

Appendix III

European patents dataset

The claims sections of the following 69 European Patents were examined for surface structure markers of claims recitation in the *alternative* vs. *cumulative*, per the provisions of the MPEP *Section 608.01(n)*.

1. **EP0946450A1** - *Hydraulic binder and cement compositions containing photocatalyst particles.*
   Cassa, L. and P. Carmine (1999). Hydraulic binder and cement compositions containing photocatalyst particles (European Patent No. 0946450A1). European Patent Office. https://worldwide.espacenet.com/patent/search/family/011374787/publication/EP0946450A1?q=pn%3DEP0946450A1
2. **EP2282203A1** - Method of measuring the photocatalytic activity of cementitious materials.
   ****cumulative ("and") recitation of dependent Claims #3 to #14**
   Borzetti, F. et al. (2011). Method of measuring the photocatalytic activity of cementitious materials (European Patent No. 2282203A1). European Patent Office. https://worldwide.espacenet.com/patent/search/family/041571073/publication/EP2282203A1?q=2.%20EP2282203A1
3. **EP0076069A1** - *Single channel auditory stimulation system.*
   Hochmair, I.J. and E.S. Hochmair (1983). Single channel auditory stimulation system (European Patent No. 0076069A1). European Patent Office. https://worldwide.espacenet.com/patent/search/family/023172606/publication/EP0076069A1?q=3.%20EP0076069A1
4. **EP1947966A1** - *System and method for protecting a body part.*
   Alstin, T. and A. Haupt (2008). System and method for protecting a body part (European Patent No. 1947966A1). European Patent Office. https://worldwide.espacenet.com/patent/search/family/037968058/publication/EP1947966A1?q=4.%20EP1947966A1
5. **EP3242166A1** - *Mechanism for triggering an animation.*
   Stalder, N. et al. (2017). Mechanism for triggering an animation (European Patent No. 3242166A1). European Patent Office. https://worldwide.espacenet.com/patent/search/family/055963105/publication/EP3242166A1?q=5.%20EP3242166A1

6. **EP3239786B1** - *Mechanism for driving an animation of a clock movement.*
Stalder, N. et al. (2021). Mechanism for driving an animation of a clock movement (European Patent No. 3239786B1). European Patent Office. https://worldwide.espacenet.com/patent/search/family/055862483/publication/EP3239786B1?q=6.%20EP3239786B1
7. **EP2330255B1** - *Extensible, transportable habitable cell.*
Beau, E. (2012). Extensible, transportable habitable cell (European Patent No. 2330255B1). European Patent Office. https://worldwide.espacenet.com/patent/search/family/042797173/publication/EP2330255B1?q=7.%20EP2330255B1
8. **EP3315400A1** - *Folding propeller.*
Klein, S. et al. (2018). Folding propeller (European Patent No. 3315400A1). European Patent Office. https://worldwide.espacenet.com/patent/search/family/057206090/publication/EP3315400A1?q=8.%20EP3315400A1
9. **EP3189945A1** - *Exoskeleton and method of providing an assistive torque to an arm of a wearer.*
Angold, R. et al. (2017). Exoskeleton and method of providing an assistive torque to an arm of a wearer (European Patent No. 3189945A1). European Patent Office. https://worldwide.espacenet.com/patent/search/family/057583090/publication/EP3189945A1?q=EP3189945A1
10. **EP2959770A1** - *System, especially for growing plants, comprising a water supply for which the overflow is discharged at a constant rate.*
Grimard, J-Ch. and R. Lame (2015). System, especially for growing plants, comprising a water supply for which the overflow is discharged at a constant rate (European Patent No. 2959770A1). European Patent Office. https://worldwide.espacenet.com/patent/search/family/051519044/publication/EP2959770A1?q=10.%20EP2959770A1
11. **EP2876203A1** - Supercritical CO2.
Cepi, A. (2015). Supercritical CO2 (European Patent No. 2876203A1). European Patent Office. https://worldwide.espacenet.com/patent/search/family/049626864/publication/EP2876203A1?q=EP2876203A1
12. **EP2784896B1** - System for managing electricity production and consumption.
Lamotte, G.G. (2018). System for managing electricity production and consumption (European Patent No. 2784896B1). European Patent Office. https://worldwide.espacenet.com/patent/search/family/050382349/publication/EP2784896B1?q=EP2784896B1
13. **EP1042967A1** - Footwear.
Ganon, M.H. (2000). Footwear (European Patent No. 1042967A1). European Patent Office. https://worldwide.espacenet.com/patent/search/family/023109844/publication/EP1042967A1?q=EP1042967A1
14. **EP3014245** - Biosensor based on measurements of the clustering dynamics of magnetic particles.
Donolato, M. et al. (2016). Biosensor based on measurements of the clustering dynamics of magnetic particles (European Patent No. 3014245).

European Patent Office. https://worldwide.espacenet.com/patent/search/family/048692386/publication/EP3014245A1?q=14.%20EP3014245

15. **EP2831268A1** - *Molecular code systems.*
Grass, R.N. and W.N. Stark (2015). Molecular code systems (European Patent No. 2831268A1). European Patent Office. https://worldwide.espacenet.com/patent/search/family/048044489/publication/EP2831268A1?q=EP2831268A1
16. **EP2561380A1** - *Imaging method and apparatus using shear waves.*
Montaldo, G. et al. (2013). Imaging method and apparatus using shear waves (European Patent No. 2561380A1). European Patent Office. https://worldwide.espacenet.com/patent/search/family/043416784/publication/EP2561380A1?q=EP2561380A1
17. **EP2340865A1** - *Nasal delivery device.*
Jupesland, P.J. (2011). Nasal delivery device (European Patent No. 2340865A1). European Patent Office. https://worldwide.espacenet.com/patent/search/family/026315212/publication/EP2340865A1?q=EP2340865A1
18. **EP3041883A1** - *Higher function polyether carbonate polyols obtained by use of branched molecules.*
Müller, T.E. et al. (2016). Higher function polyether carbonate polyols obtained by use of branched molecules (European Patent No. 3041883A1). European Patent Office. https://worldwide.espacenet.com/patent/search/family/049111036/publication/EP3041883A1?q=EP3041883A1
19. **EP2576881A2** - *Natural nonwoven materials.*
Hijosa, C. et al. (2014). Natural nonwoven materials (European Patent No. 2576881A2). European Patent Office. https://worldwide.espacenet.com/patent/search/family/045004476/publication/EP2576881A2?q=EP2576881A2
20. **EP2731423A1** - *Hook pod.*
Kibel, P. and B. Kibel (2014). Hook pod (European Patent No. 27314 23A1). European Patent Office. https://worldwide.espacenet.com/patent/search/family/044544597/publication/EP2731423A1?q=EP2731423A1
21. **EP2625703A1** - *Method for manufacture of an improved dye-sensitized solar cell*
Lindstroem, H. and G. Fili (2013). Method for manufacture of an improved dye-sensitized solar cell. (European Patent No. 2625703A1). European Patent Office. https://worldwide.espacenet.com/patent/search/family/044860317/publication/EP2625703A1?q=EP2625703A1
22. **EP3072083A1** - *Secure human fingerprint sensor.*
Pi, B. and Y. He (2016). Secure human fingerprint sensor (European Patent No. 3072083A1). European Patent Office. https://worldwide.espacenet.com/patent/search/family/053180278/publication/EP3072083A1?q=EP3072083A1
23. **EP1456401A2** - *Isolation and cultivation of microorganisms from natural environments and drug discovery based thereon.*

Lewis, K. (2004). Isolation and cultivation of microorganisms from natural environments and drug discovery based thereon (European Patent No. 1456401A2). European Patent Office. https://worldwide.espacenet.com/patent/search/family/026833851/publication/EP1456401A2?q=EP1456401A2

24. **EP1999248A2** - *Devices and methods for the isolation and cultivation of microorganisms.*
    Lewis, K. et al. (2008). Devices and methods for the isolation and cultivation of microorganisms (European Patent No. 1999248A2). European Patent Office. https://worldwide.espacenet.com/patent/search/family/038564126/publication/EP1999248A2?q=EP1999248A2
25. **EP1225867A1** - *Radiopaque dental materials with nano-sized particles.*
    Zhang, X, et al. (2002). Radiopaque dental materials with nano-sized particles (European Patent No. 1225867A1). European Patent Office. https://worldwide.espacenet.com/patent/search/family/023702168/publication/EP1225867A1?q=EP1225867A1
26. **EP1227782A1** - *Aesthetic dental materials.*
    Wu, D. et al. (2002). Aesthetic dental materials (European Patent No. 1227782A1). European Patent Office. https://worldwide.espacenet.com/patent/search/family/023700572/publication/EP1227782A1?q=EP1227782A1
27. **EP1229886A1** - *Clustered particle dental fillers.*
    Windisch, M.S. et al. (2002). Clustered particle dental fillers (European Patent No. 1229886A1). European Patent Office. https://worldwide.espacenet.com/patent/search/family/023700572/publication/EP1229886A1?q=EP1229886A1
28. **EP1771143A1** - Dental compositions containing nanozirconia fillers.
    Kolb, B.U. (2007). Dental compositions containing nanozirconia fillers (European Patent No. 1771143A1). European Patent Office. https://worldwide.espacenet.com/patent/search/family/034968322/publication/EP1771143A1?q=EP1771143A1
29. **EP0268946A2** - Method for separating long-chain nucleic acids.
    Henco, K. Dr. et al. (1988). Method for separating long-chain nucleic acids (European Patent No. 0268946A2). European Patent Office. https://worldwide.espacenet.com/patent/search/family/006314555/publication/EP0268946A2?q=EP0268946A2
30. **EP1861886A1** - Organic photoactive component.
    Pfeiffer, M. et al. (2007). Organic photoactive component (European Patent No. 1861886A1). European Patent Office. https://worldwide.espacenet.com/patent/search/family/036577398/publication/EP1861886A1?q=EP1861886A1
31. **EP2408401A1** - Methods, devices, and systems for bone tissue engineering using a bioreactor.
    Vunjak-Novakovic, G. et al. (2012). Methods, devices, and systems for bone tissue engineering using a bioreactor (European Patent No. 2408401A1).

European Patent Office. https://worldwide.espacenet.com/patent/search/family/042709998/publication/EP2408401A1?q=EP2408401A1

32. **EP1488468A2** - *Transparent, thermally stable light-emitting component comprising organic layers.*
 Blochwitz-Nimoth, J. et al. (2004). Transparent, thermally stable light-emitting component comprising organic layers bioreactor (European Patent No. 1488468A2). European Patent Office. https://worldwide.espacenet.com/patent/search/family/028458612/publication/EP1488468A2?q=EP1488468A2
33. **EP1943520** - *An in vitro method for the prognosis of progression of a cancer and of the outcome in a patient and means for performing said method.*
 Galon, J. et al. (2008). An in vitro method for the prognosis of progression of a cancer and of the outcome in a patient and means for performing said method bioreactor (European Patent No. 1943520). European Patent Office. https://worldwide.espacenet.com/patent/search/family/036129834/publication/EP1943520A1?q=EP1943520
34. **EP2241891** - *An in vitro method for the prognosis of progression of a cancer and of the outcome in a patient and means for performing said method.*
 Galon, J. et al. (2010). An in vitro method for the prognosis of progression of a cancer and of the outcome in a patient and means for performing said method bioreactor (European Patent No. 2241891). European Patent Office. https://worldwide.espacenet.com/patent/search/family/036129834/publication/EP2241891A1?q=EP2241891
35. **EP2420836** - *An in vitro method for the prognosis of progression of a cancer and of the outcome in a patient and means for performing said method.*
 Galon, J. et al. (2012). An in vitro method for the prognosis of progression of a cancer and of the outcome in a patient and means for performing said method bioreactor (European Patent No. EP2420836). European Patent Office. https://worldwide.espacenet.com/patent/search/family/036129834/publication/EP2420836A2?q=EP2420836
36. **EP1355666** - Use of repulsive guidance molecule (RGM) and its modulators
 Mueller, B. K. et al. (2003). Use of repulsive guidance molecule (RGM) and its modulators (European Patent No. 1355666). European Patent Office. https://worldwide.espacenet.com/patent/search/family/008170794/publication/EP1355666A2?q=EP1355666
37. **EP2767834** - Quantitative standard for mass spectrometry of proteins.
 Mann, M. et al. (2014). Quantitative standard for mass spectrometry of proteins (European Patent No. 2767834). European Patent Office. https://worldwide.espacenet.com/patent/search/family/044484002/publication/EP2767834A2?q=EP2767834
38. **EP2633912B1** - Device for separating by vertical filtration of biological particles contained in a liquid.
 Paterlini-Brechot, P. (2016). Device for separating by vertical filtration of biological particles contained in a liquid (European Patent No.

2633912B1). European Patent Office. https://worldwide.espacenet.com/patent/search/family/035229619/publication/EP2633912B1?q=EP2633912B1

39. **EP1108057B1** - *Method, equipment, and reagent for cell separation.*
Bisconte de Saint-Julien, J.-Cl. and P. Paterlini (2008). Method, equipment, and reagent for cell separation (European Patent No. 1108057B1). European Patent Office. https://worldwide.espacenet.com/patent/search/family/009529872/publication/EP1108057B1?q=EP1108057B1
40. **EP1383926B1** - *Prenatal diagnosis method on isolated foetal cell of maternal blood.*
Paterlini-Brechot, P. (2015). Prenatal diagnosis method on isolated foetal cell of maternal blood. separation (European Patent No. 1383926B1). European Patent Office. https://worldwide.espacenet.com/patent/search/family/008862866/publication/EP1383926B1?q=42.%2
41. **EP2202361** - *Mould for manufacturing concrete cubipods*
Corredor Molguero, A. and C. F. Menendez Diaz (2010). Mould for manufacturing concrete cubipods (European Patent No. 2202361). European Patent Office. https://worldwide.espacenet.com/patent/search/family/040410159/publication/EP2202361A1?q=EP2202361
42. **EP2766166B1** - *Apparatus for processing plastic material.*
Feichtinger, K. and M. Hackl (2015). Apparatus for processing plastic material (European Patent No. 2766166B1). European Patent Office. https://worldwide.espacenet.com/patent/search/family/047142843/publication/EP2766166B1?q=EP2766166B1
43. **EP2558263B1** - Apparatus for processing plastic material.
Weigerstorfer, G. et al. (2014). Apparatus for processing plastic material (European Patent No. 2558263B1). European Patent Office. https://worldwide.espacenet.com/patent/search/family/044209669/publication/EP2558263B1?q=EP2558263B1
44. **EP2766157B1** - Apparatus for processing plastic material.
Feichtinger, K. and M. Hackl (2015). Apparatus for processing plastic material (European Patent No. 2766157B1). European Patent Office. https://worldwide.espacenet.com/patent/search/family/047142833/publication/EP2766157B1?q=EP2766157B1
45. **EP2766158B1** - Apparatus for processing plastic material.
Feichtinger K. and M. Hackl (2015). Apparatus for processing plastic material (European Patent No. 2766158B1). European Patent Office. https://worldwide.espacenet.com/patent/search/family/047142834/publication/EP2766158B1?q=EP2766158B1
46. **EP2766159** - Apparatus for processing plastic material.
Feichtinger K. and M. Hackl (2015). Apparatus for processing plastic material (European Patent No. 2766159B1). European Patent Office. https://worldwide.espacenet.com/patent/search/family/047142835/publication/EP2766159A1?q=pn%3DEP2766159A1

47. **EP1188368** - *A construction for automatically milking animals.*
Fransen, R. I. J. et al. (2002). A construction for automatically milking animals (European Patent No. 1188368). European Patent Office. https://worldwide.espacenet.com/patent/search/family/019772092/publication/EP1188368A1?q=EP1188368
48. **EP0951651** - *A sensor apparatus, as well as a method of determining the position of an object, in particular a teat of an animal to be milked.*
Fransen, R. and A. Van Der Lely (1999). A sensor apparatus, as well as a method of determining the position of an object, in particular a teat of an animal to be milked (European Patent No. 0951651). European Patent Office. https://worldwide.espacenet.com/patent/search/family/019765517/publication/EP0951651A1?q=EP0951651
49. **EP1221282** - *A device for and a method of cleaning a milking machine, and a milking machine.*
Van Der Lely, A. (2002). A device for and a method of cleaning a milking machine, and a milking machine (European Patent No. 1221282). European Patent Office. https://worldwide.espacenet.com/patent/search/family/019772694/publication/EP1221282A1?q=EP1221282
50. **EP1163843** - *Method of increasing the utilization capacity of the implement.*
Van Der Lely, A. (2001). Method of increasing the utilization capacity of the implement (European Patent No. 1163843). European Patent Office. https://worldwide.espacenet.com/patent/search/family/019771537/publication/EP1163843A2?q=EP1163843
51. **EP2531022** - *Method and device for destroying parasites on fish.*
Beck, E. (2012). Method and device for destroying parasites on fish (European Patent No. 2531022). European Patent Office. https://worldwide.espacenet.com/patent/search/family/044534926/publication/EP2531022A1?q=51.%20EP2531022
52. **EP1996453** - Antifouling fibre coatings for marine constructions.
Breur, H.J.A. (2008). Antifouling fibre coatings for marine constructions (European Patent No. 1996453). European Patent Office. https://worldwide.espacenet.com/patent/search/family/036915752/publication/EP1996453A1?q=EP1996453
53. **EP1832186** - Energy absorbing material and corresponding method of manufacturing.
Palmer, R.M. and P.C. Green (2007). Energy absorbing material and corresponding method of manufacturing (European Patent No. 1832186). European Patent Office. https://worldwide.espacenet.com/patent/search/family/009928316/publication/EP1832186A2?q=EP1832186
54. **EP2063435** - Novel polymer electrolyte and electrochemical device.
Yoshino, A. and H. Shobukawa (2009). Novel polymer electrolyte and electrochemical device (European Patent No. 2063435). European Patent Office. https://worldwide.espacenet.com/patent/search/family/039183717/publication/EP2063435A1?q=EP2063435

55. **EP2063436** - *Polymeric electrolyte, method for production thereof, and electrochemical element.*
Yoshino, A. and H. Shobukawa (2009). Polymeric electrolyte, method for production thereof, and electrochemical element (European Patent No. 2063436). European Patent Office. https://worldwide.espacenet.com/patent/search/family/039183738/publication/EP2063436A1?q=EP2063436
56. **EP1806595** - *Estimating distance to an object using a sequence of images recorded by a monocular camera.*
Stein, G.P et al. (2007). Estimating distance to an object using a sequence of images recorded by a monocular camera (European Patent No. 1806595). European Patent Office. https://worldwide.espacenet.com/patent/search/family/037888143/publication/EP1806595A1?q=EP1806595
57. **EP1741079** - *Collision warning system.*
Stein, G.P et al. (2007). Estimating distance to an object using a sequence of images recorded by a monocular camera (European Patent No. 1741079). European Patent Office. https://worldwide.espacenet.com/patent/search/family/034960526/publication/EP1741079A1?q=EP1741079
58. **EP2702137** - *Method for making dehydrated mycelium elements and product made thereby.*
Bayer, E. and G. Mcintyre (2014). Method for making dehydrated mycelium elements and product made thereby (European Patent No. 2702137). European Patent Office. https://worldwide.espacenet.com/patent/search/family/047021633/publication/EP2702137A1?q=pn%3DEP2702137A1
59. **EP2094856** - *Method for producing grown materials and products made thereby.*
Bayer, E. et al (2009). Method for producing grown materials and products made thereby (European Patent No. 2094856). European Patent Office. https://worldwide.espacenet.com/patent/search/family/039512340/publication/EP2094856A2?q=EP2094856
60. **EP2450453** - *Method for the replication, amplification, or sequencing of a DNA template.*
cumulative ("and") recitation of the final dependent Claim #40
Salas Falgueras, M. et al. (2012). Method for the replication, amplification or sequencing of a DNA template (European Patent No. 2450453). European Patent Office. https://worldwide.espacenet.com/patent/search/family/043411512/publication/EP2450453A2?q=EP2450453
61. **EP2450436** - *Phage phi 29 DNA polymerase chimera.*
cumulative ("and") recitation of the final dependent Claim #51
Salas Falgueras, M. et al. (2012). Phage phi 29 DNA polymerase chimera (European Patent No. 2450436). European Patent Office. https://worldwide.espacenet.com/patent/search/family/043410525/publication/EP2450436A1?q=EP2450436
62. **EP1970380** - *Inhibitor of the uracil-DNA glycosylase enzyme and uses thereof.*

Serrano de las Heras, G. et al. (2008). Inhibitor of the uracil-DNA glycosylase enzyme and uses thereof (European Patent No. 1970380). European Patent Office. https://worldwide.espacenet.com/patent/search/family/038217718/publication/EP1970380A1?q=EP1970380

63. **EP0527728** - *(in vitro) DNA synthesis reactions using phi 29 DNA polymerase and a DNA fragment encoding said polymerase.*
Blanco, L. et al. (1993). DNA synthesis reactions using phi 29 DNA polymerase and a DNA fragment encoding said polymerase (European Patent No. 0527728). European Patent Office. https://worldwide.espacenet.com/patent/search/family/023281085/publication/EP0527728A1?q=EP0527728
64. **EP2304961** - *Rate-distortion defined interpolation for video coding based on fixed filter or adaptive filter.*
Ye, Y. and M. Karczewicz (2011). Rate-distortion defined interpolation for video coding based on fixed filter or adaptive filter (European Patent No. 2304961). European Patent Office. https://worldwide.espacenet.com/patent/search/family/040688433/publication/EP2304961A1?q=EP2304961
65. **EP2074828** - *Efficient significant coefficients coding in scalable video codecs.*
Karczewicz, M. (2009). Efficient significant coefficients coding in scalable video codecs (European Patent No. 2074828). European Patent Office. https://worldwide.espacenet.com/patent/search/family/039286551/publication/EP2074828A2?q=EP2074828
66. **EP2165542** - *Adaptive coefficient scanning in video coding.*
Ye, Y. and M. Karczewicz (2010). Adaptive coefficient scanning in video coding (European Patent No. 2165542). European Patent Office. https://worldwide.espacenet.com/patent/search/family/040132401/publication/EP2165542A2?q=EP2165542
67. **EP1057204B1** - *Device for correcting third-order spherical aberration in a lens, especially the objective lens of an electronic microscope.*
Haider, M. and S. Uhlemann (2006). Device for correcting third-order spherical aberration in a lens, especially the objective lens of an electronic microscope (European Patent No. 1057204B1). European Patent Office. https://worldwide.espacenet.com/patent/search/family/007855390/publication/EP1057204B1?q=EP1057204B1
68. **EP1012866B1** - *Method for eliminating first, second and third-order axial image deformations. during correction of the third-order spherical aberration in electron optical systems.*
Haider, M. and S. Uhlemann (2007). Method for eliminating first, second and third-order axial image deformations. during correction of the third-order spherical aberration in electron optical systems (European Patent No. 1012866B1). European Patent Office. https://worldwide.espacenet.com/patent/search/family/007841589/publication/EP1012866B1?q=EP1012866B1

69. **EP1112348** - *Use of growth factors and hormones for expansion of mammalian cells and tissue engineering.*
    Freed, L.E. et al. (2001). Use of growth factors and hormones for expansion of mammalian cells and tissue engineering (European Patent No. 1112348). European Patent Office. https://worldwide.espacenet.com/patent/search/family/022282845/publication/EP1112348A2?q=pn%3DEP1112348A2

Appendix IV

Cited US Code, rules, regulations, and administrative instructions

US Constitution [Transcript]

https://www.archives.gov/founding-docs/constitution-transcript

Supreme Court decision

Diamond v. Chakrabarty, 447 U.S. 303 (Supreme Court 1980). https://supreme.justia.com/cases/federal/us/447/303/

US Case Law

Application of Borkowski, 422 F.2d 904, 164 U.S.P.Q. (BNA) 642. (C.C.P.A. 1970). https://casetext.com/case/application-of-borkowski

Chef America, Inc. *vs*. Lamb-Weston, Inc. 358 F.3d 1371, 1372, 69 USPQ2d 1857 (Fed. Cir. 2004). https://casetext.com/case/chef-america-inc-v-lamb-weston-inc

Gillette Co. v. Energizer Holdings Inc., 405 F.3d 1367, 1371-73, 74 USPQ2d 1586, 1589-91 (Fed. Cir. 2005). https://casetext.com/case/gillette-co-v-energizer-holdings-inc

Martek Biosciences v. Nutrinova, 579 F.3d 1363 (Fed. Cir. 2009). https://casetext.com/case/martek-biosciences-v-nutrinova

PPG Industries v. Guardian Industries, 156 F.3d 1351, 1354, 48 USPQ2d 1351, 1353-54 (Fed. Cir. 1998). https://casetext.com/case/ppg-industries-v-guardian-industries

Title 35 - United States Code

35 US Code (USC) - Patents. https://www.uspto.gov/web/offices/pac/mpep/mpep-9015-appx-l.html

35 USC 101 - Invention patentable. https://www.uspto.gov/web/offices/pac/mpep/mpep-9015-appx-l.html#d0e302376

35 USC 102 - Conditions for patentability; novelty. https://www.uspto.gov/web/offices/pac/mpep/mpep-9015-appx-l.html#al_d1fbe1_234ed_52

35 USC 103 - Conditions for patentability; non-obvious subject matter. https://www.uspto.gov/web/offices/pac/mpep/mpep-9015-appx-l.html#al_d1fbe1_19797_b0

35 USC 112 - Specification. https://www.uspto.gov/web/offices/pac/mpep/mpep-9015-appx-l.html#d0e302824912

35 USC 112 (a) - Best mode requirement and obligation to disclose. https://www.uspto.gov/web/offices/pac/mpep/mpep-9015-appx-l.html#d0e302824912

35 USC 113 - Drawings. https://www.uspto.gov/web/offices/pac/mpep/mpep-9015-appx-l.html#d0e302850

35 USC 154 (a) (1) - Contents and term of a patent; provisional rights. https://www.uspto.gov/web/offices/pac/mpep/mpep-9015-appx-l.html#d0e303482

35 USC 154 (a) (2) - Contents and term of a patent; provisional rights. https://www.uspto.gov/web/offices/pac/mpep/mpep-9015-appx-l.html#d0e303482

35 USC 154 (a) (4) - Contents and term of a patent; provisional rights. https://www.uspto.gov/web/offices/pac/mpep/mpep-9015-appx-l.html#d0e303482

35 USC 161 - Patents for plants. https://www.uspto.gov/web/offices/pac/mpep/mpep-9015-appx-l.html#d0e304416

35 USC 171 - Patents for designs. https://www.uspto.gov/web/offices/pac/mpep/mpep-9015-appx-l.html#d0e304480

35 USC 173 - Term of a design patent. https://www.uspto.gov/web/offices/pac/mpep/mpep-9015-appx-l.html#d0e304510

Title 37 - Code of Federal Regulations

Code of Federal Regulations (CFR) Title 37. https://www.uspto.gov/web/offices/pac/mpep/mpep-9020-appx-r.html

37 CFR 1.52 - Language, paper, writing, margins, read-only optical disc specifications. https://www.uspto.gov/web/offices/pac/mpep/mpep-9020-appx-r.html#d0e318327

37 CFR 1.71 (a), (b), (c) - Detailed description and specification of the invention. https://www.uspto.gov/web/offices/pac/mpep/mpep-9020-appx-r.html#d0e320131

37 CFR 1.72 (a), (b) - Title and abstract. https://www.uspto.gov/web/offices/pac/mpep/mpep-9020-appx-r.html#d0e320224

37 CFR 1.73 - Summary of the invention. https://www.uspto.gov/web/offices/pac/mpep/mpep-9020-appx-r.html#d0e320249

37 CFR 1.74 - Reference to drawings. https://www.uspto.gov/web/offices/pac/mpep/mpep-9020-appx-r.html#d0e320259

37 CFR 1.75 - Claim(s). https://www.uspto.gov/web/offices/pac/mpep/mpep-9020-appx-r.html#d0e320269

37 CFR 1.76 - Application Data sheet. https://www.uspto.gov/web/offices/pac/mpep/mpep-9020-appx-r.html#plt_d0e320348
37 CFR 1.81 - Drawings required in patent application. https://www.uspto.gov/web/offices/pac/mpep/mpep-9020-appx-r.html#aia_d0e320940
37 CFR 1.83 - Content of drawing. https://www.uspto.gov/web/offices/pac/mpep/mpep-9020-appx-r.html#d0e320967
37 CFR 1.84 - Standards for drawings. https://www.uspto.gov/web/offices/pac/mpep/mpep-9020-appx-r.html#d0e320999
37 CFR 1.154 - Arrangement of application elements in a design application. https://www.uspto.gov/web/offices/pac/mpep/mpep-9020-appx-r.html#d0e324243

Manual of Patent Examining Procedure (MPEP)

MPEP Manual of Patent Examination Procedure. Ninth Edition, Revision 10.2019, Last Revised June 2020. https://www.uspto.gov/web/offices/pac/mpep/index.html
MPEP-Subject Index A. https://www.uspto.gov/web/offices/pac/mpep/mpep-index-a.html
MPEP - Section 301 Ownership/Assignability of Patents and Applications. [R-10.2019]. https://www.uspto.gov/web/offices/pac/mpep/s301.html
MPEP - Section 301 I. Ownership. https://www.uspto.gov/web/offices/pac/mpep/s301.html
MPEP - Section 602.01 Naming the Inventor; Inventor's Oath or Declaration. [R-07.2022]. https://www.uspto.gov/web/offices/pac/mpep/s602.html#ch600_d1ff64_24f27_297
MPEP - Section 608 Disclosure. [R-11.2013]. https://www.uspto.gov/web/offices/pac/mpep/s608.html
MPEP - Section 608.01 Specification. [R-10.2019] V. Filing of non-English applications. https://www.uspto.gov/web/offices/pac/mpep/s608.html#d0e42440
MPEP - Section 608.01 (c) Background of the Invention. [R-07.2015]. https://www.uspto.gov/web/offices/pac/mpep/s608.html#d0e44561
MPEP - Section 608.01 (d) Brief Summary of Invention. [R-07.2015]. https://www.uspto.gov/web/offices/pac/mpep/s608.html#d0e44589
MPEP - Section 608.01 (f) Brief Description of Drawings. [R-10.2019]. https://www.uspto.gov/web/offices/pac/mpep/s608.html#d0e44626
MPEP - Section 608.01 (g) Detailed Description of Invention. [R-10.2019]. https://www.uspto.gov/web/offices/pac/mpep/s608.html#d0e44731
MPEP - Section 608.01 (h) Mode of Operation of Invention. [R-11.2013]. https://www.uspto.gov/web/offices/pac/mpep/s608.html#d0e44799
MPEP - Section 608.01 (i) Claims. [R-08.2012]. https://www.uspto.gov/web/offices/pac/mpep/s608.html#d0e44872
MPEP - Section 608.01 (m) Form of Claims. [R-10.2019]. https://www.uspto.gov/web/offices/pac/mpep/s608.html#d0e45061

MPEP - Section 608.01 (n) Dependent Claims. [R-10.2019]. https://www.uspto.gov/web/offices/pac/mpep/s608.html#d0e45256

MPEP - Section 608.01 (o) Basis for Claim Terminology in Description. [R-07.2015]. https://www.uspto.gov/web/offices/pac/mpep/s608.html#d0e46173

MPEP - Section 901.01 Canceled matter in U.S. patent files. [R-08.2017]. https://www.uspto.gov/web/offices/pac/mpep/s901.html#d0e110030

MPEP - Section 901.05 Foreign patent documents. [R-08.2017]. https://www.uspto.gov/web/offices/pac/mpep/s901.html#d0e110750

MPEP - Section 901.05 (b) Other Significant Data. [R-08.2012]. https://www.uspto.gov/web/offices/pac/mpep/s901.html#d0e112731

MPEP - Section 901.05 (d) Translation. [R-10.2019]. https://www.uspto.gov/web/offices/pac/mpep/s901.html#d0e113207

MPEP - Section 901.06 Nonpatent Publications. [R-08.2012]. https://www.uspto.gov/web/offices/pac/mpep/s901.html#d0e113237

MPEP - Section 1502.01 Distinction Between Design and Utility Patents. [R-07.2015]. https://www.uspto.gov/web/offices/pac/mpep/s1502.html#d0e150263

MPEP - Section 1601 Introduction: The Act, Scope, Type of Plants Covered. [R-11.2013]. https://www.uspto.gov/web/offices/pac/mpep/s1601.html

MPEP - Section 1851 Identification of Patent Documents. [R-07.2015]. https://www.uspto.gov/web/offices/pac/mpep/s1851.html

MPEP - Section 2107 Guidelines for examination of applications for compliance with the utility requirement. [R-11.2013]. https://www.uspto.gov/web/offices/pac/mpep/s2107.html

MPEP - Section 2111 Claim Interpretation; Broadest Reasonable Interpretation. [R-10.2019]. https://www.uspto.gov/web/offices/pac/mpep/s2111.html

MPEP - Section 2111.01 Plain Meaning. [R-10.2019]. https://www.uspto.gov/web/offices/pac/mpep/s2111.html#d0e200409

MPEP - Section 2111.01 IV. Applicant may be own lexicographer and/or may disavow claim scope. [R-10.2019]. https://www.uspto.gov/web/offices/pac/mpep/s2111.html#d0e200409

MPEP - Section 2111.03 Transitional phrases. [R-08.2017]. https://www.uspto.gov/web/offices/pac/mpep/s2111.html#d0e200824

MPEP - Section 2117 Markush Claims. [R-07.2022]. https://www.uspto.gov/web/offices/pac/mpep/s2117.html

MPEP - Section 2141.03 Level of ordinary skill in the art. [R-10.2019]. https://www.uspto.gov/web/offices/pac/mpep/s2141.html#d0e209300

MPEP - Section 2164 The Enablement Requirement. [R-11.2013]. https://www.uspto.gov/web/offices/pac/mpep/s2164.html

MPEP - Section 2164.01 Test of Enablement. [R-08.2012]. https://www.uspto.gov/web/offices/pac/mpep/s2164.html#d0e215268

MPEP - Section 2164.01 (a) Undue experimentation factors. [R-08.2012]. https://www.uspto.gov/web/offices/pac/mpep/s2164.html#d0e215360

MPEP - Section 2164.02 Working Example. [R-11.2013]. https://www.uspto.gov/web/offices/pac/mpep/s2164.html#d0e215531
MPEP - Section 2165 The Best Mode Requirement. [R-08.2017]. https://www.uspto.gov/web/offices/pac/mpep/s2165.html

Appendix V

Cited European Patent Convention rules and administrative instructions

European Patent Convention (EPC)

EPC Part II. Chapt. III. Article 65 - Translation of the European patent. https://www.epo.org/en/legal/epc/2020/a65.html

Agreement on the application of Article 65 EPC - London Agreement (Oct. 17, 2000). https://www.epo.org/law-practice/legal-texts/london-agreement.html

Agreement on the application of Article 65 of the Convention on the grant of European patents.

(Full-text pdf version in French, German and English). https://documents.epo.org/projects/babylon/eponet.nsf/0/7FD20618D28E9FBFC125743900678657/$File/London_Agreement.pdf

EPC Part III. Chapt. II. Rule 41(2)(b) - Request for grant (re. title of the invention). https://www.epo.org/law-practice/legal-texts/html/epc/2020/e/r41.html

EPC Part III. Chapt. II. Rule 42 - Content of the description. https://new.epo.org/en/legal/epc/2020/r42.html

EPC Part III. Chapt. II. Rule 43 - Form and content of claims. [English]. https://www.epo.org/law-practice/legal-texts/html/epc/2020/e/r43.html

EPC (French Version) Convention sur le brevet européen (CBE) Troisième Partie, Chapt. II. Règle 43 - Forme et contenu des revendications. [French]. https://www.epo.org/law-practice/legal-texts/html/epc/2020/f/r43.html

EPC (German version) Europäisches Patentübereinkommen Dritter Teil, Kapitel II. Regel 43 - Form und Inhalt der Patentansprüche. [German]. https://www.epo.org/law-practice/legal-texts/html/epc/2020/d/r43.html

EPC Part III. Chapt. II. Rule 49 - Presentation of the application documents. https://www.epo.org/law-practice/legal-texts/html/epc/2020/e/r49.html

EPC European Guidelines for Examination

European Guidelines for Examination in the European Patent Office. Guidelines for Examination - List of contents (March 2023). https://www.epo.org/law-practice/legal-texts/html/guidelines/e/index.htm

Guidelines for Examination - Alphabetical Keyword Index. https://new.epo.org/en/legal/guidelines-epc/2023/k.html
Guidelines for Examination - Part A. Chapt. III. 7.1 Requirements (for titles). https://www.epo.org/law-practice/legal-texts/html/guidelines/e/a_iii_7_1.htm
Guidelines for Examination - Part F. Chapt. IV Claims. https://www.epo.org/law-practice/legal-texts/html/guidelines/e/f_iv.htm
Guidelines for Examination - Part F. Chapt. IV. 3.4 Independent and dependent claims. [English]. https://www.epo.org/law-practice/legal-texts/html/guidelines/e/f_iv_3_4.htm
Directives relatives à l'examen pratiqué - Partie F. Chapt. IV. 3.4 Revendications indépendantes et revendications dépendantes. [French]. https://www.epo.org/law-practice/legal-texts/html/guidelines/f/f_iv_3_4.htm
Richtlinien für die Prüfung - Teil F. Kapitel IV. 3.4 Unabhängige und abhängige Patentansprüche. [German]. https://www.epo.org/law-practice/legal-texts/html/guidelines/d/f_iv_3_4.htm
Guidelines for Examination - Part F. Chapt II. 4.3 Background Art. https://new.epo.org/en/legal/guidelines-epc/2023/f_ii_4_3.html
Guidelines for Examination - Part F. Chapt. IV. 4.20 "Comprising" *vs.* "consisting of". [English]. https://www.epo.org/law-practice/legal-texts/html/guidelines/e/f_iv_4_20.htm
Directives relatives à l'examen pratiqué - Partie F. Chapt. IV. 4.20 Sens des termes "comprenant" et "constitué de". [French]. https://www.epo.org/law-practice/legal-texts/html/guidelines/f/f_iv_4_20.htm
Richtlinien für die Prüfung - Teil F. Kapitel IV. 4.20 "umfassen" gegenüber "bestehen aus". [German]. https://www.epo.org/law-practice/legal-texts/html/guidelines/d/f_iv_4_20.htm
Guidelines for Examination - Part F. Chapt II - Annex 2 Units recognized in international practice and complying with Rule 49(2). https://www.epo.org/law-practice/legal-texts/html/guidelines/e/f_iia2.htm
Guidelines for Examination - Part F. Chapt. II, Annex 2, 4. Units and names of units permitted in specialized fields only. https://new.epo.org/en/legal/guidelines-epc/2023/f_iia2_4.html#GLF_CIIA2_4
Guidelines for Examination - Part F. Chapt. II. 4.13 Physical values, units. https://new.epo.org/en/legal/guidelines-epc/2023/f_ii_4_13.html

Appendix VI

Cited WIPO Patent Cooperation Treaty rules, guidelines, and administrative instructions

International Patent Classification System (IPC). https://www.wipo.int/classifications/ipc/en/

Administrative Instructions under the Patent Cooperation Treaty. https://www.wipo.int/pct/en/texts/ai/ai_index.html

Administrative instructions under the Patent Cooperation Treaty, Section 103 - Languages of the forms used by the international authorities. https://www.wipo.int/pct/en/texts/ai/s103.html

Patent Cooperation Treaty (PCT) (as in force April 1, 2002)

Patent Cooperation Treaty (PCT) - List of contents. https://www.wipo.int/pct/en/texts/articles/atoc.html

PCT Article 17 - Procedure before the International Searching Authority. https://www.wipo.int/pct/en/texts/articles/a17.html#_17

PCT Article 18 - The International Search Report. https://www.wipo.int/pct/en/texts/articles/a18.html

PCT Article 46 - Incorrect translation of the international application. https://www.wipo.int/pct/en/texts/articles/a46.html#_46

Regulations under the Patent Cooperation Treaty (as in force July 1, 2022)

Regulations under the Patent Cooperation Treaty - Table of contents. https://www.wipo.int/pct/en/texts/rules/rtoc1.html

Regulations under the PCT - Rule 4.3 Title of the invention. https://www.wipo.int/pct/en/texts/rules/r4.html

Regulations under the PCT - Rule 5 The Description. https://www.wipo.int/pct/en/texts/rules/r5.html#_5

Regulations under the PCT - Rule 6 Form and content of claims. [English]. https://www.wipo.int/pct/en/texts/rules/r6.html#_6

Règlement d'exécution du PCT - Règle 6 Forme et contenu des revendications. [French]. https://www.wipo.int/pct/fr/texts/rules/r6.html

Reglamento del PCT - Regla 6 Reivindicaciones. [Spanish]. https://www.wipo.int/pct/es/texts/rules/r6.html

Regulations under the PCT - Rule 6.4 (a) Dependent claims. [English]. https://www.wipo.int/pct/en/texts/rules/r6.html#_6
Règlement d'exécution du PCT - Règle 6.4 (a) Revendications dépendantes. [French]. https://www.wipo.int/pct/fr/texts/rules/r6.html
Reglamento del PCT - Regla 6.4 (a) Reivindicaciones dependientes. [Spanish]. https://www.wipo.int/pct/es/texts/rules/r6.html
Regulations under the PCT - Rule 10 Terminology and signs. https://www.wipo.int/pct/en/texts/rules/r10.html
Regulations under the PCT - Rule 12 Language of the international application and translations for the purposes of international search and international publication. https://www.wipo.int/pct/en/texts/rules/r12.html#_12
Regulations under the PCT - Rule 37 Missing or defective title. https://www.wipo.int/pct/en/texts/rules/r37.html#_37
Regulations under the PCT - Rule 48.3 Languages of publication. https://www.wipo.int/pct/en/texts/rules/r48.html#_48_3_a

WIPO Standards

About WIPO Standards. https://www.wipo.int/standards/en/
List of WIPO Standards, Recommendations and Guidelines: Part 3 of the *Handbook on Intellectual Property Information and Documentation.* https://www.wipo.int/standards/en/part_03_standards.html
Liste des normes recommandations et principes directeurs de l'OMPI. Partie 3 du Manuel sur l'information et la documentation en matière de propriété intellectuelle. [French]. https://www.wipo.int/standards/fr/part_03_standards.html
Lista de Normas, Recomendaciones y Directrices de la OMPI. Parte 3 del Manual de Información y Documentación en materia de Propiedad Intelectual. [Spanish]. https://www.wipo.int/standards/es/part_03_standards.html
WIPO Standard ST. 9 - Recommendation concerning bibliographic data on and relating to patents and SPCS. [English]. https://www.wipo.int/export/sites/www/standards/en/pdf/03-09-01.pdf
OMPI ST. 9 - Recommandation concernant les données bibliographiques qui figurent sur les brevets ou qui se rapportent aux brevets ou aux CCP. [French]. https://www.wipo.int/standards/fr/pdf/03-09-01.pdf
OMPI Norma ST. 9 - Recomendación relativa a los datos bibliográficos contenidos en los documentos de patente y en los CCP o en documentos relacionados con ellos. [Spanish]. https://www.wipo.int/standards/es/pdf/03-09-01.pdf
WIPO Standard ST. 12/A - General guidelines for the preparation of abstracts of patent documents. [English]. https://www.wipo.int/standards/en/pdf/03-12-a.pdf
OMPI Norme ST.12/A - Principes directeurs de caractère général relatifs à la préparation des abrégés de documents de brevet. [French]. https://www.wipo.int/standards/fr/pdf/03-12-a.pdf

OMPI Norma ST.12/A - Directrices generales para la preparación de resúmenes de documentos de patentes. [Spanish]. https://www.wipo.int/standards/es/pdf/03-12-a.pdf

WIPO Standard ST. 14 - Recommendation for the inclusion of references cited in patent documents. https://www.wipo.int/export/sites/www/standards/en/pdf/03-14-01.pdf

OMPI Norme ST.14 - Recommandation sur l'indication des références citées dans les documents de brevet. [French]. https://www.wipo.int/export/sites/www/standards/fr/pdf/03-14-01.pdf

OMPI Norma ST.14 - Recomendación para la inclusión de las referencias citadas en los documentos de patente. [Spanish]. https://www.wipo.int/export/sites/www/standards/es/pdf/03-14-01.pdf

WIPO Standard ST. 15 - Guidelines for the wording of titles of inventions in patent documents. https://www.wipo.int/export/sites/www/standards/en/pdf/03-15-01.pdf

OMPI Norme ST. 15 - Principes directeurs sur la rédaction des titres d'invention dans les documents de brevet. [French]. https://www.wipo.int/export/sites/www/standards/fr/pdf/03-15-01.pdf

OMPI Norma ST.15 - Directrices para la redacción de títulos de invenciones en documentos de patentes. [Spanish]. https://www.wipo.int/export/sites/www/standards/es/pdf/03-15-01.pdf

WIPO Standard ST. 16 - Recommended standard code for the identification of different kinds of patent documents. https://www.wipo.int/export/sites/www/standards/en/pdf/03-16-01.pdf

OMPI Norme ST.16 - Code normalisé recommandé pour l'identification de différents types de documents de brevet. [French]. https://www.wipo.int/export/sites/www/standards/fr/pdf/03-16-01.pdf

OMPI Norma ST.16 - Código normalizado para la identificación de los diferentes tipos de documentos de patente. [Spanish]. https://www.wipo.int/export/sites/www/standards/es/pdf/03-16-01.pdf

PCT International Search and Preliminary Examination Guidelines (as in force July 1, 2022)

PCT International Search and Preliminary Examination Guidelines - Table of Contents. https://www.wipo.int/pct/en/texts/ispe/index.html

Patent Cooperation Treaty (PCT) International Search and Preliminary Examination Guidelines. Part I, Introduction and Overview. Chapt. 2 Overview of the International Search Stage. https://www.wipo.int/pct/en/texts/ispe/2_10_12.html

PCT International Search and Preliminary Examination Guidelines Part II, Chapt. 4.05 Background art. https://www.wipo.int/pct/en/texts/ispe/4_02_27.html#_4_05

PCT International Search and Preliminary Examination Guidelines. Part II International Application Chapter 5.24 Open and closed claims. [English]. https://www.wipo.int/pct/en/texts/ispe/5_20_28.html

OMPI - Directives concernant la recherche internationale et l'examen préliminaire international selon le PCT. Deuxième partie. La demande internationale. Chapitre 5.24 Revendications de type ouvert ou fermé. [French]. https://www.wipo.int/export/sites/www/pct/fr/docs/texts/ispe-11.pdf

OMPI - Directrices de búsqueda internacional y de examen preliminar internacional del PCT. Parte II Solicitud internacional. Capítulo 5.24 Reivindicaciones de tipo abierto y cerrado. [Spanish]. https://www.wipo.int/export/sites/www/pct/es/docs/texts/ispe.pdf

PCT - International Search and Preliminary Examination Guidelines. Part V. Written opinion/international preliminary examination report. Chapt. 17. Content of Written Opinions and the International Preliminary Examination Report. 17.52 Language of the Written Opinion and the International Preliminary Examination Report. https://www.wipo.int/pct/en/texts/ispe/17_09_55.html#_17_52

Guidelines and Manuals of National/Regional Patent Offices

WIPO - Guidelines and manuals of national/regional patent offices. [English]. https://www.wipo.int/patents/en/guidelines.html

OMPI - Directives et manuels des offices de brevet nationaux et régionaux. [French]. https://www.wipo.int/patent-law/fr/guidelines.html

OMPI - Directrices y manuales de las oficinas nacionales/regionales de patentes. [Spanish]. https://www.wipo.int/patent-law/es/guidelines.html

WIPO Patent Drafting Manual. (English). https://www.wipo.int/edocs/pubdocs/en/wipo-pub-867-22-en-wipo-patent-drafting-manual.pdf

Manuel de l'OMPI pour la rédaction des brevets. (French). https://www.wipo.int/edocs/pubdocs/fr/patents/867/wipo_pub_867.pdf

Manual de la OMPI de redacción de solicitudes de patente. (Spanish). https://www.wipo.int/edocs/pubdocs/es/patents/867/wipo_pub_867.pdf

Index

Pages in *italics* refer to figures, pages in **bold** refer to tables, and pages followed by n refer to notes.